IDMS/R

A Professional's Guide to
Concepts, Design and
Programming

IDMS/R

A Professional's Guide to Concepts, Design and Programming

Larry E.Towner

Intertext Publications
McGraw-Hill Book Company
New York, N.Y.

Library of Congress Catalog Card Number 88-82420

10 9 8 7 6 5 4 3 2 1

ISBN 0-07-065087-X

Intertext Publications/Multiscience Press, Inc.
One Lincoln Plaza
New York, NY 10023

McGraw-Hill Book Company
1221 Avenue of the Americas
New York, NY 10020

IDMS/R, IDMS/DC, IDMS/Architect, IDD, OLQ, ADS/O, CULPRIT, OLM, IDB, and ASF are trademarks of Cullinet Software, Inc. Automate Plus and LSDM are the trademarks of Learmonth & Burchett Management Systems (LBMS), Inc.

To those true professionals who gave of their time and talents to organize and manage the IDMS User Association, not for personal gain but to benefit each and every user of the product; the best of the unsung heros of the IDMS user community:

George Bentley
Bill Coward
John Cwi
Jim Emerson
Jim Gilliam
Barry Groves
Paul King
John Lindsey, Jr
Jerry McColough
Ken Paris
Jack Peck
Frank Sweet
Yvonne Towner

Contents

Foreword

IDMS is one of the most versatile DBMS products on the market. Since its first availability in 1974, IDMS has grown in both capabilities and flexibilities. The product has been expanded through release after release. While this growth is generally acknowledged as a major strength of the product, it can also present a painful orientation to the novice user.

This book on IDMS/R is an accumulation of many tips, procedures, and guidelines organized to make IDMS easier and more effective to use. I hope that this book will help both the novice and experienced user alike to make a great product perform even better. Unfortunately, I had to draw the line somewhere in order to complete the book. There are some topics that would have justified a book by themselves. Conversely, I elected to treat some subjects briefly because their current use is limited.

The book is divided into three parts. The first, Logical Database Design, describes some proven approaches to the initial design process which is so important to a successful database implementation.

Part Two, Physical Database Design, delves in detail into the intricacies of designing the physical IDMS database. The logical designs are converted into IDMS physical structures. This section concentrates on the network database structure and the "conventional" database design. After much soul-searching and agonizing, I decided not to include specific chapters on IDB and ASF in the book. While there are many reasons, the principal considerations were usage and change. Both features are still evolving at a rapid pace. Virtually anything I would put in this book about IDB and ASF would be obsolete in a short time. Since my objective was to identify principles and techniques that transcend individual product releases, I felt that it would be better to concentrate at a different level.

Part Three, Database Access And Maintenance, delves into the physical use of the database. This will cover a combination of program design, development, and performance considerations.

Acknowlegements

It would be impossible to name all of the people who, over the past 10 years, have contributed to the knowledge that has been concentrated in this book. A few special people, though, deserve individual mention:

Bill Potter, a close friend who is one of the most knowledgeable IDMS internals specialists in the country;

Paul King, as the long-time Chairman of the TAC Committee of the IDMS User Association, was responsible for guiding the IDMS enhancement recommendation process; and

Barry Groves, who is embarrassed when called an IDMS guru, a title that he has clearly earned.

Introduction

This book on IDMS/R tries to accomplish two related but somewhat contrasting goals: 1) a tutorial for the novice user, and 2) a reference guide for the more experienced. The approach used is to present the text as a tutorial heavily laced with examples and illustrations while including a very detailed index to permit quick reference to specific topics.

The book has been subdivided into three parts:

1. Logical Database Design. This part explores the analysis and design activities that are essential to an effective and efficient database implementation. It briefly describes the use of a development methodology to define the analysis techniques that have proven their worth in IDMS design teams.
2. Physical Database Design. Knowledge of the subtleties of physical design in the IDMS world is essential to the implementation of an effective database application. This section details many of those subtleties to help you implement a good database.
3. Database Access and Maintenance. This part goes into detail about the data manipulation language (DML) associated with IDMS, a description of currency, and backup and recovery. Special facilities, such as Automatic Systems Facility (ASF), the Information Database (IDB), Central Version (CV), and On-Line Query (OLQ) are discussed in this section.

While separately formatted, the three parts are presented in a logical progression of information. The body of the book is supported by extensive appendices that provide a condensation of many of the techniques and standards recommended within the body. A detailed glossary of terms followed by the index completes the book.

The Use of DBMS in Application Development

Application definition, scheduling and costing, development, and implementation in the database arena is more complex, typically, than for individual file-oriented approaches. Why, then, is everyone touting database? There are many reasons. The most important, from a management viewpoint, is the cost of the application system development life cycle (SDLC).

The cost of data processing software development is skyrocketing. A labor intensive function, skilled programmers are difficult to find and attract; the result is high salaries. There is a saying that nothing is impossible with a computer. Basically that is true if accompanied by a blank check. Blank checks, however, are becoming a thing of the past when budgeting the data processing resource.

Database management systems (DBMS) are expensive to purchase and to use. Why, then, does management buy them? The principal reason is that, properly used, DBMS can control the SDLC costs of application software. DBMS accomplishes this by introducing an environment of standardized development and implementation which makes software easier to design, develop, and maintain.

The increasing complexity and volume of data applied to computers has, for many organizations, reached a point where the development of "state of the art" applications is no longer cost-effective. It is one thing to develop a series of file-type applications, each separately residing on magnetic tape or disk and processed in "batch" mode. It is another thing entirely to merge several related applications into an integrated database, disk resident, which may be processed by either batch or interactive remote terminals. While a majority of programmers can develop the file-type applications, only the more highly skilled have the experience to develop the database type of applications without the assistance of specialized software.

The key to cost-effective application development using a DBMS is standardization of the process. The DBMS lends itself readily to standardization, in fact enforcing standards through its data dictionary and development tools. A great deal of time will be devoted to the implementation of such standards throughout the book.

The Database Environment

It is essential that the company establish the proper environment for the use of DBMS if its utilization is to be successful. Two primary steps, establishing the data/database administration function and defining installation standards and conventions are necessary before installing and using the DBMS software.

The Data/Database Administration Function

It is very important that the decision to utilize DBMS be accompanied by the establishment of the data/database administration function. Central control of the DBMS environment is critical to its long-term success. It is useful at this point to distinguish between a data administrator and a database administrator. A "standard" definition is difficult because different authors have placed the two positions at different levels. For this discussion, assume that the database administrator reports to the data administrator.

Data Administrator. The Data Administrator is the custodian and coordinator of corporate data. This may, and often does, include all data whether supported by database or by "conventional" software. The Data Administrator should report to the highest levels of corporate management, not to data processing management.

Database Administrator. The Database Administrator is responsible for the design, definition, support, security, and integrity of databases, principally those residing in DBMS-driven systems. The database administrator maintains the corporate data dictionary and consults with users and system developers to ensure that new developments and enhancements for existing systems are in sync with operational systems.

It is not uncommon for the two positions to be merged and placed under a single group. The size of the data processing function in the company often dictates how the functions are organized.

LOGICAL DATABASE DESIGN

While oriented to IDMS, this book explores logical database design techniques that could be applied to any of the database structure types. The material is focused toward the developer of database applications.

Development Methodologies

Methodology *is another of the buzzwords that has been receiving a large amount of press in recent years. And for good reason. Numerous case studies and testimonials have firmly established that the use of a consistent approach to software development will result in improved quality and timeliness of system development.*

While this book does not in itself describe a methodology, it provides background material and techniques that may be applied to any development methodology. The book does refer frequently to a development methodology marketed by Learmonth & Burchett Management Systems.[1]

The first chapters of this book provide building block information and techniques that are used as we actually begin the logical design process in Chap. 9. For the experienced database developer, much of the information in the first eight chapters will be reference material; you are, however, encouraged to review it in detail.

Value of Pictures

"A picture is worth a thousand words" is a cliche that has been used for centuries. When attempting to communicate with users, the data processing professional frequently has difficulty establishing the desired results to be achieved from a new application system. DP terminology is as foreign to the customer as the customer's terminology is to the analyst.

Road signs have evolved from words to pictures over the past 10 years to provide a common language for all drivers. Pictures can also provide a common language between the customer and analyst.

---

[1]   Learmonth & Burchett Management Systems, Houston, TX. markets the LBMS Structured Development Method (LSDM) and its supporting PC-based software package, AUTOMATE Plus. In the author's opinion, this is one of the most effective database design methodologies available.

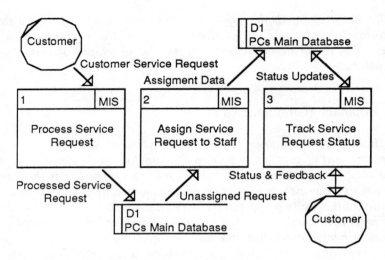

Figure 1   Service Request Data Flow Diagram.

Some pictures, however, are better than others. One of the major assets of data flow diagrams (DFD) has been the ease with which they can be understood by both the analyst and customer. We can improve on the DFD by using symbology that is universally understood. Figure 1 demonstrates a process where the customer calls in a service request. Using DFDs, the process is clearly described. Figure 2, on the

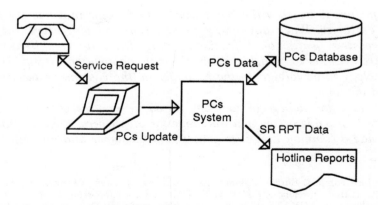

Figure 2   Service Request Pictorial Diagram.

other hand, illustrates the same process using icon-type symbols. When describing the process to customer management, the second illustration is more easily understood.

The preceding pictorials were both produced by Automate, further demonstrating its capability.

1

Data

The data processing world has been making a dramatic change in philosophy during the last five years. This change, traumatic to many, has turned the emphasis in application software development from focusing on the specific needs of a single application to the general data needs of the organization. The focus has turned to *data functionality* instead of *application functionality*.

The availability of large-scale integrated database products is certainly one of the contributing factors to this change in philosophy. Prior to the inception of DBMS, those who had the foresight to see the change simply did not have the facilities to implement multiuser databases.

Data: Resource Or Asset

With the advent of DBMS products such as IDMS, the tools became available to bring related data together. Early users found that data redundancy was reduced while the integrity of the data was increased by using a DBMS. As more and more of us began to use these tools, we found a subtle but even more compelling reason for data integration.

Through the 1970s, most companies looked at data as a resource from which to produce reports about various facets of company operation. Data, in this form, provided after-the-fact records of the status of company activities. Little consideration was made of the use of the data to measure trends or highlight strategic possibilities.

The advent of database management systems (DBMS) allowed the association of data in ways never before economically available. In companies where DBMS was being used heavily, management found that strategic information was *more accurate and quickly available.* Interrelated data was now available in ways that were previously too cumbersome to consider. These "new" combinations of data gave management a better perspective on the company and its competitive position.

Suddenly the complexion of data changed; it bloomed from a lot of printing to an asset of the organization. Data became a key to the growth and, in many cases, the survival of the organization.

It is important to note, however, that this growth occurs *only when upper management understands the potential of data* to enhance the organization position. This is a selling job that rests primarily with the DP manager. The DBMS vendors will "help" with the process; beware, however, of too much help. There are few things worse than being sold a pie in the sky and then not being able to deliver.

Multiple Uses of Data

In the early years of data processing, data associated with an application, such as payroll, was used exclusively for that purpose. Even before DBMS, users found that there were other uses for data that were not directly associated with the application the data was created for. For example, payroll data could be used to produce a mailing list for the company to send material to the employee's home.

Integration

The earliest attempts at integration of data from separate applications were often frustrating and expensive. The payroll and personnel departments, for example, often have overlapping data. But if the only data element that can be used as a key between them, i.e., the employee number, is formatted differently, sharing of their data becomes difficult.

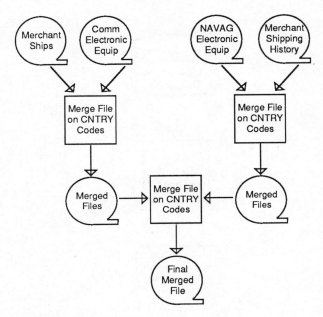

Figure 1-1   Bringing File Data Together.

This problem was compounded many times over in most companies. The availability of data dictionaries seemed to emphasize the problem rather than solve it. For example, at the Navy where I initially installed IDMS in 1975, we found that we had 43 (yes, 43) different ways to identify the two-character code that identifies the countries of the world.

This confusing situation consistently proved costly. The only way that management could get a composite report of activities associated with a particular country was by writing special programs to extract and gather the data into a single file. Figure 1-1 illustrates this kind of activity.

Many times the extracted data didn't match on corresponding fields. Because individual files were updated by different people at different times, data was rarely in synchronization. A question of which data was right frequently arose; management began to distrust all of the data.

With the arrival of DBMS, it was necessary to straighten out this confusion. A consistent definition of data elements and records was required before we could proceed further in the process of integrating

Figure 1-2 An Example Of Integrated Data.

data. The database administrator (DBA) became a key person in these early days, assisting the individual users and development teams in establishing order in the data definition arena.

Integration eliminated many of the problems associated with separate files. Of major interest to management was the reduction in time and cost to produce a shared-data report; the improved credibility of the data was also a significant point. Figure 1-2 illustrates the difference when the same kind of report is drawn from an integrated database.

The Information Utility

We are rapidly moving toward the next stage of data processing, the information utility. Here, the data of the company has been integrated and made generally available to end users. The emphasis changes again, from integration and data gathering to distribution of the data to those who need it.

   The increasing availability of personal computers and micro-mainframe communications makes it possible to extract portions of the database, download it, and manipulate the information on the PC.

   Before we can realize this level of capability, we must be sure that our databases are designed in the most effective manner. Where possible, data redundancy should be eliminated; where it must remain, redundancy has to be controlled and well documented. End users must be able to understand what the database has to offer if they are to use it effectively.

2

Database Structures

Once involved with a DBMS, we have a tendency to ignore or discount the availability of data structures other than those supported by our DBMS. Our focus narrows and our users often suffer. We build all applications to fit the DBMS, regardless of the applicability of the DBMS to the task. It is patently foolish to use IDMS to maintain a simple mailing list of 100 names; the development and support costs would far outweigh any benefits derived. A mailing list as a byproduct of a customer database is a different story.

The point here is that we must not forget the availability of other data structures that have their place in our data world. Flat files are not bad just because they are old; there are places where the flat file is the best possible solution to a specific data handling need. As part of our analysis of an application, we must consider all structure alternatives and pick the most cost-effective one that fits the overall data architecture of the organization.

Five Principal Data Structures

There are five types of data structures that are commonly used in software packages today:

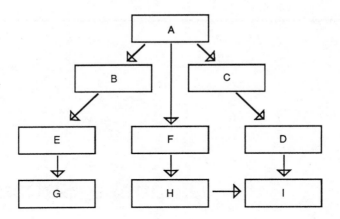

Figure 2-1 Network Data Structure.

1. *Flat File.* The flat file data structure dates back to the beginning of data processing. The original punched card was a flat file. The name is derived from the one-dimensional nature of the file. Each file record contained a consistent number of data elements that were only associated with other elements in the same file.

   The interesting phenomenon about flat files is that the description also fits the relational database. The principal difference between a flat file and a relational database is that the latter was designed more scientifically (using normalization of data) and contains a wide variety of on-line tools to make it easier to use. Figure 2-4 therefore can be used as an illustration of flat files, too.

2. *Network.* The network data structure is a comprehensive arrangement of data that permits relating data in the same form that it actually occurs in the "real world." Ideally, with this structure, data relationships can be created without forcing the program developer to traverse long or illogical paths to reach related information. Figure 2-1 illustrates the network format.

   The networking of data permits the database designer to physically associate data records with each other through data paths (*sets* in IDMS) that provide the most direct access possible. This has the effect of minimizing the amount of input/output (I/O) activity and improving database application

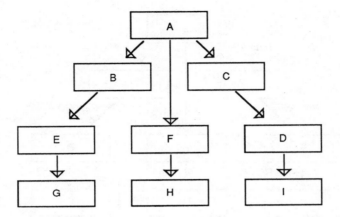

Figure 2-2   Hierarchical Data Structure.

performance. A subtle side effect reduces the amount of path traversing logic within the application program because the network enforces data association rules.

3. *Hierarchical.* The hierarchical data structure is also known as the *tree structure* since it resembles the inverted trunk and branches of a tree. With this structure, a subset of a network, data on one branch can be reached from a point on another branch only by returning to the closest common junction and traversing the data on the branch containing the desired data. Figure 2-2 illustrates the hierarchical format.

Figure 2-3 illustrates the functional differences between network and hierarchical formats. The network structure provides a direct path between records H and I (path HI), while the hierarchical structure requires that the user navigate back to the common record A (path ACDI) and walk through record F to reach H (path AFH), a significant performance overhead. The dotted line identifies the path required for a hierarchical DBMS to move from record I to record H; the asterisk line shows the more direct path permitted by a network data structure.

The hierarchical data structure, lacking the direct data association capabilities of the network, requires increased program logic to locate and verify data outside of the branch of the tree where the program is working.

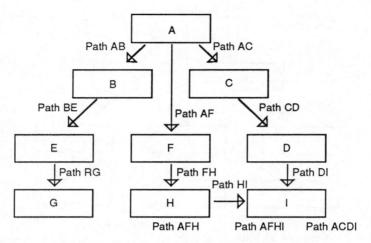

Figure 2-3 Hierarchical vs. Network Data Structure.

4. *Relational.* "Relational" has become the buzzword of database in the 1980s. Vendors (if they market such a thing) would have us believe that unless a database is relational, it is worthless. Many vendors, whose packages are not really relational, market them as "relational like." The relational concept, illustrated in Figure 2-4, has gained considerable attention because it is "user friendly," another buzzword that has caught on. The users of microprocessors have made the concept popular, even if only a few micros or their programs can truly be called friendly.

The relational structure is best described as a two-dimensional array or table. It is made up of a series of columns (*data elements*) and rows (*records*). Theoretically, the data elements should be related to each other so that all elements are primarily dependent upon the key and there are no repeated elements.

In reality, the designer of small databases that stand alone doesn't worry about the niceties of format. The database is designed to meet a need without respect for the "purity" of design.

The relational structure is actually a flat file, a throwback to second-generation sequential tape systems with a direct access wrinkle. The only real structural difference is that relational

ANDERSON	WILLIAM	K	84221	WASHINGTON	DC	20015	BLD	BLUE	A
JONES	ROBERT	A	23233	CHICAGO	IL	60604	BRN	BLUE	A
WILSON	JUDITH	M	44212	NEW YORK	NY	10019	BLK	HZL	C
ARDMORE	ROGER	C	22124	LOS ANGELES	CA	90009	BRN	GRN	C
WATSON	BETTY	Q	12765	SPOKANE	WA	98204	BLD	GRN	B

PRIMARY
KEY

Figure 2-4 Relational Data Structure.

databases do not permit repeating data groups, frequently found in sequential tape files.

The simplicity of the file structure is the greatest asset, and also the greatest liability of the relational DBMS. The ease with which the structure can be modified, new structures can be created, and an end user can create small databases is based on the structure's simplicity. The liability comes from the amount of computer resources required to handle the data during the use of multiple databases; as the volume and size of database use grow, system responsiveness degrades.

The relational structure has one major drawback: It does not handle high volumes of data very well, the normal occurrence in business data processing. Its update speed is simply too slow for many of the applications where it would be most useful. As a result, most relational databases are restricted to small subsets of the large-scale production databases in use in most businesses.

5. *Inverted list*. The inverted list data structure may be implemented in either "full" or "partial" form. The basic structure is characterized by the removing of selected data fields, such as person identifier, from the data record itself and placing that information in a separate file, called a list. Through pointers, the list entry for each succeeding person identifier is linked to the data record to which it belongs.

A *full* inverted structure places ALL fields into lists and the data record is nothing more than a stub to link everything together.

A *partial* inverted structure places only those fields that the database designer sees as potential entry or query points into

ORIGINAL RECORD

JONES	ROBERT	A	23233	CHICAGO	IL	60604	BRN	BLUE	A
WILSON	JUDITH	M	44212	NEW YORK	NY	10019	BLK	HZL	C

PARTIALLY INVERTED RECORD

JONES	ROBERT	A	CHICAGO	60604	BRN	BLUE	A	1
WILSON	JUDITH	M	NEW YORK	10019	BRN	HZL	C	2

INVERSION LISTS

PERSON #   STATE

1	23233
2	44212

1	IL
2	NY

Figure 2-5   Inverted List Data Structure.

lists. This approach has been implemented commercially several times. The principal hazard within inverted structures, as a family, is that update speed is sacrificed significantly for on-line retrieval speed. Because all of the data associated with an entry is not colocated (some of it is in the lists), batch or high-volume retrieval is severely affected.

In general, then, inverted file systems serve well in an environment where there is little update (as a percentage of the file size) but large volumes of on-line retrieval. Figure 2-5 illustrates a partial inverted file structure. The original record contains last name, first name, initial, person number, city, state, zip code, hair color, eye color, and job code. The design calls for direct access to the record by person number and state.

The partially inverted record removes the person number and state from the physical database record and places them in separate lists. Each list value is tied to the database record through pointers (1 and 2). As you can see, it is necessary to access the database record and both lists to retrieve the complete information on either person.

Interestingly enough, inverted structures may be associated with network and hierarchical structures. In fact, several of the principal implementations of inverted database packages are organized as either network or hierarchical in the manner in which the principal data records are stored.

Referential Integrity

Referential integrity is a topic that has received an increasing amount of attention as the popularity of relational DBMS has grown. A great deal of emphasis has been placed stating that without referential integrity a relational DBMS can be hazardous to your data. The referential integrity problem, however, has been with us for years. The reason it has not surfaced before is that most hierarchical and network DBMS implementations more or less automatically took care of the issue. In this section, we will explore referential integrity in both relational and network environments.

What Is Referential Integrity?

Referential integrity refers to maintaining integrity within a physical database through the reference (hence, the term referential) keys that tie the database together. In a relational DBMS, the *name* of a key field in one table must match the *name* of another key field in a second table in order to join the two tables together. Changing the *name* of *either* key field in either table prevent the DBMS from locating the common elements required for a join.

Referential integrity, therefore, is *CRITICAL* to the ability to navigate through a database. Without this feature, the database can be reduced to a hodgepodge of related but unrelatable data in a short time.

Referential Integrity in a Network Environment

Referential integrity is provided automatically within the schema of a network database. The set structure ensures that related data are linked. This, of course, is one of the criticisms of network DBMS. The physical linking of related data makes database structure changing more difficult and time consuming. The tradeoff is that less programming and system activity is required to maintain referential integrity so the DBMS typically performs better.

Communication between databases within the network environment, however, does require that the database developer provide for referential integrity. The access keys (CALC keys in IDMS) within each database must be compatible. Compatibility normally means

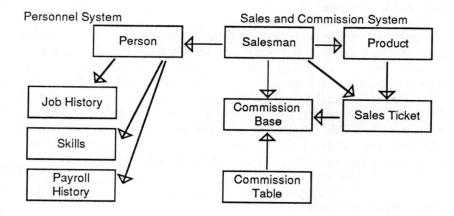

Figure 2-6   Cross Database Linking.

that they must be of the same format (alpha, numeric) and the same length. With this level of compatibility, the same key value in one database may be used to access another database.

The name of the key element is not as important in the network environment as in the relational because the DBMS relies on the application software to supply the key access logic. From a data administration standpoint, however, consistency of element names across databases is almost as important as the consistency of the data element structure. Figure 2-6 illustrates the cross database linking via common data elements.

Even within the same application database, multiarea databases may require referential keys. Cross-area sets are a problem because of the domino effect of an area recovery. Many developers avoid cross-area sets by establishing *tie point records* between two areas. We will discuss this record structure in detail in the book on physical design. Figure 2-7 shows a tie point data relationship within the same database across two areas.

As we can see from Figure 2-7, there is increased processing and space overhead from the use of tie point records. The advantages often outweigh the disadvantages, particularly in very large physical databases where backup and recovery of the entire database cannot be performed simultaneously.

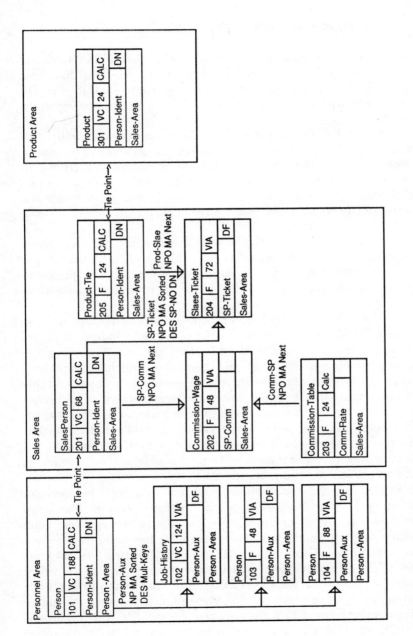

Figure 2-7 Tie Point Record Structure.

Referential Integrity in a Relational Environment

At the time of this writing, the only pure relational DBMS that had implemented some form of referential integrity was SUPRA from Cincom. A form of referential integrity is present in Datacom DB (ADR) that partially meets requirements; some programming assistance is required.

The relational DBMS cannot be considered an effective production tool for an organization without implementing referential integrity. This implementation may be either automatic within the DBMS itself (obviously the most desirable approach) or it may be implemented through the application software. Implementing through the application software has three major drawbacks:

1. *It is much more costly.* The programming effort required grows exponentially as the number of tables in the database increases. The skill, and associated salary cost, of the programmers required to support this software is much higher than average.

2. *It reduces design flexibility.* THE major selling feature of relational DBMS is its ease of use, ease of change, and its flexibility. As the number of tables in a database increases, the ability to change the database decreases. Each change to a table must be carefully evaluated to ensure that another table is not impacted. Changing the name or structure of a *foreign key* will have disastrous effects on the linkage between tables. (A foreign key is a field in one relational table that is present to provide access to another relational table. It is called a foreign key to differentiate it from the *primary key*, which is the access key for the table itself.)

   Figure 2-8 illustrates three relational tables: a person file; an office location file; and types of an employee file. The office location and types of employee files are reference files, each with a single primary key. The person file has one *primary key,* the last name of the person. It also contains two *foreign keys,* the CITY (which corresponds to the *primary key* of the office location file) and EMPLOYEE TYPE (corresponding to the *primary key* of the types of employee file). If we were to change the name of the CITY field in the person file, the relational DBMS would not be able to join the person file with the office location file.

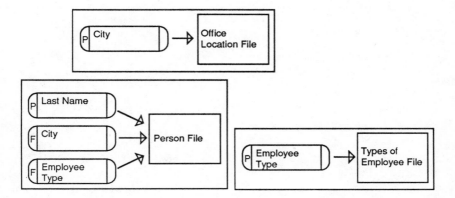

Figure 2-8   Relational Table Interfacing.

3. *Multiuser control is difficult.* If a relational DBMS has multiple users, each with the ability to modify the database structure, controlling those changes is very difficult. For example, let's say that we have a personnel locator file. Its primary key is the payroll number, a field of six numeric digits.

   Many other relational users join with this file to get personnel information. The number of actual users is unknown to the maintainers of the locator file. Because of company growth, it is necessary to change the structure of the payroll number in the locator file to nine alphanumeric characters. The company now uses Social Security numbers to identify the employees. The name of the primary key in the locator file is changed from PAYROLLID to SSNO. The other users of the locator file suddenly find the file unavailable.

   Where this kind of database use occurs, and it is very common, referential integrity is absolutely essential. There is no way to effectively administer the change otherwise. Keeping a list of users is ineffective because there will always be some user who does not register.

Referential integrity implemented to prevent these problems automatically renames and restructures the foreign keys of any relational table that points to a table where the primary key has been renamed or restructured. This capability requires an active data dictionary where all relationships are recorded automatically.

3

Data Modeling

Data modeling is an integral part of the logical design of a database structure. The data model becomes the road map of the organization's data and its functional interaction with each segment of the organization. This chapter will explore the principal considerations associated with the creation of the organization data model.

Why A Data Model?

Ten years ago data processing applications were built to support a specific user with little concern or desire to share the data with anyone else. In fact, many users were extremely reluctant to share data. Data ownership was the common attitude of the day, with turf battles erupting when other organizations intruded on what one area considered "its data."

Data models were frequently employed to illustrate just how much data was replicated between organizations. It was often found that data was shared in subtle ways, even though not through official channels. Organization management, often reluctantly, began to recognize that there were certain data items that were used across organization lines.

The next step was to identify the data that was being shared. Inconsistencies were often found; the size and format of the data varied by application and organization.

Forward-thinking data administrators have long realized that integrated database software development can be done most effectively if a master plan is employed; piecemeal database application development achieves little improvement in processing effectiveness unless each piece fits an overall puzzle. The organization data model resulted from this need to see the "big picture."

Key Data Attributes

Every organization has several key data elements, or attributes, that bind its data together. These attributes are the threads of the organization's data cloth. They are the keys to associating the rest of the data in a logical manner.

Key data attributes that can be found in nearly every organization include: general ledger account, employee number, part number, customer identifier, and organizational unit identifier. It is not unusual for each organizational level to have its own key attributes that are unique to that level.

Corporate Data

At the top level of the organization, key attributes are those that are implemented uniformly across all subdivisions of the organization. The general ledger account and organizational unit identifier will nearly always be uniform across the entire organization. Employee number and customer identifier should also be uniform; they must be uniform if centralized payroll and billing are used.

Where the same type of data is present in more than one subdivision of an organization, a uniform definition is desirable and may be mandatory. Part numbers, for instance, may be defined differently *only* if no division shares parts with another.

Divisional Data

Let's assume, for a minute, that one division of our organization builds motor homes and that another division creates semiconductor devices. It would appear that the product lines of the two divisions are so diverse that it would not be necessary for them to share a common part number configuration. Digging deeper, however, we find that the motor homes use an electronic ignition system and emergency flasher built by the semiconductor device division.

We can justifiably argue that the part number for the flasher should be the same in both divisions, eliminating duplication of data. Some consideration must be made, however, of the nature of each division's business. The semiconductor division may require only a short sequential part number to adequately catalog its products.

The motor home division, on the other hand, may wish to assign its part numbers to provide visible indication of the level of assembly in the bill-of-materials for its motor homes. What is an end product for the semiconductor division is just one of many components that go into a motor home.

If the semiconductor division only needs an eight-character part number while the motor home division needs 15 characters, seven characters are wasted on each semiconductor part number if a uniform format is enforced. The nature of the business must be actively considered before forcing uniformity on all business organizations.

What *should* happen, however, is the assignment of a unique name to each division's part number if they are allowed to define them separately. Both *must not* be named "part number." Using the division acronym or functional abbreviation as part of the name will make it unique and easily understood, e.g., "SC-PART-NUM," "MH-PART-NUM."

Application Data

Data attributes associated only with a software application must be carefully reviewed to ensure that the data does not exist elsewhere. *Truly unique data at the application level is somewhat rare.*

	PERS	PAYRL	SALES	ACCTG	CREDIT	INVEN	MFG
PERSON IDENT	C	U	U	U			
GEN LED ACCT #		U	U	C	U	U	U
ORGAN IDENT	U	U	U	C			
PART NUMBER			U	U		U	C
BIN LOCATION						C	U
CUSTOMER #				C	U	U	U

Figure 3-1   Data Association Array.

Data definition and association at the application level is a challenge to Data Administrators. At this level, the number of elements expands rapidly; it is very easy to have the same data named several ways. At our Navy installation, many years ago, we had 43 different ways to describe the code associated with a country; so-called *independent* applications utilized whatever name came into the mind of its developer. Integrating these applications into a single database required the reeducating of many users as well as achieving agreement on the name, size, and definition of this and several other elements.

The Data Array

The first step in building a data model is to identify those data attributes that are present in the organization and who uses them. A two-dimensional matrix is constructed with the data attribute running down the left side and the organizational units across the top. (See Figure 3-1.) The organization that creates a certain data attribute is indicated by placing a "C" at the point where the attribute and organization cross. Using organizations are indicated by a "U" at the cross point.

This can be an extensive and time-consuming project. Many interviews are usually necessary. Existing processes, automated and manual, must be reviewed. Politics frequently get involved when organizations are suspicious of each other. It is not unusual for management to initially disbelieve the results of the project. If the organization can afford it, an outside consulting firm with no biases should be considered; they will usually be accepted by all parties as a neutral observer. Even a high-level effort by a *qualified* consultant will cost between $75,000 and $100,000. I emphasize qualified because many consulting firms simply do not have the experience to attack such an undertaking effectively. One of the Big Eight accounting firms or a nationally known software consulting firm is the best source of qualified data modelling analysts.

The Logical Data Model

A logical data model is a data road map, identifying the data attributes (elements) that tie together a series of data entities (groups of like data). Said another way, the data model shows how the data of an organization works together.

The data model provides a picture of how data flows through the subject data areas of an organization. It supplies a game plan for the automating of organization data management, identifying which subject areas are dependent on others for data and should therefore be developed first. The interfaces between software applications is clearly specified, reducing problems of handshaking between applications.

For practical purposes, there are three levels of logical data model:

1. *The corporate data model.* The highest level model illustrates the relationship between major subject data areas within the complete corporation/organization. *All* major subject data areas required by the corporation to perform its stated business functions are shown on a single diagram.
2. *The subject data model.* This level of the model explodes one of the subject data areas into more detail. The subject data model is often notable because most of the key attributes linking the model entities together use the same attribute.
3. *Application data model.* Many subject data models are large and complex enough that they must be broken into separate subareas for development. This model level is more detailed, breaking into data entities that can realistically be defined into physical data records. Here the key attributes represent physical data that ties the entities together.

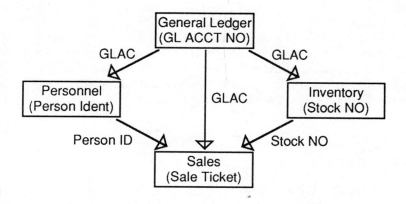

Figure 3-2   Corporate Data Model.

It is possible for a subject model and application model to be at the same level. When this occurs, the subject model key attributes will vary between entities. Figure 3-4 will illustrate this phenomenon.

The Corporate Data Model

A corporate or organization-wide data model is essential to long-term, cost effective data management. While individual databases can be established and maintained without such a model, it will be very difficult over the long term to expand and integrate databases without a model to provide the guidance needed to tap the full potential of a corporate-wide data management plan.

The corporate data model groups data into subject areas at a very high level. At this level, the model will closely mirror many of the elementary functions performed by a company, such as finance, personnel, sales, manufacturing, etc. Figure 3-2 illustrates such a data model.

In Figure 3-2, we find that each of the "islands" of data (subject data areas) are linked by *key attributes*, data elements which provide threads of continuity between each subject data area. Looking at the model, we can see that development of the personnel area requires

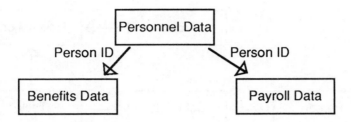

Figure 3-3   Personnel Subject Data Model.

an interface to the general ledger through the ledger account number. Payroll will be charged against a cash account and be posted to a number of other accounts, such as gross pay, federal tax, FICA, etc.

The payroll number of sales employees who are on bonus or commission will be required when posting sales. Therefore, both sales and personnel areas require the payroll number. Sales requires general ledger accounts for sales and commissions.

Our model should be organizationally independent. Separating the inventory function into an independent department from manufacturing does not affect the way manufacturing and inventory data interrelate. It *does* affect who uses the data and the manner in which it is used. Once completed, the corporate data model will largely remain stable over time; it will change when the nature of the business changes. If our software company decided to switch to selling groceries, the project management subject data area would probably disappear.

Subject Data Model

Each of the major subject data areas in Figure 3-2 may be further exploded to identify more detail. The personnel subject data model is illustrated in Figure 3-3. Here we break out the components of the personnel model into personnel data, payroll, and benefits.

Of significance to this, and other, subject data areas is the use of the same key attribute to associate the major sub subject areas. As a general rule of thumb, a sub subject area does not belong to a subject

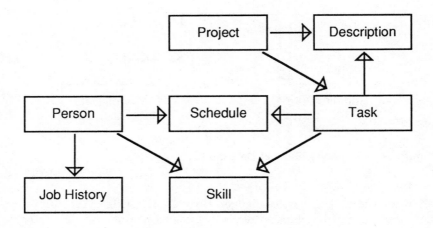

Figure 3-4   Application Data Model.

area unless its principal interface key attribute is the same as all other sub subject areas in that subject area. A different key attribute normally signals that a different data subject drives the sub subject and it should be associated with a different subject area.

Application Data Model

The application data is that portion of the corporate data model which is the basis for a specific software development effort. Using the project management subject data area, illustrated in Figure 3-4, we see that the overall project management area combines pieces from the personnel area (person data, job history, skills inventory) with the management of a project.

As shown in Figure 3-4, linkage entities are included in the data model at this level. While these are really pseudo entities — they don't exist logically — they improve the quality of the diagram and illustrate the specific many-to-many relationships which exist within the logical structure. Double-pointed arrows, frankly, do not do a good job of anything except reducing the number of lines on a diagram.

4

Data Structuring

The logical data model identifies the relationship between the subject data areas and the detail data entities of the organization. As part of that model, it is necessary to define the subtleties of the data relationships. These subtleties are reflected in the structures that the data assumes to accomplish the purpose for which it was created.

This chapter will address six structural conditions that are present in every data model and some of the considerations that must be made in order to properly define the functional use of the data. The six structure conditions are:

1. *Independent data.* Some data entities stand by themselves, dependent on nothing and not requiring any other data to be present in order to exist. This type of structural condition is the exception and truly exists only rarely. What frequently appears to be independent data at the beginning of a data model definition turns out to be either owner or operational data.
2. *Owner data.* As its name implies, some data entities own others. Owning, in this case, means there are some entities in the model that cannot exist without the presence of the owner data. In some circles, this data is referred to as *parent* data.
3. *Member data.* This data, sometimes called *child* to further emphasize its dependence, requires owner data in order to exist. It is possible for member data to also act as owners of other

member data. When this occurs, a hierarchical data relationship is formed.

4. *Optional data.* We can assume that most data structures in the model are required in order to accurately represent the actual business data. While that assumption is certainly valid in some cases, it is often surprising to find how frequently the presence of data is optional. By optional, we mean that the data (most of the time it is member data) does not have to be present for the model to be functional. Optional data is nice-to-have data that adds value to an application but which does not cripple to application if not present.

5. *Data entry points.* Every data structure must have one or more entry points. The definition of an entry point establishes conditions on the model. It is usually not practical to have an entry point that occurs at member data unless that data is also owner data.

6. *Operational data.* Every application has special access conditions where a second entry point is desired or data groupings by special values are required. Operational data, usually in the form of secondary indexes, provides the means for satisfying the special access conditions. Operational data, as the name implies, is present only to meet physical operational requirements for data access; the data itself is usually duplicated within the entity to which the operational data is linked.

Independent Data

We frequently encounter situations where a data entity exists that does not appear to be related to any other entities. By definition, this data is termed *independent.* As the model definition continues, however, the data usually changes its form and becomes the owner or member of some other data entity.

Independent data usually exists as physical rather than logical data simply because completely independent logical data just does not exist in the real world. Physically, independent data exists as control records that occur as one-of-a-kind (OOAK) records in a database. These OOAK records usually contain control information

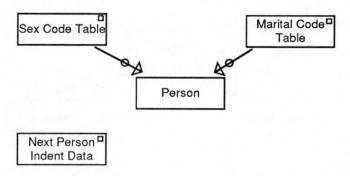

Figure 4-1   Independent Logical Data.

such as the next account number to be assigned, the last billing cycle posted, etc.

Even in the physical world, these records are not truly independent. The next account number to be assigned is dependent upon a project record where the most recent account number is used. Figure 4-1 illustrates such a data entity and its subtle relationship to other data.

Owner Data

Owner, or parent, data supports member data. These two structural constructs are mutually dependent. There is no reason for owner data to exist unless it has member data to depend on it. Without at least one member data entity, the owner data becomes independent data.

In practical application, owners always have at least one member defined. There may be no occurrences of the member data existing at some point in time but at least the data structure allows for potential member occurrences. Figure 4-2 shows an owner entity with members. As the figure shows, the removal of the PERSON data would leave the JOB HISTORY and SKILLS data without something to relate to. Conversely, the presence of only the PERSON data doesn't accomplish much except to provide a lookup table.

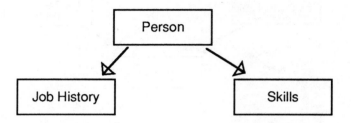

Figure 4-2   Owner Logical Data.

Member Data

Member data has little purpose unless accompanied by *owner* data. JOB HISTORY and SKILLS entities in Figure 4-2 have no meaning unless linked to the PERSON owner. It is common for member data to also be owners of other members. Figure 4-3 illustrates the JOB DESCRIPTION member associated with the JOB HISTORY. The description entity provides the ability to add comments and descriptive information to each job assignment.

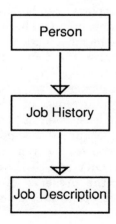

Figure 4-3   Member/Owner Logical Data.

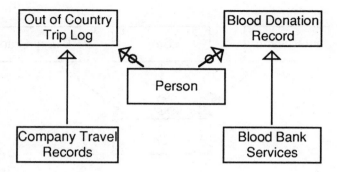

Figure 4-4   Optional Logical Data.

Optional Data

We frequently want to add frosting to the cake by including extra data that is nice to have but which is not essential to the function for which the subject data area was designed to support. It may be nice, for example, to include education history on a person within the database. But unless education information is somehow necessary to the process of managing a person, the information is not critical to the functioning of the business process supported by the database.

This optional data must be carefully monitored to prevent it from cluttering up the database and obscuring the real purpose of the principal data. It is not unusual to find a database application bogged down in developing software to support data that is only marginally useful. Optional data may well account for half of the development effort.

Figure 4-4 illustrates optional data associated with the PERSON entity. As you can see, much of this data is not related to normal personnel management. Arguments can be made for each optional entity; the main point, however, is that the personnel department could manage the employee's records effectively without *any* of this information.

Data Entry Points

Every data model will have one or more commonly used points of entry. Each entry point typically occurs with an *owner entity*.

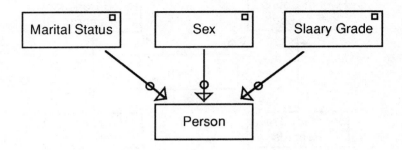

Figure 4-5   Operational Data Logical Data.

Through this owner, access can be made quickly to any of the member entities associated with the owner. The entry point, then, serves two purposes: 1) it provides access to the data structure; and 2) it serves as valid substantive data to the user. The payroll number is the *key attribute* for entry into the PERSON entity; it also is useful information about the person and the payroll number resides with the rest of the person data.

Translated into a physical network database, the entry point occurs with a CALC record with the CALC key field providing a direct entry into the database. Again, most entry point records are owner records.

Operational Data

As the use of data increases, additional ways of accessing the data are required. On-line database access requires response times that preclude scanning the entire database to locate one or a few occurrences of data. Additional entry points are provided through the use of *operational data entities.*

This data structure is called *operational* because it adds nothing to the data model itself. Operational data simply provide the means to access the data structure from another angle. Physically implemented, operational data is found as secondary indexes. Figure 4-5 illustrates the use of operational data against the PERSON entity. In this example, the operational data permit direct access of those PERSON entity occurrences that contain a particular sex, marital, or salary grade code.

5

Data Flow

Many of the design methodologies available today provide excellent facilities for defining the *structure* of data and its relationship to other data. Very few, however, account effectively for the *flow* of the data from one point to another.

The accurate description of the flow of data is the key to successful database design. Overlooking this key requirement can easily lead to a database design that appears to work well when first implemented but gradually degrades as the database matures. This is where the *two-year syndrome* originates. It usually takes about two years for the database to bog down into unacceptable performance levels.

This chapter will discuss the essentials of data flow and its effect on database design. The critical elements of entry points and cascading hierarchical structure on the flow of data will also be covered in detail.

Data Volume

Why should we worry about data volume during logical design? Volume is a physical characteristic that should not affect the logical design. Ideally, this is true. But, since we do not live in the ideal world, many physical aspects of database design intrude on the logical. If we ignore these physical elements, the transition from logical design to physical database will be made that much more difficult.

The ultimate size of the database will affect the manner in which it is accessed. A very small database may be *swept*, read from beginning to end to locate desired data. Sweeping the database is a procedure often used for batch reporting; it is seldom used for on-line reporting.

As the physical volume of data grows, sweeping the database becomes less and less desirable. On-line reporting and retrieval, therefore, requires that additional entry points and secondary indexes be established to provide high-speed access to the database.

Planning For Growth

Few databases are static. They typically grow over time. The rate of growth is very important to overall design. When designing the data structure, it is necessary to understand how big the database will be at its inception and how big it will be at the end of 2 years. In some cases, a 5-year estimate may be desirable too. As we will find later when discussing physical area sizing, this growth rate must be carefully factored into the definition of database areas.

Databases grow for several reasons. The most common, of course, is the addition of new data. New data, as defined here, is data unrelated to that of the same type already in the database. For example, it may be the adding of a new customer account or a new work project. Neither of these are related to existing accounts or projects.

The next most common reason for growth is updating existing information. Adding more lines of narrative to an existing description is a good example. Updating the dates on a project already in the database will not cause the database to grow (unless the empty field has been compressed).

Audit trails or transaction history data can cause a high-volume database to explode in size almost overnight. If, for example, updating the dates on a project requires that we keep a copy of the prior dates for historical purposes, the most common approach is to clone the entire record and track it chronologically. Where such changes are frequent, the size of the database can double very quickly.

Controlling Growth

While some aspects of controlling database growth seem to be beyond the scope of logical designers, there are many decisions about data that can affect the way the physical database grows. Let's review a few:

1. *Repetitive data.* Lines of text, for example, can be handled singly or in multiple line groups. Where the volume is low, single line records are more flexible. As the volume increases, the overhead of key information associated with each line becomes excessive. The number of lines in a multiple line group depends on the manner in which the data will be displayed or used. It may also be practical to limit the total number of lines that may be associated with a single logical owner. Figure 5-1 illustrates both single- and multiple-line text records.
2. *Historical data.* In some systems, the user wants to be able to retrieve history data to see what happened in the past for a particular event, such as a project. Controlling growth of this history data can be done in several ways including a combination of different options. For example:

   a. *Limit duration.* A simple rule may be established that limits the retention of historical data to a specific period of time, say 6 months. When such a limitation is implemented, the record must contain a date that can be used for the purge process. Two approaches may be used:

      1) *Last update date.* This date field identifies the date when the record was last updated. Purging takes place at a specified number of days after the update date. This is the most flexible of the two approaches as the purge period can be changed without having to modify the database.
      2) *Purge date.* The date field identifies the specific date when the record is to be purged. When retention dates are specified by law or policy, this approach ensures retention of the data until the period passes.

```
01   SINGLE-LINE-TEXT.
     03   TEXT-IDENT.
          05   TEXT-TYPE          PIC X.
          05   TEXT-SEQ           PIC 999.
     03   DATE-TEXT.
          05   CENT-YR-TEXT.
               07   CENT-TEXT     PIC 99.
               07   CENT-YR       PIC 99.
          05   CENT-MONTH         PIC 99.
          05   CENT-DAY           PIC 99.
     03   TEXT-LINE               PIC X(60.)


01   MULTI-LINE-TEXT.
     03   TEXT-IDENT.
          05   TEXT-TYPE          PIC X.
          05   TEXT-SEQ           PIC 999.
     03   DATE-TEXT.
          05   CENT-YR-TEXT.
               07   CENT-TEXT     PIC 99.
               07   CENT-YR       PIC 99.
          05   CENT-MONTH         PIC 99.
          05   CENT-DAY           PIC 99.
     03   LINES-USED              PIC 99.
     03   TEXT-BLOCK.
          05   TEXT-LINE          PIC X(60) OCCURS 10.
```

Figure 5-1   Repetitive Text Record Options.

b. *Limit scope.* Not every data item within the database must be retained for historical purposes. Select only those that are critical. Figure 5-2 illustrates the retention of PER-SON-ADDR data while ignoring data from the PERSON record itself.

c. *Split functions.* Figure 5-3 shows a conventional PROJECT record structure. Note that if a clone is made of this record for historical purposes, all data elements within the record must be replicated.

In addition, the developer has the choice of either writing a clone with all of the current fields and then writing an

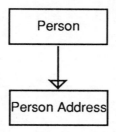

Figure 5-2   Limited Scope History Retention.

updated primary record or of replicating the linkages with those records associated with the PROJECT record. Obviously, these approaches can lead to extra record occurrences that are necessary only on rare occasions. Figure 5-4 illustrates the PCS approach to using an EVENT record to identify common data for similar functions and placing the project data in a subordinate record where it can be copied easily for historical purposes.

d. *Split data.* Within each record that is to be retained for history is some data that either does not change or whose

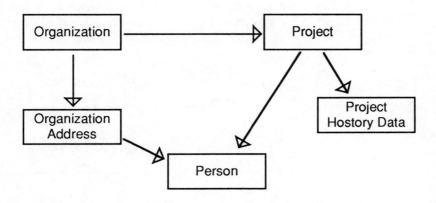

Figure 5-3   Conventional Data History Approach.

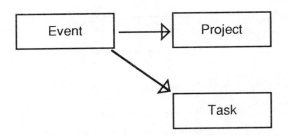

Figure 5-4   Split Function Data History Approach.

change is irrelevant to historical retention. Break the record into two segments to avoid duplicate data. Figure 5-5 illustrates this approach that is followed with the PROJECT record of the PCS database.

3. *Audit data.*   Auditors frequently want to be able to follow a trail of transactions from the current status to a point of origin. Depending on the type of data, this may require retention of past transaction results for many years. It is obviously not economically practical to retain all of that data within the database. The most cost-effective way to retain such data is on magnetic tape. We will discuss the physical aspects of this retention later. For now, the logical design should include one or more independent record definitions that contain all of the

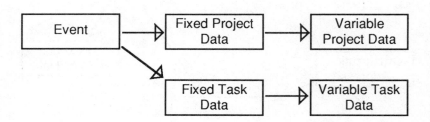

Figure 5-5   History Retention.

audit data requirements. These records will be stored separately from the normal database.

Data Frequency

How often data is presented to the database can have a dramatic effect on the design. Large bulk batch updates, for example, can be presorted to apply the data in the most efficient way possible. Low volume ad hoc on-line updates, on the other hand, must be able to efficiently update single items. The two approaches often suggest data structures that conflict with each other.

Batch Considerations

Since batch data can be presorted, the database structure does not have to be concerned as much with the efficiency of the structure. It is common to have batch preparation programs use a hashing routine (such as IDMSCALC) to compute the logical location of the data to be loaded and sort the data in the order of the location. This dramatically speeds up data loading because the physical actions of the disk drive are optimized.

On-Line Considerations

The picture is quite different in the on-line world. Here, response time is important. Batch users submit their jobs and walk away, not expecting output for some time. They only become concerned if processing costs rise beyond acceptable limits or output is not ready several hours later.

On-line data handling requires a data structure matched to the processing patterns if optimal response times are to be achieved. Modifying or deleting a data record, for example, requires that the data be retrieved first. Adding, conversely, requires no preretrieval of data. Where 80 percent of the database activity is changing, deleting, or retrieving data, the data structure must be optimized toward retrieval; additions are permitted to suffer in order to support the majority profile.

Entry Point Impacts

Entry points are the standard navigational doors to the database. The number of entry points needed within a database varies by the volume of data within the database. Since entry points, in IDMS, are CALC records, they cause clustering of data. The size of the data cluster, the entry point record and normal member occurrences, has a direct relationship to the size of the database page.

It is important that sufficient entry point records be defined to adequately access the data. It is better to err in the direction of too many entry points than too few. Be careful to avoid sorted relationships between the entry point records; they cause performance bottlenecks.

Cascading Hierarchical Structures

When defining hierarchical structures that descend beyond two levels (owner to owner/member to member), it is important that thought be given to the access time required to reach the lowest level. The volume of data associated with each record in the hierarchy will directly affect the design of the hierarchy.

Figure 5-6 illustrates a four-level hierarchy. If B has 10 occurrences, C has 10 occurrences, and D has 10 occurrences, then the *average* number of reads to locate a specific desired occurrence of D is 250 (5 x 5 x 5). This is clearly unacceptable for on-line operation. An increase in the number of occurrences in either the first or second levels of the hierarchy will make the delay even greater.

To reduce the average records read, it will be necessary to sort at least one of the links. It will be better to sort two. If the data volume will be quite high within the structure, all three link levels should be sorted.

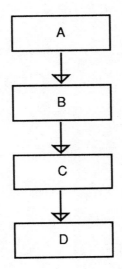

Figure 5-6   Cascading Hierarchical Structure.

6

Data Life Cycle

The life cycle of data is sequence of events that occurs from the time a particular data item is created until it is deleted from the database. This cycle can be very simple: store, modify, delete; it can also be very complex: store, modify multiple times, archive, delete. This chapter will look at the impacts on the design of a database that are caused by the defined life cycle of its data.

Data Creation

The life cycle of a data item begins at its creation in the database. This sounds simple enough; however, there are a number of conditions that must be considered before the event takes place:

1. *Valid contents*. Does the content of the data item meet validation criteria, range of data, and proper mode (alpha or numeric)?
2. *Redundancy*. Is there data already in the database that is redundant to that being entered?
3. *Cross dependency*. Does this data's validity depend on the presence of other data in the database containing a specific value?

4. *Required vs. optional.* Under some circumstances, a value must be present in order for the data item to be considered valid.
5. *Default value.* Frequently a default value may be identified that will be used if the operator does not enter a value.
6. *Data source.* Data may originate from external sources such as input transactions or it may be generated by the software.

Data Use

What are we going to do with all this data we're loading to the database? Such a simple question deserves a simple answer, but the answer is seldom simple. Some of the data loaded to the database will never be used; some will be used constantly.

This discussion focuses on how the way we use data will also affect the logical structure of the database. Generally static data that is seldom required need not be at your fingertips, unless when you need it you must have the data *NOW!* Data that represents history is seldom required rapidly; such data may be placed in a less responsive environment.

Data maintained on-line, on the other hand, usually requires a faster response time; the premise is that if updated on-line, then it is likely to be required on-line. Such an assumption needs clarification though. Within each application are data items that exist logically and are updated with all of the other data but are seldom modified. These low usage items may be handled differently than their higher use cousins.

Data Modification

Modifying data, while appearing simple, can often be very complex. In a database environment, we must consider much more than the simple replacement of data within the record. Here are the major items to be reviewed as part of defining the modification process:

1. *Locating the data.* The record containing the data to be changed must be located and retrieved. Unless the data to be changed is the key, key data must be included in the process so that the record can be found.

2. *Verifying the data.* The new data must meet the validation and verification criteria for the field being modified. This may require checking the data value against values in other database records.
3. *Historical audit trail.* Some applications require that the data modifications be traceable to the originator and a record kept of when the change was made. Other requirements may include retaining the previous values for a period of time.
4. *Authority to make change.* Many applications restrict change authority to specific persons. Some change authority even goes to the point where a person may change a field if its value is within a specific range. For example, a clerk can change a price as long as it is less than $5.00; a manager must make all changes over that value. Or the clerk may change a price plus or minus $1.00 from the current price; the manager must make all changes beyond that range.

Data Deletion

Most of the considerations listed previously for data modification also apply to deletion. The principal consideration for deletion, however, is whether the data is actually removed from the database.

Many conditions within an integrated environment may make physical deletion of data from the database difficult. The integrity of the data picture can be damaged if certain data is removed, i.e., when an employee quits. Removing the physical record from the database will disrupt statistical data associated with the project on which the person was working. It would cause a discrepancy in the payroll system (the company still has to issue W2s to the person at the end of the year).

In cases such as these, the physical record remains in the database; a flag is placed within the record to identify its logical status.

The other consideration is linked to the first, when to purge all of those logically deleted records. Using the preceding examples, the person record could be physically removed from the database when the project to which the person was assigned is completed or at the end of the tax year, whichever occurs last. We would still have to design the data structures so that any statistical information about the project would be retained even after deletion of the person data.

Often we will find that it is impractical to ever physically delete the data. If, for example, we wanted to retain project statistics indefinitely for use in estimating future work, the person data might be critical to those statistics (skill level, experience data). When this occurs, the logical design should separate the critical data from the optional. Then the optional data could be deleted when it is no longer required. Another option is to delete the field values that are no longer required and let the DBMS compress the physical record to reduce storage usage.

Data Archiving

Some data retains a measure of usefulness for many years. It needs to be available but not on-line. Data handling rules may stipulate that data remain on-line for two years, then be available for retrieval for an additional five years.

Archiving procedures and software must be developed that transfer data periodically to magnetic tape. This tape data must be kept in a format that permits easy reloading to the on-line database or reading from the archive file. Keep in mind that archiving requires more than just transferring a record to tape.

Archiving a CALC record is a simple process, as long as it isn't owned by any other record. The entire record is copied to tape. It can be retrieved and reloaded to the database without depending on other data.

A VIA record or a CALC record owned by another record must include key values from the owner record. This will permit the data to be properly connected to its owners. Care must be taken to ensure that the owner record occurrences are present in the database before restoring the member data.

7

Security

Back in the "old days," people from the payroll department wheeled their cart of tapes and forms into the computer room, took over the computer, and ran the company payroll. The run completed, they picked up their tapes, forms, checks, trash, and departed. This was a very positive form of data security. No one except those from the payroll department could get access to their data.

In today's increasingly integrated environment, it is not practical to permit such independent operation. The payroll department staff needs and wants access to data supplied by other departments, data that they can receive in machine-readable form faster and more accurately than the manual methods previously employed.

The integration of data places an enormous burden on data administration personnel to define and structure databases to ensure the security of sensitive data. Governmental regulations require that some data, especially that associated with people, be heavily restricted.

Integration also concentrates the essential data of an organization in a single location, accessible through a single medium. In the past, separate systems provided a measure of security because it was difficult to gather together all of the material necessary to compromise a company; integration has eliminated that barrier.

Database design must take the sensitivities of different data into consideration, often specifying that certain data is to be isolated and controlled at a level beyond that of the remainder of the database.

Security Levels

Security is implemented at many levels; actual implementation may encompass multiple levels concurrently. Each level has a measure of overhead that must be accepted in order to implement the desired security. The following list of security levels begins with the least costly:

1. *Hardware access security.* The valid users of data are permitted to have access to the computer as a whole. This may be by having a key to a terminal or the room in which the terminal is located. Once access is obtained, all data within the computer is available.
2. *Hardware signon security.* A valid user may sign onto the computer, usually into a certain facility like TSO or IDMS. Once signed on, the user may access all data associated with that facility. Security facilities such as ACF2 or Top Secret are the most frequently used for controlling access at this level.
3. *Menu security.* Once signed onto the computer, the user is presented with a menu of those activities that may be accessed. The user may be restricted to one or more different applications and their databases. Once signed onto an application, all data within that application is available. Passwords are the most frequently used control facility at this level.
4. *Transaction security.* The user is restricted, within an application, to certain transactions. Within the transaction, the user may perform all functions and access all data. This level of security may have its own password protection.
5. *Function security.* The user is permitted to execute a transaction but cannot perform all functions associated with the transaction. For example, the user may execute the update person transaction but may only change a person's data.
6. *Area security.* The user is restricted to a specific subset of the database. Within that area, all data may be accessed. This is

frequently implemented in IDMS through use of subschema registration.

7. *Record type security.* The user can process only specific record types, such as the person or organization records, within the database. This technique may be implemented through subschema registration but may require a large number of specialized subschemas.

8. *Record occurrence security.* The user may access only specific record occurrences of a record type. This can be a very expensive security process. The user is assigned an access code that is matched to a key value stored in the record. If the codes match, the user is granted access.

9. *Record content security.* The most difficult and expensive to implement, this level of security restricts users to certain data elements within a record. It can be implemented by use of segmented records within a subschema but often requires many subschemas to control the access of many users.

An offshoot of this process restricts user access to a record if certain field values are not within a specified range. For example, payroll clerks can look at person data only when the grade level of the person is below that of managers; the department manager can look at all person data. This implementation requires extensive software support. It can be supported by use of database procedures in IDMS, protecting the security from tampering by application programmers.

Designing for Security

Integrated databases *must* be designed to secure the data within to the level required by law and company policy. This means that a combination of the preceding security levels will be employed. Security processing overhead can be minimized if the requirements are designed into the data structures from the beginning.

The remainder of this chapter will identify design processes that may be included in the initial design of an application to take advantage of natural security capabilities.

Menu Security

A number of menu systems have been designed for the IDMS environment. One that I submitted to the User Association Contributed Program Library several years ago uses the data dictionary to control user signon and access to applications. Access to transactions and to functions within the transactions is also addressed by this facility. It has the disadvantage, however, of system overhead into the dictionary; large numbers of applications and users also make it difficult to maintain the security parameters.

Menus will be discussed in more detail later in the Cookbook. From a security standpoint, a menu should display to the operator only those options that the operator is authorized to use. Including other options will irritate the operator when the options abort; it will also encourage some operators to attempt to penetrate the option. This is a case of what the operator doesn't know won't hurt either the operator or the system.

Transaction Security

Transactions may be secured by placing security checking software at the start of the transaction. If the transaction is menu-driven, include it only for those authorized. Much of the security considerations are identical to menu security.

Function Security

Individual functions, such as add, change, and delete, may be easily controlled by inserting calls to security checking software at the beginning of the function logic.

Area Security

Area security is the highest level security capability that is directly related to logical design. Certain sensitive data, such as personnel job and salary history, can be separated from the remainder of the personnel data and stored as a separate record type in its own database area. From a logical design, this data is shown as a separate entity associated with the person entity.

Record Type Security

Restricting access to a specific record type may be accomplished by area security or by placing special controls on the record in the subschema.

Record Occurrence Security

The structure of a record can be important when designing a record for security. One example uses the first three positions of a record to store a security key, which a generic database procedure matches to the user. If the user key matches, access or updating is permitted.

This level of security involves matching users and individual record occurrences in what can be a very expensive operation. I/O activity must be avoided at all costs or the process will quickly bring the computer to its knees.

Record Content Security

This approach is best implemented by separating those sensitive elements into a separate record type that can be controlled by less expensive processes. If that cannot be accomplished, however, be prepared for expensive and difficult work to implement content security.

Most content security systems require that the system have available more information about the operator than is provided in the normal signon. A personnel file access is often needed, especially if access is partially dependent on the job title or level of the operator. Comparison to data fields is necessary beyond that visible to the operator. The data record in question must be retrieved and tested prior to making it available to the operator (and the program being used by the operator). Database procedures are nearly always used in this situation because they hide the validation process from even the programmer.

8

Audit Requirements

As the scope of database applications expands, the integration of data frequently intrudes on the financial and asset domain of corporate or private auditors. The combination of previously independent data files may act to break down a set of checks and balances that existed in batch file mode.

Of particular concern to the auditor is the ease with which the user can navigate through sensitive data. Security of data that had been previously maintained by physically locking up a reel of tape now must be supported by the DBMS and its associated facilities.

Next is the concern for the safety of the data itself. Again, tape files could be locked in fireproof vaults. On-line disk storage is most often found in large difficult-to-move cabinets that cannot be easily protected or secured. Backup and recovery of the data becomes an important consideration; will the DBMS provide sufficient protection to insure that organization's valuable data assets are not lost or destroyed?

Audit Trails

Those applications that deal with the organization's physical assets, especially money and inventory, are always subject to penetration and fraud. The auditor uses audit trails to detect unauthorized use of the data. Depending on the type of data, audit trails will take several forms. The logical design of the database must consider these alternatives.

Long Term On-line History

This mode of audit trail simply retains data in the database for extended periods of time. Instead of physically deleting obsolete data, the record is flagged as deleted and ignored by the normal processing software.

This mode also requires that the database records contain elements that record the date, time, and person updating the record. The rationale or authorization for the transaction may also be required (what triggered the update to the database).

The advantage of this mode of audit trail is the ease with which it may be accessed by the auditor. A special program to look at all data instead of only active data can be written to supply the auditor with detail information.

There are several disadvantages: 1) The amount of on-line disk storage required is frequently several times that where only current data is stored; 2) Fraudulent activity can be directed against the history too, rendering the audit trail ineffective; 3) Audit data and live data comingle, eliminating any checks and balances that might be accomplished with the audit data physically stored elsewhere.

For the most part, then, long-term on-line history is not a favored method of establishing an audit trail. It is certainly one of the easiest and quickest to implement.

The DBMS Journal

Nearly all DBMS products have a journal file that contains images of the database records that have been updated in one way or another. The IDMS journal, for example, records a combination of the image of the record prior to its change (before image) and the image after the change (after image). New records have only the after image, deletions only the before image.

The journal is ultimately recorded on magnetic tape. It is usually stored away from the immediate computer location to make sure it survives any calamity that might befall the computer center. The journal, plus a snapshot of the database, can be used to rebuild a destroyed or damaged database.

It is possible for the auditor to use the journal to trace activity against certain portions of the database. It certainly will not be easy. Let's assume that our DBMS has created an average of six journal tapes a day (a small number in some installations), six days a week. Thirty-six tapes a week are accumulated. Over a year's time 1872 tapes would be created. If an auditor wished to review all of the transactions for a particular application for one year, the huge volume of tape to be passed could make the job impractical.

The journal as an auditor's tool, therefore, is limited in its usefulness unless a number of special programs are written to extract data regularly for those applications where auditing is expected. Such programs must be controlled carefully so that the extracted data cannot be tampered with and unauthorized activity covered up.

Special Audit Files

There are several ways to create special audit trail files from a DBMS. Some examples will be described in detail in the book on physical design. Basically, however, the application design includes the creation of external database records or files that are loaded with audit trail data. This information is then used directly by auditors to reconstruct transactions.

Special Considerations

Audit trails must be tailored to the application. No one "standard" technique works for all software. The complexity and depth of security of the database must be carefully matched to the *actual working requirements* of the user. Too much control will inhibit the use of the system and burden its processing with unnecessary CPU overhead.

9

Preparing The Logical Design

Every system, regardless of its size, should be completely analyzed and designed before development begins. Database applications especially need this definition because the scope of a system can easily expand at the whim of its users and developers. Since the cast of characters often changes before an application is completed, the definition assists in holding the perspective and continuity of the system at a constant level.

Unfortunately, it is frequently not possible to complete analysis and design before development starts. The users often balk at the lead time required. For this reason, and to involve the user community more heavily, prototyping is often employed to accelerate the analysis and design process.

Looking ahead, the remainder of this chapter will be devoted to the initial analysis associated with the development of a proposal, identifying and categorizing the system's users, strategy for interviewing, and the preparation of DFDs from the results of the interviews. When these functions have been completed, the background of the proposed system should have been defined. We will then be ready to proceed with the details of logical system design.

Top-Down vs Bottom-Up Design

While most of today's experts agree that top-down analysis and design is the most desirable for integrated database development, there is still a lot of controversy. The basis for this controversy is the desires of the user; few are enlightened, understanding, or patient enough to accept the time required to perform effective top-down development.

Our Changing World

Our business environment is changing at an increasing pace. Fifty years ago, the structure of an organization changed only to accommodate new products or growth; some had never altered their organization chart. Thirty years ago, changes in the business forced organization restructures every five years or so. Today, it is not unusual to see significant organization structure changes every six to 12 months. Application development tasks extending beyond that time frame may well be implemented for a new organization that operates in a way different from the new software.

This phenomenon has led to a dramatic change in software development philosophies. Prototyping has become a necessity in many cases. Development methodologies have been altered to include prototyping and increased user involvement. Bottom-up design has increased because time and resources are not available to "do it right."

The emergence of Computer Assisted Software Engineering (CASE) tools is one example of the industry's attempt to provide a solution to the increasing cost and complexity of software development. For the first time, CASE tools provide us with the ability to get a grasp on the complete data picture and show promise to helping develop quality applications quicker.

Bottom-Up Development

In most installations, a wealth of DP applications are already in use. While they are often overlapping and occasionally conflicting, these applications provide the basis for a comprehensive design of the organization's overall data structure.

The Data Administrator can establish the beginning of the corporate data model, quicker and less costly, through the logical integrating of these existing applications. Once completed, this bottom-up design can be smoothed and enhanced by selectively applying top-down information to those areas that are not yet defined or need additional definition.

The System Proposal

When developing new applications, it is essential that a firm documented basis for the systems direction be provided. The remainder of this chapter will address the preparation of a description, clearly understood by both user and developer, that builds the foundation of the application. *Changes undoubtedly will occur as the development progresses*, but the presence of a baseline system document will prevent the direction of the application from straying too far.

The system proposal is directed at management. It should be used as a communications tool to inform management of the size, scope, and boundaries of the system. It is essential that the proposal be clear, concise, and conservative. The plan should contain, as a minimum:

1. *The purpose of the system.* Why is this project being initiated? What will it accomplish in improving the operating capability of the organization?
2. *The scope of the system.* What areas of the organization will be affected by the system? Will the system integrate or interface with other existing or planned systems?
3. *The cost of the system.* How many persons will be required? What computer and support resources are necessary? Don't forget the background costs of training, travel, headhunter fees, etc. Be conservative. Allow adequate lead times, particularly the time necessary to hire and bring aboard skilled database and teleprocessing professionals. It takes an average of 90 to 120 days to locate and bring on board this type of person.
4. *When the system will be available.* How soon will management see visible results from their investment? If the system is to be developed in phases, identify each clearly by the functions that will be available and when. Be sure to provide a Gantt chart of

the schedule and describe the features in terms that user management will understand.

Subsystem Specifications

On all but the smallest systems, subsystems should be defined that group the logical divisions of the system's functions. Each subsystem should be described in the same terms as the system plan defined earlier.

This permits management to assess the impacts and payoffs of each segment of the system, establishing priorities and (if resources are too tight) identifying those portions of the system that may be deferred to a later date. Be sure to indicate the dependency between subsystems. It can be embarrassing if management relegates a critical subsystem to a low priority.

The System's Users

Database systems are, or should be, unique in the manner in which they serve the user community. Conventional file-oriented systems typically serve a very focused user. Database systems, properly designed, can serve not only multiple users, but multiple *levels* of users.

The user levels operating within a database application system can be generally grouped into four classes, each with their own needs and expectations of the system:

1. Executive management. These users, at the vice-president level and above, are primarily concerned with summarized data that identifies trends and data that can be used for planning and decision making purposes. Summary reports of very high level, simulations, and ad hoc "what if" queries characterize this level of user.

    Executive management also has little desire to understand the technical aspects of an application, but is very interested in its cost/benefit analysis and the impact on the competitive position of the organization.

2. Middle management. These users, ranging from second-level managers to those just below the executive management level, require a wider variety of information. They are concerned with trends of their particular area of the business while needing to stay in touch with many of the current and dynamic aspects of the business. Summary reports focused to their area, standard queries of repetitive nature, and ad hoc business status queries are common for this level of user.

   The middle manager, frequently on a budget, will be interested in the operational costs of the application system once it has reached production. The cost of enhancements will be important as this manager will frequently be looking for more information as time goes by.

3. First-level management. These users are much more concerned with the progress of individual tasks under their immediate responsibility. They desire detail reports of productivity and performance of their personnel, scheduling of their tasks, and the results of the work unit. Ad hoc requirements are few. Most interactive data requirements can be supported by predefined dialogs, some with variable replacement capabilities.

   The first-level manager is the key to any system success. The system *must* serve this manager, or at least be perceived as serving this manager. The "What will it do for me?" or "How will this system give me something for the work I have to do to feed it?" type of questions are common and should be expected.

4. The individual worker. This user is concerned with the immediate tasks at hand. Reports are limited to the status of those assigned tasks and a tickler of upcoming tasks. Little, if any, ad hoc querying is required. Where the individual worker utilizes the computer and the database as part of job performance, printed reports and predefined on-line transactions predominate.

   The individual worker is second only to the first-level manager in importance to the system's success. The computer can be a friend, a tool to make the work easier and the worker look better to the boss. If the worker perceives the application as a threat, it will be overtly or covertly sabotaged to remove the threat. *The best computer system is one that is transparent to the worker's performance of their job.*

User Interview Strategy

Interview strategies must, of necessity, vary by the category of user that is to be interviewed. It is important that the approach be tailored to the results expected. It would be useless, for example, to ask a corporate president to describe the detailed information required by a clerk or engineer to perform their jobs.

While you may feel that going into detail about interviewing strategy is overkill or apple pie and motherhood, the information gathered from the user (at all affected levels) is absolutely key to the long-term success of the application. Data gathering cannot be haphazard if it is to be complete. The interview will be more successful if you plan and tailor it to fit the person being interviewed.

The Interviewee List

The list of interviewees changes depending on the type of application system being developed. The basic rule is: The interviewee list should contain representatives from all areas of the organization that will be affected by the system or its upgrade. If the president of the company is directly affected by the system, then the list begins there.

It is dangerous to ignore *any* level of user at the outset. The entire database design can be invalidated if one class of user suddenly identifies requirements that cannot be readily met by the design.

As each level of user is interviewed, a pictorial of the system and its processes should be developed. This pictorial is frequently referred to as a Data Flow Diagram (DFD) and we will consider this the basic pictorial description of a system throughout the book. [1]

This pictorial is reviewed with the interviewees and modified until it represents a true picture of the business process being automated and the relationship to the system *at that level*. Interviews at succeeding lower levels within the organization should expand on the

---

[1]   The structured analysis technique has proved quite successful for the top-down interview approach. There are several methodologies marketed in the country today, each of which has its good and bad points. Throughout the Cookbook, the illustrations associated with the analysis and design functions will be prepared using AUTOMATE Plus/IDMS Architect.

DFD, exploding it to increasing levels of detail corresponding to the organizational view of the processing.

Depending on the vendor, the highest level of DFD is identified as either *level zero* or *level one*. In the Cookbook, we will identify the highest level of DFD as *level zero*.

When interviewing is complete, we should have a level of DFD for each level of user personnel interviewed. The actual number of levels should seldom exceed four; if it does, the DFD will get bogged down in detail.

Interview Results

The following list, while not all-inclusive, identifies some of the major items that should result from each level of interview. The system requirements specification should be updated to reflect these results.

Executive Management

A level zero DFD must result from these interviews. Where executive management provides more details of the component processes, e.g., the high-level breakdown of the personnel department into staffing, payroll, benefits, etc., a level one DFD may also result. Such a level one diagram will be expanded further than interviews at the next level occur.

Executive management should define:

1. *The primary business objective(s)* to be satisfied by the proposed system.
2. *The areas of the organization* that will be affected by the system.
3. *The person(s) who are responsible* for each area that will be affected by the system. This represents much of the shopping list for the next level of interviews.
4. *The types of information and scenarios* of what executive management expects from the system and the responsiveness to inquiry they require.

5. *The level of management commitment and support* that the project can expect in terms of priorities, personnel, and other resources, including financing.

Middle Management

This class of management may encompass several physical layers of supervision within the organization. Each layer must be interviewed. Their contributions, in addition to expanding the DFDs, should include:

1. *A view of the interface* of the manager's area of responsibility with the system.
2. *A view of the interface* between the manager's area of responsibility and other managers at peer level. This adds important insight into the actual workings of the organization at this management level. There are subtleties that must be observed when discussing this point with the interviewee. Valuable keys to organizational politics surface that can have a significant effect on the potential success of an application system that crosses the lines of managers authority.
3. *The expectation of the manager* of the support that the system will provide. This should be as specific and as detailed as possible without getting out of perspective. Follow-up interviews can fill in additional details.

The contribution of each manager should be used to update the DFDs. Normally these DFDs should be at level one. Where successive layers of middle management exist for an area, however, it is possible that the DFD may extend to level two.

First-Level Management

The first-level manager, as we said before, is the key to the success of the system. This manager will have the greatest amount of detail to contribute to the design of any management level. The DFDs of previous levels should be reviewed and enhanced during the interviews. It is possible, even probable, that this manager will find the perceptions of higher level managers to be incorrect when it comes to what the system should do or how the business is conducted.

When that occurs, it is important to identify the anomalies and resolve them at all levels. Be careful not to place any manager at risk by creating controversy during this resolution process.

The first-level manager should provide:

1. *A view of the manager's interface* with the system.
2. *A detailed view of the expectations* of the manager with regard to what support the system will provide. This should include detailed data views, data manipulations, and other considerations that will affect the manager's ability to utilize the system's data.
3. *Physical considerations* (equipment locations, space etc.) which may affect the manager's ability to use the system.
4. *Equipment requirements* to effectively utilize the system. This includes terminals, printers, forms, etc.

Data requirements at the detail element level are required. However, it is a good idea to complete DFDs first and then get into the details during follow-up interviews.

This level of user is very busy with day-to-day concerns. Be extra considerate of their time and keep interviews concise and short.

The Individual Worker

While the first-level manager is singularly key to the success or failure of an application system, the individual worker who must supply data to the database will have the most intimate and continuing contact with the system. The needs of this worker must also be recognized and supported. Just as this worker's supervisor must see benefit from the system, so must the worker at the point of data entry.

The interview of the individual worker(s) should identify:

1. *The specifics of the worker's job.*
2. *The data that the worker requires* to perform the job and the source(s) of that data. Where possible, specifics and copies of forms associated with this data should be included.

3. *The products of the workers efforts.* Identify specific data which results from the efforts and where it goes.
4. *N Specific areas where the system can improve the productivity* of the worker. Identify what the system can do to make it worth the worker's while to support it.

The individual worker is the most frequently overlooked user when it comes to system definition. Usually tasked most heavily to supply data to the system, this level of worker often receives little consideration when designing support features.

PHYSICAL DATABASE DESIGN

Physical database design should just be a logical extension of the logical design if all of the rules have been followed. The problem most DBAs have is that they haven't been introduced to the rules. As a result, physical databases are often created by rote and as a result of experiencing problems with database performance.

This book first introduces the housekeeping activities associated with building a physical database. The features of IDD that enhance and document the design are reviewed in detail. Many techniques and procedures designed to make the job of physical design easier are described.

We then go into physical design in depth. Many types of data structures are dissected and their inner workings explained. Where multiple approaches to solving a problem are available, the most commonly used will be reviewed.

Most importantly, we will walk from the logical to the physical data structure. With the use of the LBMS methodology, this transition is made easier and more effective.

10

Classes and Attributes

It may seem strange that we begin a book on physical design with a chapter on data dictionary classes and attributes. *The data dictionary is critical to effective physical design.* The class/attribute facility provides the dictionary with a cross reference road map that enhances effective use of the dictionary as it becomes larger and more complex.

Classes

What is a Class? What makes it so important? When should it be used? These are a few of the questions frequently asked about classes that this chapter will address.

What is a Class?

A class is a dictionary entity that permits the user to identify a major category or group to which other dictionary entities will belong. The term *APPLICATION* may be identified as a class. It is, in turn, broken into numerous *attributes*, each one a different database application supported by the dictionary. A class, then, is primarily an organizing tool to assist in reporting specialized orders of data in the dictionary; a class functions much like a secondary index.

What Makes It So Important?

The class provides the dictionary user with the ability to group similar characteristics of dictionary contents. The dictionary may be searched on a characteristic without regard to which entities in dictionary are related to that characteristic. For example, the *APPLICATION* class mentioned above can be used as the basis for a dictionary report that will list all elements, record, maps, dialogs, and other entities that are associated with each individual application in the dictionary.

When Should Classes Be Used?

It might seem that classes can be used to set up many different relationships throughout the dictionary. While this is true, too many classes linked to dictionary entities can complicate the dictionary, particularly if an application is to be migrated from one dictionary to another.

The number of classes used in the dictionary should be limited to those that can provide the greatest advantage to dictionary reporting. A list of recommended classes is provided later in this chapter.

Attributes

An attribute is a subset of a class, as used within the IDD. Normally it is the attribute, rather than the class, that is connected to other dictionary entities.

Using our class example of *APPLICATION* above, each attribute of that class would be the acronym of a specific application. Our case study application, *PCS,* would therefore be an attribute to *APPLICATION.*

```
ADD ATTRIBUTE IS EVENT-EXPL WITHIN CLASS IS SCHEMA-SET
APPLCATION IS PCS
COMMENTS
'THIS SET PROVIDES THE ABILITY TO RELATE MULTIPLE EVENTS'
-'OF DIFFERENT TYPES, SUCH AS PROJECTS TO TASKS.'
```

Figure 10-1 SCHEMA-SET Class Example.

Examples Of Classes And Attributes

APPLICATION. This class identifies all of the application projects being developed under IDMS. Its attributes identify the individual application projects, such as *PCS* in our case study. By associating the attribute to each of the dictionary entities within an application, a single list containing all of the elements, records, processes, programs, maps, and tables can be created.

This list is very useful in the management of the project. You can quickly review everything under development for a project. When it comes time to transfer the project materials from one dictionary to another, the list can be used as a basis for the dictionary transfer commands.

If you are using the DME editor product from DBMS, Inc., you can use *APPLICATION* to provide a list of all modules in a particular application for quick selection.

SCHEMA-SET. This class fills a gap in the IDD entity capability. While a set is implicitly defined as part of the schema structure, there is no way for us to explicitly define a set prior to schema compilation. There is no way, for that matter, of enhancing the description of a set after compilation.

Each attribute of the SCHEMA-SET class is a physically defined set. The purpose and conditions of each set definition are included as text. The attribute is then linked to each record that participates in the set, either as owner or member. The text describes the individual relationship in detail.

Properly used, this class provides detailed documentation of the set structure and the basis for schema source definition. Figure 10-1 illustrates how the SCHEMA-SET class is used.

MESSAGE-DEFINED. The message area of the dictionary is physically separate from message area of the main dictionary. Because of this, there is no class-attribute link to messages. This class is intended to provide that link for documentation and control purposes.

One of the essentials of good dialog documentation is to identify the messages used by the dialog. This can be done by textual documenting or by using the class-attribute. The class-attribute is preferable for two reasons:

1. *The message need only be documented once.* Special uses of the message in the dialog can be described in the text portion of the class/attribute relationship.
2. *Reviewing the message attribute* identifies all of the dialogs that use the message. If the text of the message is to be changed, the impact on the overall system can be assessed quickly.

Figure 10-2 illustrates the use of the class-attribute arrangement.

PFKEYS. This class was originally installed to support the PF-key display facility that appears at the bottom of the screen in our case study. Use of the class has progressed, however, to management of PF-key usage. Reviewing the individual attributes by the dictionary administrator (PF1, PF2, etc.) quickly identifies that dialogs use the keys. Again, the impact of a potential change of PF-key usage can be readily assessed. Figure 10-3 illustrates the use of this class.

RECORD-ID. This class is used primarily for documenting the advance assignment of schema record identifiers to records in the dictionary. Individual attributes are the identifier numbers (1401, 4101, etc.). An attribute report will also quickly identify overlapping use of the identifiers.

LOCATION-MODE. This class, like the RECORD-ID class, is used to document the record that will appear in a schema. The attributes are always CALC, VIA, DIRECT, SEQUENTIAL.

RECORD-FORMAT. This is the third in the series of descriptive classes associated with schema records. The attributes are FIXED, VARIABLE, and VARIABLE-COMPRESSED.

```
ADD CLASS MESSAGE-DEFINED
   DELETION LOCK IS ON
   COMMENTS
   'THIS CLASS PROVIDES THE ABILITY TO ASSOCIATE MESSAGES WITH'
  -'APPLICATIONS, MODULES, MAPS, AND PROGRAMS.  SINCE THE'
  -'MESSAGE ENTITY ITSELF DOES NOT HAVE A CLASS-ATTRIBUTE'
  -'LINK, THIS CLASS SUBSTITUTES.'
ATTRIBUTES ARE MESSAGE IDENTIFIERS.'.

ADD ATTRIBUTE DC930001 WITHIN CLASS MESSAGE-DEFINED  APPLICATION
IS PCS
COMMENTS 'ORGANIZATION NOT FOUND IN DATABASE'.
```

AFTER LINKING TO MODULES AND PROGRAMS, DISPLAY:

```
ADD ATTRIBUTE DC930001 WITHIN CLASS MESSAGE-DEFINED  APPLICATION
IS PCS
COMMENTS 'ORGANIZATION NOT FOUND IN DATABASE'
MODULE SCAPC002 VERSION 26 LANGUAGE IS PROCESS
   TEXT IS 'ORGANIZATION NOT FOUND IN DB'
MODULE SCAPP060 VERSION 26 LANGUAGE IS PROCESS
   TEXT IS 'ORGANIZATION NOT FOUND IN DB'
PROGRAM SCADS060 VERSION 26
   TEXT IS 'ORGANIZATION NOT FOUND IN DB'.
```

WITHIN MODULE SCAPP060, THE ATTRIBUTE IS SHOWN AS:

```
ADD MODULE NAME SCAPP060 VERSION IS 26 LANGUAGE IS PROCESS
MODULE DESCRIPTION 'PCS ORGANIZATION CMTS PREMAP'  APPLICATION
IS PCS
MESSAGE-DEFINED IS DC930001
   TEXT 'ORGANIZATION NOT FOUND IN DB'.
```

Figure 10-2   Message-Defined Class Example.

The preceding three classes described are illustrated in Figure 10-4 as part of the description of a PCS record.

```
ADD CLASS NAME IS PFKEYS   DELETION LOCK IS ON
ADD ATTRIBUTE PF1 WITHIN CLASS PFKEYS
COMMENTS 'PROGRAMS USING PF1'.
```

DISPLAY OF ATTRIBUTE WILL SHOW PROGRAMS USING PF1

```
ADD ATTRIBUTE PF1 WITHIN CLASS PFKEYS
COMMENTS 'PROGRAMS USING PF1'
PROGRAM IS SCADS070 VERSION 26 TEXT IS 'F1:HELP'
PROGRAM IS SCADS060 VERSION 26 TEXT IS 'F1:HELP'
```

WITHIN PROGRAM LISTING OF SCADS060, PF KEYS ARE SHOWN:

```
ADD PROGRAM NAME SCADS060 VERSION 26 . . .
PFKEYS IS PF1 TEXT IS 'F1:HELP'
PFKEYS IS PF2 TEXT IS 'F2:INSERT' . . .
```

Figure 10-3   PFKEYS Class Example.

CATEGORY. This class replaces ELEMENT DESIGNATOR. It was created so that a category of data could extend beyond data elements. A single class eliminated the need for multiple classes, one for each entity. Several of the attributes to this class are discussed below.

PRIMARY ELEMENT. This class identifies all of the data elements within the dictionary that are classed as *primary*. The primary elements are those that are used as the basis for all other element definitions. *MONTH* and *DAY* are typical primary elements.

STANDARD ELEMENT. The class identifies those data elements that have been approved as an installation standard. In contrast to the PRIMARY ELEMENT, this attribute is limited to those that have passed a formal standardization process.

Element and record data descriptors identify elements, element groups, and records. Some of the most common ones are: **TEXT,**

```
ADD RECORD NAME IS PCS-ORGAN VERSION 1
RECORD DESCRIPTION 'ORGANIZATION MASTER RECORD'
APPLICATION IS PCS
RECORD-ID IS 4130
LOCATION-MODE IS CALC TEXT 'PCS-ORGAN-IDENT DN'
RECORD-FORMAT IS VARIABLE-COMPRESSED.
```

Figure 10-4   Record Definition With Special Classes.

SUBSCRIPT, POINTER, DBKEY, NUMBER, COUNTER, DATE, TIME, KEY, JUNCTION, and **NEST**. Linking elements and records to descriptors (more than one may be associated with an individual element or record) makes locating generic types of data easier. It also enhances the documentation with minimal effort.

11

User-Defined Comments And Nests

User-Defined Comments

The User-Defined-Comment (UDC) is one of the most powerful documentation tools provided within IDD. Unfortunately, the UDC gets little attention. In the examples following, we will use UDCs for both specialized comments and for dialog driving data.

TEST-PLAN provides a description of the process and dialog test plan. The programmer and analyst may include detailed tests to be performed against each process and dialog. The results of the tests are also entered. See Figure 11-1 for an abbreviated example.

```
MODIFY PROGRAM IS SCADS020
TEST-PLAN
'EXECUTE DAILOG, ATTEMPT:
-'   1.  ADD PROJECT THAT ALREADY EXISTS - (ERROR)'
-'   2.  CHANGE NON-ESISTING PROJECT - (ERROR)'
-'   3.  DELETE NON-EXISTING PROJECT - (ERROR)'
-'   4.  CHANGE EXISTING PROJECT WITH ALL PRIORITY CODES'
-'   5.  CHANGE EXISTING PROJECT WITH ALL TYPE CODES'
-'   6.  CHANGE EXISTING PROJECT WITH ALL STATUS CODES'
-'   7.  CHANGE EXISTING PROJECT WITH INVALID PRIORITY CODES'
-'       (ERROR)'
-'  8.  CHANGE EXISTING PROJECT WITH INVALID TYPE CODES'
-'  9.  CHANGE EXISTING PROJECT WITH INVALID STATUS CODES'
-' 10.  ATTEMPT TO DELETE PROJECT OTHER THAN CLOSED'
-'       OR CANCELLED.'
```

Figure 11-1   UDC TEST-PLAN Example.

PROGRAM-FUNCTIONS describes the functions that a program or dialog is to perform. It permits using the dictionary as the repository of program specifications prior to actual coding (see Figure 11-2).

PROGRAM-HELP is the basic source of information for the integrated HELP facility described elsewhere in the Cookbook. An un-

```
MODIFY PROGRAM SCADS020 VERSION IS 1
PROGRAM-FUNCTION
'THIS  DIALOG  ADD,  CHANGES,  AND  LOGICALLY'
-'DELETES  PROJECTS  FROM  THE  PCS  DATABASE'
-'THE  DIALOG  STORES  AN  EVENT  RECORD  AND  A  PROJECT'
-'MEMBER  RECORD.'
-'PROJECT  IDENTIFIERS  MUST  BE  UNIQUE  AND  ARE  ASSIGNED'
-'IN  SEQUENTIAL  ASCENDING  ORDER  BY  TESTING  THE  PROJECT'
-'IDENTIFIER  INDEX  FOR  THE  LAST  ENTRY.'.
```

Figure 11-2   UDC PROGRAM-FUNCTION Example.

```
MODIFY   PROGRAM   SCADS020   VERSION   IS   1
PROGRAM-HELP
   'TRANSACTION PURPOSE:    UPDATE THE PROJECT'
   -'   DATA WITHIN THE ROJECT CONTROL SYSTEM (PCS)'
   -'   DATABASE.'
   -'PROCESSING OPTIONS:'
   -'   PF1 - HELP'
   -'   PF2 - ADD DESCRIPTION'
   -'   PF3  - ASSOCIATE ORGANIZATIONS'
   -'   PF4 - ASSIGN PEOPLE'
   -'   PF6 - PREPARE REPORTS'.
```

Figure 11-3   UDC PROGRAM-HELP Example.

limited number of lines of formatted text may be prepared, which is then displayed whenever the operator presses PF1 (see Figure 11-3).

MESSAGE-HELP extends the HELP facility, displaying information to the operator about a specific message that has occurred as part of application processing. Depending on the programmer's desires, this text may be displayed instead of the PROGRAM-HELP data when the operator presses PF1 (see Figure 11-4).

```
MODIFY   MESSAGE   DC910326
MESSAGE-HELP
   'THE   DATABASE   RECORD   REQUESTED   BY   THIS'
   -'TRANSACTION   CANNOT   BE   LOCATED   IN   THE'
   -'DATABASE. REVIEW   YOUR   INPUT   DATA   AND   TRY'
   -'AGAIN.   IF   THE   PROBLEM   REPEATS,   ATTEMPT   TO'
   -'RETRIEVE   THE   DATA   USING   THE   "INQ"   OPTION.'.
```

Figure 11-4   UDC MESSAGE-HELP Example.

```
MODIFY  ELEMENT  PROJ-BEGIN-DATE  VERSION  1
ELEMENT-HELP
   'THIS  ELEMENT  CONTAINS  THE  DATE  WHEN  THE'
   'PERFORMANCE  OF  THE  PROJECT  ACTUALLY'
 -'BEGAN,  USING  THE  FORMAT  YY/MM/DD.'
```

Figure 11-5   UDC ELEMENT-HELP Example.

ELEMENT-HELP is also an extension of the HELP facility, permitting the operator to display information about a specific data element (see Figure 11-5).

ELEMENT RANGE DESCRIPTION overcomes a shortcoming of IDD, the inability to include descriptive comments about the data element range clauses. This UDC covers that requirement, permitting extensive comments about each range value (see Figure 11-6).

VALIDATION-CRITERIA separates element specifications for the validation of data element contents from normal comments. Here we specifically identify those conditions that the programmer must support logically to ensure the integrity of data (see Figure 11-7).

```
MODIFY  ELEMENT  PROJ-BEG-MONTH  VERSION  1
RANGE-DESCRIPTION
   'THIS  ELEMENT  HAS  A  VALID  RANGE  OF  1  THRU  12'
 -'CORRESPONDING  TO  THE  MONTHS  OF  A  YEAR.'.
```

Figure 11-6   UDC RANGE-DESCRIPTION Example.

```
MODIFY ELEMENT PROJ-BEG-DAY VERSION 1
VALIDATION-CRITERIA
   'THE ELEMENT HAS VALID RANGES DEPENDING ON'
  -'THE CONTENT OF PROJ-BEG-MONTH AND PROJ-BEG-CENT-YR:'
  -' 1. IF MONTH = 04, 06, 09, OR 11, THE VALID RANGE'
  -'        IS 01-30.'
  -' 2. IF MONTH = 02 AND CENT-YR IS EVENLY'
  -'        DIVISIBLE BY 4, THE VALID RANGE IS 01-29;'
  -'        OTHERWISE THE VALID RANGE IS 01-28.'.
```

Figure 11-7   UDC VALIDATION-CRITERIA Example.

PROGRAM-OPTION is an example of using the facility as the data
source of control information used by a dialog. The two-level controller gets its menu data from this UDC. The advantages are several:
(1) the documentation of the program is enhanced, (2) the program
may be generalized to accept an array, (3) the array can be easily
changed, and (4) it is not necessary to build an auxiliary file for the
array data (see Figure 11-8). The disadvantage of this UDC is that a
dictionary access is required to read the array, presenting a potential
bottleneck in high-usage environments.

```
MODIFY  PROGRAM  SCADM000 VERSION  1
PROGRAM-OPTION
     '00,SCADS005,TERMINATE  PROCESSING'
   -'01,SCADS030,ORGANIZATION  MAINTENANCE'
   -'02,SCADS020,PROJECT  MAINTENANCE'
   -'03,SCBDS010,TASK  MAINTENANCE'
   -'04,SCBDS040,MILESTONE  MAINTENANCE'
   -'05,SCADS310,PERSON  MAINTENANCE'
   -'06,SCADS070,ORGANIZATION  REPORTS'
```

Figure 11-8   UDC PROGRAM-OPTION Example.

```
MODIFY PROCESS SCAPR030 VERSION 1
INCLUDED-MODULE SY2PR002 V 1 TEXT 'HELP'
INCLUDED-MODULE SCAPC001 V 1 TEXT 'DATE VALIDATE'
INCLUDED-MODULE SCAPC002 V 1 TEXT 'TYPE VALIDATE'.
```

Figure 11-9   An Example Of UDN INCLUDED-MODULE.

Reporting From UDCs

The data dictionary structure under which the user-defined comment
is established permits reporting all of a particular UDC as a group.
Each UDC is identified as an *attribute* within the class *USER-
DEFINED-COMMENT*. Each time a particular UDC occurs, TEST-
PLAN for example, a junction is created within the dictionary to the
entity under which the comment is entered. This connection permits
us to run a class-attribute dictionary report and print the details of
all test plans.

User-Defined-Nests

The User Defined Nest (UDN) facility permits assigning a logical association between occurrences of the same dictionary entity. This
facility takes advantage of the nest record that exists for most principal entities within IDD. Some examples are of this:

INCLUDED-MODULE. This UDN identifies the link between a
process and an INCLUDEd routine, which is also a process. ADSO
does not create the dictionary link between a process and the one it
includes, so this UDN accomplishes the task. Again, the approach
serves the dual purpose of enhancing documentation and identifying
all of the places an included module is used (see Figure 11-9).

```
MODIFY ELEMENT PERSON-SALARY-RATE VERSION 1
DEPENDENT-ELEMENT
    'THE VALUE OF THIS FIELD MUST BE WITHIN THE RANGE OF'
  -'VALUES ASSOCIATED THE SALARY-GRADE FIELD CONTENTS'
  -'UNLESS THE SALARY-RATE-EXCEPTION FIELD IS SET'
  -'TO A VALUE OF 1.'
```

Figure 11-10   UDN DEPENDENT-ELEMENT Example.

DEPENDENT-ELEMENT. It is not unusual for the presence of a data element occurrence to be dependent on the occurrence of another element elsewhere in the database. For example, the value of a weekly salary field may be dependent upon the pay grade field that identifies the minimum and maximum salary amounts for that pay grade. The weekly salary field is dependent upon the pay grade field (see Figure 11-10).

12

General Naming Conventions

Back in the early days of IDMS few of us fully understood the need for standards, particularly standard naming conventions. Unfortunately, it took some real life trauma to bring home the need to define our standards *before* we got in the middle of a database implementation.

Our Cullinet (then Cullinane) reps told us that standards were essential to the effective use of database. Chaos would result, we were told, if we did not implement effective standards before designing our first database. Unfortunately for many, no one explained what standards to use.

This chapter describes successful baseline standards for IDMS usage. While there are others around, and some are better for individual situations and environments, these have worked well in several different installations.

Standardized Format

A basic naming format, eight characters long, can be used to support a majority of the entities used by IDMS in program development. Properly used, this format will establish a thread of reference between program entities, making visual reference easy. Figure 12-1 illustrates the format. By establishing a set of naming criteria within

A B C D E 000

WHERE:

1. A — identifies the major organization developing software, as-signed by Data Administration.
2. B — identifies the major application project within the or-ganization, assigned by Data Administration.
3. C · — identifies the subsystem within the major application project, assigned by the project manager.
4. D — identifies the entity being named, fixed by standard.
5. E — identifies a subset of the entity being defined, fixed by standard.
6. 000 — a unique identifier of the entity occurrence, assigned by the project manager.

Figure 12-1   The Program Entity Naming Convention.

the standard, it is possible to easily identify those entities that par-ticipate within an application. Figure 12-2 provides an example.

The primary feature of this naming approach is that complete separation of development projects is assured while minimizing the amount of interaction necessary between DBA and development staffs. With each group responsible for specifying certain of the name characters, a majority of the detail assignments are performed by the application staff, reducing the bureaucracy to a minimum.

Record And Element Naming

There are more "standards" for naming data elements and records than we can discuss. I have reviewed, and used, several over the years. Each has its good and bad points.

Before we look at a standard, let's look at the audience. Who will view the elements and records? There are some key considerations based on the answer to that question:

1. *The system developers (DBAs, analysts, programmers) will have intimate contact* with the most detailed element in the applica-

Dialog	SCADS130
Premap Process	SCAPP130
Enter Response Process	SCAPR130
Add Response Process	SCAPR131
Change Response Process	SCAPR132
Delete Response Process	SCAPR133
Inquiry Response Process	SCAPR134
Dialog Work Record	SCARW130
Map	SCAM0130
Map Work Record	SCARM130
Edit Table	SCATE130
Edit Table 2	SCATE131
Decode Table	SCATC130

Figure 12-2   ADSO Entity Assignment Example.

tion. For them, structured naming conventions and abbreviations are acceptable.

2. *End users who are permitted to utilize direct query facilities, such as OLQ and OLE, will not recognize or understand the use of records and elements that are too cryptic. For this group, names must be meaningful.*

3. *The users of formatted transactions require meaningful literal extensions of the elements* to identify what data to enter. The actual name of the data elements and records is of little concern.

The elusive happy medium can be achieved through using some of the following points (although not all will be applicable in every instance):

1. *Elements should be defined in a hierarchy.* The base of the hierarchy is the so-called primary or standard element. This element name provides the principal description of the data purpose, format, and function. Extensions of the element name are created for schema and work records that must contain the element. (The extensions, called *synonym extensions*, group together all the records containing the element under a common prefix while maintaining each record's unique identifier.)

2. *The maximum length of a primary* element should be 24 bytes. Since the COBOL compiler limit is 30 bytes, this leaves 6 bytes for the synonym extension.

3. *Synonym extensions should prefix the element. This permits easy stripping of the prefix for end-user display purposes.*

4. Synonym prefixes should make the use of the element quickly understood (see Figure 12-3). Suggested prefixes include:

   a. *S0000-* is a schema record element, with the digits identifying the record ID of the schema record. For flexibility in changing the record IDs without affecting the application code, you might consider using the last three digits of the record ID only. Therefore, a record ID of "1204" might use a prefix of "S0204." This is only valid if the system uses record IDs in the same thousand range.

   b. *W-* is used for work record elements.

   c. *M-* is used for map work record elements.

   d. *S-* is used for scratch work record elements.

   e. *Q-* is used for queue work record elements.

5. *The name of the element may be broken into sections*, separated by hyphens. Each section should be meaningful to the casual viewer. As a general rule, the element should not contain more than five segments; the fewer the number of segments, the easier it is to read. Remember that you can categorize elements through use of the ELEMENT DESIGNATOR class. This class permits adding grouping to an element that does not have to be present in the element name. For example, the element PART-NUMBER is an access key to the database. The element can be identified by ELEMENT DESIGNATOR IS KEY with the need to add KEY to the element name.

6. *Record names should be meaningful* while remaining within the 16-byte limit imposed by IDMS. Where the same record name may be used for multiple applications, the simple use of a prefix to make it unique is often desirable to avoid confusion.

7. *Check the reserve word list* for both elements and records to ensure that you do not use a COBOL or IDMS reserved word. These errors show up long after you are down the development path and require a lot of rework to correct.

Schema Record Prefix

```
ADD REC PCS-DESCR-DETL V 1.
  02   S4104-PCS-DETAIL-SEQ              PIC 99999.
  02   S4104-PCS-DESCRIPTION-TEXT.
    03   S4104-PCS-TEXT-LINE             PIC X(60) OCCURS 10.
```

Work Record Prefix

```
ADD REC SCARW000 V 1.
  02   W-SUBA                            PIC S9(8) COMP VALUE +1.
  02   W-SUBB                            PIC S9(8) COMP VALUE +1.
  02   W-SUBC                            PIC S9(8) COMP VALUE +1.
  02   W-SUBD                            PIC S9(8) COMP VALUE +1.
  02   W-UDC-IDENT                       PIC (32).
```

Map Work Record Prefix

```
ADD REC SY1RM001 V 1.
  02   M-SUB10                           PIC S9999 COMP.
  02   M-PFKEY-LINE.
    03   M-PFKEY-GROUP OCCURS 5.
      04   M-PFKEY-INDICATOR             PIC XXX.
      04   M-PFKEY-TEXT                  PIC X(8).
```

Scratch Work Record Prefix

```
ADD REC SZGRS001 V 1.
  02   S-SUB1                            PIC S9999 COMP.
  02   S-DIALOG-IDENT                    PIC X(8).
  02   S-DIALOG-VERS                     PIC S9999 COMP.
  02   S-DIALOG-TITLE                    PIC X(40).
```

Queue Work Record Prefix

```
ADD REC SZGRQ001 V 1.
  02   Q-SUB1                            PIC S9999 COMP.
  02   Q-DIALOG-IDENT                    PIC X(8).
  02   Q-DIALOG-VERS                     PIC S9999 COMP.
  02   Q-DIALOG-TITLE                    PIC X(40).
```

Figure 12-3 Synonym Prefix Examples.

The bottom line for element and record naming is to establish a convention that is comfortable for your environment *and then stick by it*.

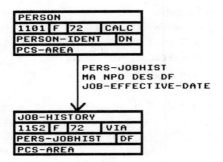

Figure 12-4   Naming Simple Owner-Member Sets.

Set Naming

The most common set naming convention, one that closely follows the way that Cullinet names the sets within the IDMS directory, uses the record names of the owner and member of the set. This is very effective for simple owner-member sets. It leaves something to be desired, however, when the set has multiple members or a special purpose.

The conventions following cover all of the common set structures. From them, you can create conventions for the exotic structures.

1. Simple owner-member sets. As mentioned previously, the most descriptive set name for a simple owner-member set is to concatenate the first seven characters of each record (beginning with the owner) and separate them with a hyphen. For example, a set between PERSON and JOB-HISTORY could be named *PERSON-JOBHIST*. Figure 12-4 illustrates this type of set.

2. Forked sets. The forked set, with multiple members, does not lend itself to the format described earlier. Since the members are all "auxiliary" to the owner, the name of the owner is concatenated with "AUX"; a set between EVENT and two or more auxiliary supporting record types would be named *EVENT-AUX* (see Figure 12-5).

3. Nest sets. Each nest structure typically has two sets: the component or explosion set and the where-used or implosion set. The explosion set should use *EXPL* as the second part of the

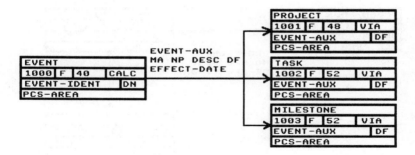

Figure 12-5 Forked Set Naming Example.

set name while the implosion set should use *IMPL*. A nest record associated with the EVENT owner, for example, would have an explosion set with the name *EVENT-EXPL* and an implosion set named *EVENT-IMPL* (see Figure 12-6).

4. Many-to-many. The many-to-many set relationship places a junction record between two principal record types. The intent, however, is to relate the principals. The naming of the sets, therefore, ideally ought to reflect the principal owners and ignore the junction. For example, a relationship between ORGAN and EVENT, shown in Figure 12-7, would have the set between ORGAN and the junction (ORG-EVENT) named *ORGAN-EVENT* and the set between EVENT and the junction named *EVENT-ORGAN*.

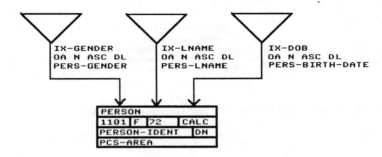

Figure 12-6 Nest Record Set Naming Example.

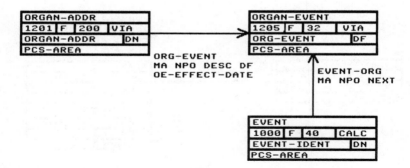

Figure 12-7   Index Set Naming Example.

5. Index sets. Index sets are a special breed. They have no real owner but need to be clearly identified as indexes. Therefore, the owner part of the name is replaced by *IX*. The use of the member record name (the one the index points to) does not work well if multiple indexes are assigned to the same record. It is more descriptive if the element on which the index depends is used. Figure 12-8 illustrates the use of this technique on the PERSON record where more than one index is present.

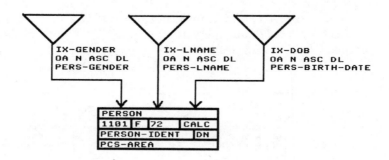

Figure 12-8   Many-To-Many Set Naming Example.

```
Area Name  =  CUSTOMER-AREA

File Name  =  CUSTOMER or

File Name  =  CUSTOMEA
              CUSTOMEB
              CUSTOMEC
```

Figure 12-9   File Name Illustration.

Areas

The area name is composed of two segments, the name itself and a suffix. The name itself is limited to eight characters in length and will correspond to the name of the principal file associated with an area. The format is:

[area name]-AREA

where

[area name] is the actual name of the area in 8 bytes or less. The name should be descriptive where possible.

AREA is the literal suffix that uniquely identifies the area from the file name.

Files

The file name for a database data set will be 1 to 8 bytes in length and be identical to the principal name of the area it supports. If an area is supported by more than one file, an alphabetic suffix will be appended to the file name. If the file name is already at 8 bytes, the eighth byte will be replaced by the suffix. Figure 12-9 illustrates the file naming convention.

13

Normalization

One of the hardest decisions about this book was where to put a chapter on normalization. While normalization is frequently included in logical design, it really does not fit there. Normalization is a physical process. While the results may have some effect on logical design, the principal beneficiary is the physical database structure.

Once the decision was made to place the chapter in the physical design book, the next question was where. Like an understanding of some data dictionary concepts will be useful to physical design, so will an understanding of the normalization process. The final decision is as you see it, preceding the definition of elements and records.

This chapter should serve not only as an introduction to normalization; but also as a way to further an understanding of the concept and why we want to normalize in the first place. Just as important, we must understand when to use normalized structures and when to ignore them. A final point: *Normalization is a tool, just one of many in the database designers kit. Used properly, it will help build a productive database structure. Used without intelligence, normalization can result in severe performance impacts.*

What Is Normalization?

We have been hearing the term for a number of years. James Martin
has been at the forefront of the movement to normalize our database
structures. Only with the increased presence of relational systems,
however, has normalization been taken seriously.

There are three common forms of normalization, known as the
first, second, and third normal form. Basically, they are progressive
stages in the analysis of data. Each succeeding stage builds on its
predecessor to more closely control and relate individual data elements. The goal is to identify data in its simplest form. Unfortunately, the process has been made more complex than needed and few
designers have really made a serious effort to normalize data.

The Three Normal Forms

We will look briefly at the three forms of normalization to gain a
basic understanding before going into the depths of the process.

First Normal Form

A record is in first normal form if it has no repeating groups. That
seems simple and it is. A first normal form record will be fixed
length (unless it is compressed). Most records defined by IDMS
DBAs qualify as first normal form (see Figure 13-1).

Second Normal Form

A record is in second normal form when:

1. *It is in first normal form.* Each succeeding form requires that
   the preceding form rules have been met.
2. *All of the elements in the record are directly dependent* on the
   key fields of the record. This assumes that the key is more
   than one field and that the remaining elements of the record
   require *all* key values in order to exist (see Figure 13-2).

```
ADD RECORD NAME IS EVENT VERSION 1
02   EVENT-IDENT.
   03    EVENT-TYPE                 PIC X.
   03    EVENT-IDENTIFIER           PIC X(12).
02   EVENT-EFF-DATE.
   03    EVENT-EFF-CENT-YR.
      04    EVENT-EFF-CENTURY       PIC 99.
      04    EVENT-EFF-YEAR          PIC 99.
   03    EVENT-EFF-MONTH            PIC 99.
   03    EVENT-EFF-DAY              PIC 99.
02   EVENT-TITLE                    PIC X(40).
02   EVENT-PRIORITY                 PIC 9.
02   EVENT-STATUS                   PIC X.
02   EVENT-EST-LABOR                PIC 9(5).
02   EVENT-EST-COMPUTER             PIC 9999.
02   EVENT-ACT-LABOR                PIC 9(5)V9.
02   EVENT-ACT-COMPUTER             PIC 9999V99.
02   EVENT-PRIME-REQUESTOR          PIC X(12).
02   EVENT-SECOND-REQUESTOR         PIC X(12).
02   EVENT-PRIME-PERFORMER          PIC X(12).
02   EVENT-SECOND-PERFORMER         PIC X(12).
```

Figure 13-1   First Normal Data Form.

Third Normal Form

A record is in third normal form when:

1. *It is in second normal form.*
2. *No nonkey field determines the value of any other nonkey field.*
   What this means is that every field in the record MUST be
   directly dependent on the key and the key MUST be a single
   field (see Figure 13-3). The third normal form, frankly, is
   easier to understand than second normal form. But many
   people get hung up on the transition from first to second form
   and never get to the third form.

```
ADD RECORD NAME IS EVENT VERSION 1
02  EVENT-IDENT.
    03   EVENT-TYPE                 PIC X.
    03   EVENT-IDENTIFIER           PIC X(12).
02  EVENT-EFF-DATE.
    03   EVENT-EFF-CENT-YR.
         04   EVENT-EFF-CENTURY     PIC 99.
         04   EVENT-EFF-YEAR        PIC 99.
    03   EVENT-EFF-MONTH            PIC 99.
    03   EVENT-EFF-DAY              PIC 99.
02  EVENT-TITLE                     PIC X(40).
02  EVENT-PRIORITY                  PIC 9.
02  EVENT-STATUS                    PIC X.
02  EVENT-EST-LABOR                 PIC 9(5).
02  EVENT-EST-COMPUTER              PIC 9999.
02  EVENT-ACT-LABOR                 PIC 9(5)V9.
02  EVENT-ACT-COMPUTER              PIC 9999V99.
```

Figure 13-2   Second Normal Form Data Structure.

Why Normalize?

Normalization is supposed to create a database structure whose elements are so tightly coupled that abnormal processing conditions cannot compromise the integrity of the database. We are familiar with the presence of validation conditions that require certain data values to be present in one database location in order that other incoming data will be valid. Properly normalized, the database contents would interrelate to minimize or eliminate such conditional situations.

Of particular interest are the problems that often occur when deleting data. Normalized data is kept within the same record. Deleting the record removes all related data, eliminating the problem of leaving data elsewhere in the database compromised because of the delete. This type of integrity control is provided today within IDMS by set structure; in most relational systems, software must provide the control if the data is not in third normal form.

Normalization, therefore, provides a form of integrity control and cross-checking. By rule, it implements the necessary processes that

```
ADD RECORD NAME IS EVENT VERSION 1
02  EVENT-IDENT.
   03  EVENT-TYPE              PIC X.
   03  EVENT-IDENTIFIER        PIC X(12).


ADD RECORD NAME IS SINGLE-EVENT VERSION 1
02  EVENT-IDENTIFIER           PIC X(12)
02  EVENT-EFF-DATE.
   03  EVENT-EFF-CENT-YR.
      04  EVENT-EFF-CENTURY    PIC 99.
      04  EVENT-EFF-YEAR       PIC 99.
   03  EVENT-EFF-MONTH         PIC 99.
   03  EVENT-EFF-DAY           PIC 99.
02  EVENT-TITLE                PIC X(40).
02  EVENT-PRIORITY             PIC 9.
02  EVENT-STATUS               PIC X.
02  EVENT-EST-LABOR            PIC 9(5).
02  EVENT-EST-COMPUTER         PIC 9999.
02  EVENT-ACT-LABOR            PIC 9(5)V9.
02  EVENT-ACT-COMPUTER         PIC 9999V99.


ADD RECORD NAME IS EVENT-REQUESTOR VERSION 1
02  EVENT-IDENTIFIER           PIC X(12).
02  EVENT-REQUEST-TYPE         PIC X.
02  EVENT-REQUESTOR            PIC X(12).


ADD RECORD NAME IS EVENT-PERFORMER VERSION 1
02  EVENT-IDENTIFIER           PIC X(12).
02  EVENT-PERFORMER-TYPE       PIC X.
02  EVENT-PERFORMER            PIC X(12).
```

Figure 13-3   Third Normal Form Data Structure.

permit relational tables to maintain data integrity. If the DBMS itself provides this integrity control, *normalization becomes an academic exercise.* Since most relational DBMSs do not provide adequate integrity control, *normalization becomes essential to relational database design.*

Normalization in Network Data Structures

Few network databases are implemented in the third normal form. It simply slows down processing too much. The first normal form, on the other hand, is the rule in network data structures. Few of us build repeating data groups anymore except to enhance processing speed, and those groups are part of multiple-occurring record types.

Planned redundancy is common throughout network databases. This is the practical way to increase performance on retrieval and to separate (segment) databases for greater flexibility.

The Normalization Process

Since each succeeding form of normalizing requires that we have achieved the previous form, the third normal form is reached by performing forms one and two first.

First Normal Form

A record, such as the ORGAN-DESCR-HDR, is a good candidate for normalization. Figure 13-4 illustrates the record in its schema form. It consists of basic header information plus 10 lines of text.

The rules for attaining first normal form are:

1. *Create a new entity for each repeating group.* This is reflected by Figure 13-5, with the 10 lines of text removed from the basic record.
2. *Define a set relationship* between the remaining part of ORGAN-DESCR-HDR and the text line record (see Figure 13-6).
3. *List the elements of the repeating group and identify its primary key.* Here we run into a problem. The text lines, as originally defined, have no key of their own. We must, therefore, establish a key. Figure 13-7 illustrates the identification of a sequence number as the unique key for each line of text.

With this last step, we have normalized ORGAN-DESCR-HDR to the first normal form. Before proceeding to the second normal form, however, we need to analyze what has happened to the record from

```
ADD RECORD NAME IS ORGAN-DESCR-HDR.
02  ORG-HDR-TYPE                          PIC X.
02  ORG-HDR-EFF-DATE.
  03  ORG-HDR-EFF-CENT-YR.
      04  ORG-HDR-EFF-CENTURY            PIC 99.
      04  ORG-HDR-EFF-YEAR               PIC 99.
  03  ORG-HDR-EFF-MONTH                  PIC 99.
  03  ORG-HDR-EFF-DAY                    PIC 99.
02  ORG-HDR-SECURITY                      PIC XX.
02  ORG-HDR-DESCR-CATEGORY                PIC X.
02  ORG-HDR-DESCR-PRIORITY                PIC 9.
02  ORG-HDR-DESCR-EFF-DATE
  03  ORG-HDR-DESCR-EFF-CENT-YR.
      04  ORG-HDR-DESCR-EFF-CENTURY      PIC 99.
      04  ORG-HDR-DESCR-EFF-YEAR         PIC 99.
  03  ORG-HDR-DESCR-EFF-MONTH            PIC 99
  03  ORG-HDR-DESCR-EFF-DAY              PIC 99.
02  ORG-HDR-LAST-UPDATE-DATE.
  03  ORG-HDR-UPDATE-CENT-YR.
      04  ORG-HDR-UPDATE-CENTURY         PIC 99.
      04  ORG-HDR-UPDATE-YEAR            PIC 99.
  03  ORG-HDR-UPDATE-MONTH               PIC 99.
  03  ORG-HDR-UPDATE-DAY                 PIC 99.
02  ORG-HDR-UPDATE-PERSON                 PIC X(10).
02  ORG-HDR-LINES                         PIC 99.
02  ORG-HDR-LINE-GROUP.
  03  ORG-HDR-LINE                        PIC X(60) OCCURS 10.
```

Figure 13-4   First Normal Form Processing Example.

the time we started the normalizing process. With this analysis it is possible to gain some insight on why some data is normalized and some left in an unnormalized format.

First, a review of the unnormalized record:

1. The inclusion of the 10 lines of text into the basic record was done to provide an initial group of lines for operator entry. In many cases, the 10 lines would be adequate for the comments to be entered.

```
ADD RECORD NAME IS ORGAN-DESCR-HDR.
02  ORG-HDR-TYPE                        PIC X.
02  ORG-HDR-EFF-DATE.
  03  ORG-HDR-EFF-CENT-YR.
      04  ORG-HDR-EFF-CENTURY           PIC 99.
      04  ORG-HDR-EFF-YEAR              PIC 99.
  03  ORG-HDR-EFF-MONTH                 PIC 99.
  03  ORG-HDR-EFF-DAY                   PIC 99.
02  ORG-HDR-SECURITY                    PIC XX.
02  ORG-HDR-DESCR-CATEGORY              PIC X.
02  ORG-HDR-DESCR-PRIORITY              PIC 9.
02  ORG-HDR-DESCR-EFF-DATE.
  03  ORG-HDR-DESCR-EFF-CENT-YR.
      04  ORG-HDR-DESCR-EFF-CENTURY     PIC 99.
      04  ORG-HDR-DESCR-EFF-YEAR        PIC 99.
  03  ORG-HDR-DESCR-EFF-MONTH           PIC 99.
  03  ORG-HDR-DESCR-EFF-DAY             PIC 99.
02  ORG-HDR-LAST-UPDATE-DATE.
  03  ORG-HDR-UPDATE-CENT-YR.
      04  ORG-HDR-UPDATE-CENTURY        PIC 99.
      04  ORG-HDR-UPDATE-YEAR           PIC 99.
  03  ORG-HDR-UPDATE-MONTH              PIC 99.
  03  ORG-HDR-UPDATE-DAY                PIC 99.
02  ORG-HDR-UPDATE-PERSON               PIC X(10)
02  ORG-HDR-LINES                       PIC 99.

ADD RECORD NAME IS ORG-HDR-LINE VERSION 1
02  ORG-HDR-LINE-GROUP.
  03  ORG-HDR-LINE                      PIC X(60).
```

Figure 13-5 Separating the Repeating Elements.

2. Placing the text lines into the header record reduces storage space requirements by eliminating set pointers.
3. The processing performance of the database is increased by permitting the entire header and 10 lines of text to be read by a single database call.

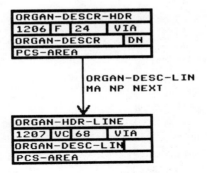

Figure 13-6   Relating Header and Repeating Elements.

4. The update program logic is more complex because the program must be able to insert and delete text within the 10 lines.

Looking at the normalized version:

1. Program logic is simplified as each line can be processed individually.
2. More than 10 lines can be stored. An odd number of lines (versus multiples of 10) does not impact storage space.
3. A line identifier is required. Without an identifier, it is possible to locate a specific line only by reading each line and checking to see if it is the one desired.
4. Processing overhead increases as more I/O requests must be made to handle the same number of lines.

```
ADD RECORD NAME IS ORG-HDR-LINE VERSION 1
02  ORG-HDR-LINE-SEQ              PIC 9999.
02  ORG-HDR-LINE-GROUP.           PIC X(60).
      03  ORG-HDR-LINE
```

Figure 13-7   Expanding The Repeating Elements.

```
ADD RECORD NAME IS ORGAN-DESCR-HDR.      PIC X.
02  ORG-HDR-TYPE
02  ORG-HDR-EFF-DATE.                     PIC 99.
    03  ORG-HDR-EFF-CENT-YR.
        04  ORG-HDR-EFF-CENTURY
        04  ORG-HDR-EFF-YEAR              PIC 99.
    03  ORG-HDR-EFF-MONTH                 PIC 99.
    03  ORG-HDR-EFF-DAY                   PIC 99.
02  ORG-HDR-SECURITY                      PIC XX.
02  ORG-HDR-DESCR-CATEGORY                PIC X.
02  ORG-HDR-DESCR-PRIORITY                PIC 9.
02  ORG-HDR-DESCR-EFF-DATE.               PIC 99.
    03  ORG-HDR-DESCR-EFF-CENT-YR.
        04  ORG-HDR-DESCR-EFF-CENTURY
        04  ORG-HDR-DESCR-EFF-YEAR        PIC 99.
    03  ORG-HDR-DESCR-EFF-MONTH           PIC 99.
    03  ORG-HDR-DESCR-EFF-DAY             PIC 99.
02  ORG-HDR-LAST-UPDATE-DATE.             PIC 99.
    03  ORG-HDR-UPDATE-CENT-YR.
        04  ORG-HDR-UPDATE-CENTURY
        04  ORG-HDR-UPDATE-YEAR           PIC 99.
    03  ORG-HDR-UPDATE-MONTH              PIC 99.
    03  ORG-HDR-UPDATE-DAYPIC 99.         PIC X(10).
02  ORG-HDR-UPDATE-PERSON
02  ORG-HDR-LINES                         PIC 99.
```

Figure 13-8   Input To Second Normal Form.

Each approach has valid plus and minus arguments. In the network database environment, most practical DBAs opt for the unnormalized record. *Either format will work however.* Relational systems *require* the normalized record.

Second Normal Form

Using our ORGAN-DESCR-HDR record again, let's look at the header portion. Figure 13-8 illustrates this part of the record.

To make a record conform to second normal form:

```
ADD RECORD NAME IS ORGAN-DESCR-HDR.
02  ORG-HDR-TYPE                          PIC X.
02  ORG-HDR-EFF-DATE.
   03  ORG-HDR-EFF-CENT-YR.
      04  ORG-HDR-EFF-CENTURY            PIC 99.
      04  ORG-HDR-EFF-YEAR               PIC 99.
   03  ORG-HDR-EFF-MONTH                 PIC 99.
   03  ORG-HDR-EFF-DAY                   PIC 99.
02  ORG-HDR-SECURITY                     PIC XX.
02  ORG-HDR-DESCR-CATEGORY               PIC X.
02  ORG-HDR-LAST-UPDATE-DATE.
   03  ORG-HDR-UPDATE-CENT-YR.
      04  ORG-HDR-UPDATE-CENTURY         PIC 99.
      04  ORG-HDR-UPDATE-YEAR            PIC 99.
   03  ORG-HDR-UPDATE-MONTH              PIC 99.
   03  ORG-HDR-UPDATE-DAY                PIC 99.
02  ORG-HDR-UPDATE-PERSON                PIC X(10).
02  ORG-HDR-LINES                        PIC 99.
ADD RECORD NAME IS ORG-HDR-PRIORITY VERSION 1
02  ORG-HDR-TYPE                         PIC X.
02  ORG-HDR-DESCR-PRIORITY               PIC 9.
02  ORG-HDR-DESCR-EFF-DATE.
   03  ORG-HDR-DESCR-EFF-CENT-YR.
      04  ORG-HDR-DESCR-EFF-CENTURY      PIC 99.
      04  ORG-HDR-DESCR-EFF-YEAR         PIC 99.
   03  ORG-HDR-DESCR-EFF-MONTH           PIC 99
   03  ORG-HDR-DESCR-EFF-DAY             PIC 99.
```

Figure 13-9 Creating The Second Normal Structure.

1. *Identify any element that is dependent on only part of the key.* In our example, the key fields are ORG-HDR-DESCR-CATEGORY and ORG-HDR-DESCR-PRIORITY. The element ORG-HDR-DESCR-EFF-DATE is dependent on ORG-HDR-DESCR-PRIORITY, but not on ORG-HDR-DESCR-CATEGORY.

2. *Remove these elements and form a new record.* Figure 13-9 shows our header now broken into two pieces: the original header and the priority section.

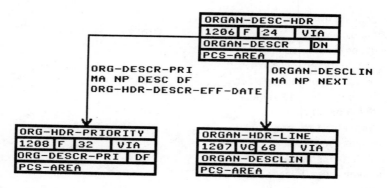

Figure 13-10   The Second Form Result.

Now, to recap, let's look at the complete record structure in Figure 13-10. Our original record has been broken into three segments.

Again, we need to analyze what has happened to our data. The practical result of achieving second normal form has been to:

1. *Separate the priority data from the header.* The priority code and its date have become a separate record, linked on a one-to-one relationship with the original header.
2. *As a separate record, an I/O is required* to retrieve the priority data. Performance of processing of the record has been reduced.
3. *The priority may be searched separately.* If we were to need to look up organization descriptions by their priority, this separation *might* be useful.

Third Normal Form

Third normal form is attained by:

1. *Remove nonkey elements that relate to other nonkey elements.* In our example, Figure 13-11 separates the LAST-UPD-PERSON from the record because it is dependent on LAST-UPD-DATE, not on the key DESCR-CATEGORY.

```
ADD RECORD NAME IS ORGAN-DESCR-HDR.
02   ORG-HDR-TYPE                          PIC X.
02   ORG-HDR-EFF-DATE.
   03   ORG-HDR-EFF-CENT-YR.
       04   ORG-HDR-EFF-CENTURY            PIC 99.
       04   ORG-HDR-EFF-YEAR              PIC 99.
    03   ORG-HDR-EFF-MONTH                PIC 99.
    03   ORG-HDR-EFF-DAY                  PIC 99.
02   ORG-HDR-SECURITY                     PIC XX.
02   ORG-HDR-DESCR-CATEGORY               PIC X.
02   ORG-HDR-LINES                        PIC 99.


ADD RECORD NAME IS ORG-HDR-PRIORITY VERSION 1
02   ORG-HDR-TYPE                         PIC X.
02   ORG-HDR-DESCR-PRIORITY               PIC 9.
02   ORG-HDR-DESCR-EFF-DATE.
   03   ORG-HDR-DESCR-EFF-CENT-YR.
       04   ORG-HDR-DESCR-EFF-CENTURY     PIC 99.
       04   ORG-HDR-DESCR-EFF-YEAR        PIC 99.
    03   ORG-HDR-DESCR-EFF-MONTH          PIC 99.
    03   ORG-HDR-DESCR-EFF-DAY            PIC 99.
ADD RECORD NAME IS ORG-HDR-UPDATE VERSION 1
02   ORG-HDR-TYPE                         PIC X.
02   ORG-HDR-LAST-UPDATE-DATE.
   03   ORG-HDR-UPDATE-CENT-YR.
       04   ORG-HDR-UPDATE-CENTURY        PIC 99.
       04   ORG-HDR-UPDATE-YEAR           PIC 99.
    03   ORG-HDR-UPDATE-MONTH             PIC 99.
    03   ORG-HDR-UPDATE-DAY               PIC 99.
02   ORG-HDR-UPDATE-PERSON                PIC X(10).
```

Figure 13-11   Achieving Third Normal Form.

2. *Create a new entity and relationship with these elements.* Our record structure is now shown by Figure 13-12. The person field stands off with the update date.

Our final analysis shows that we now could maintain an update history if we so desired. The final third normal form of the ORGAN-

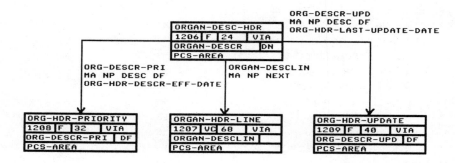

Figure 13-12   Resulting Third Normal Structure.

DESCR-HDR record is five records. Unfortunately, we are not done
with the process. Each of these created records must have a key field
that links them to the root header record. In the case of the ORGAN-
DESCR-HDR, the primary key of the owning ORGANIZATION
record is a 40-byte name. This will cause the normalized structure to
occupy significantly more disk space.

While the freedom to develop ad hoc structures is one of the pluses
of a relational system, it may actually require much more disk space
than an equivalent network structure. Obviously, in our example, a
4-byte pointer dbkey occupies much less space than a 40-byte name.
Further, changing the name in a relational system will be a time-
consuming and painful process because of the number of places the
name value is used. The same key in a network system will be
changed only a few times at the most.

14

Data Elements

The data element is the smallest uniquely identifiable piece of a database. Elements can be grouped together to define associations and for special processing. When we speak of a data element, however, we are basically talking about a specific and unique piece of database designed to hold a bit of information.

Grouping Elements By High-Level Use

We will be discussing a wide variety of types and formats of data elements. Before that, however, we need to look at some general categories of elements. Elements may be grouped in these categories for ease of identification and use.

Common Elements

Common elements are those whose *structural definition* does not vary across the database. They are used as a basis for the SAME AS clause to replicate a common definition or structure, reducing data entry effort and ensuring a consistent definition throughout the dictionary. An example of a common element may be MONTH, that

```
ADD ELEMENT NAME IS MONTH VERSION IS 1
ELEMENT DESCRIPTION IS 'THE CALENDAR MONTH WITHIN YEAR'
CATEGORY IS COMMON-ELEMENT
PICTURE IS 99
RANGE IS 01 THRU 12
COMMENTS
'A NUMERIC VALUE NORMALLY FOUND IN COMBINATION WITH'
-'YEAR AND DAY, AS PART OF A DATE.'
ELEMENT-HELP
'THE MONTH OF THE YEAR, WITH A VALID RANGE OF 01-12.' .
```

Figure 14-1   Common Element Example.

could be commonly defined as a two-digit element with a valid range of 1 through 12 (see Figure 14-1).

Standard Elements

Standard elements differ from common elements in that a standard element identifies the installation's standardization of a type of element or element group. BIRTH-DATE, for example, may be defined as being composed of YEAR, MONTH, and DAY, in that order.

The elementary components of BIRTH-DATE are common elements. The combination of those elements into BIRTH-DATE describes what the use of the elements will be in all cases where BIRTH-DATE is used. Every place in the database where a birth date is desired uses the standard element with a synonym prefix (see Figure 14-2).

Use of standard elements ensures that a consistency of *definition* exists across the entire database.

Generic Elements

Generic elements are very similar to standard elements. The primary difference is that they fall into groups whose individual members vary in detail definition. An example of a generic element group would be COUNTERS. Generic elements are associated with an ELEMENT DESIGNATOR and frequently include a standard

```
ADD ELEMENT NAME IS BIRTH-DATE VERSION IS 1
ELEMENT DESCRIPTION IS 'DATE OF BIRTH OF A PERSON'
CATEGORY IS STANDARD-ELEMENT
SUBORDINATE ELEMENTS ARE   YEAR   MONTH   DAY
COMMENTS
'THIS GROUP ELEMENT CONTAINS THE DATE OF BIRTH OF'
-'A PERSON IN THE DATABASE.  IT IS COMPOSED OF '
-'YEAR/MONTH/DAY USING A FORMAT YYMMDD.'
VALIDATION-CRITERIA
'THE STANDARD DATE VALIDATION IS PERFORMED ON THIS'
-'ELEMENT GROUP.'
ELEMENT-HELP
'THE FIELD CONTAINS THE DATE OF BIRTH OF A PERSON'
-'WITHIN THE PCS DATABASE.  IT IS FORMATTED YYMMDD'
-'WITHOUT SEPARATIONS BETWEEN THE DATE SECTIONS.' .
```

Figure 14-2   Standard Element Example.

prefix or suffix in the element name to identify its generic association, e.g., TRANSACTION-CTR (see Figure 14-3).

Structure Elements

Structure elements are those whose presence in the database is required primarily to assist in the association of other elements, groups, and records. An example of a structure element is a flag that

```
ADD ELEMENT NAME IS TRANSACTION-CTR VERSION IS 1
ELEMENT DESCRIPTION IS 'COUNT OF TRANSACTIONS PROCESSED'
CATEGORY IS GENERIC-ELEMENT TEXT 'CTR'
PICTURE IS 9(4)
USAGE IS COMP
COMMENTS
'THE FIELD CONTAINS A COUNT OF THE NUMBER OF '
-'TRANSACTIONS PROCESSED DURING THE DESIGNATED TIME'
-'PERIOD IDENTIFIED BY TRANSACTION-PERIOD.' .
```

Figure 14-3   Generic Element Example.

```
ADD ELEMENT NAME IS ASSOC-TYPE VERSION IS 1
ELEMENT DESCRIPTION IS 'FLAG DEFINING TYPE OF ASSOCIATION'
PICTURE IS X
RANGE IS 'A' THRU 'D'
VALUE IS SPACES
CATEGORY IS STRUCTURE-ELEMENT
COMMENTS
'THE FIELD IDENTIFIES THE NATURE AND RELATIONSHIP'
-'BETWEEN AN ORGANIZATION AND A PERSON.'
VALIDATION-CRITERIA
'STANDARD TABLE - SZDTE120'
RANGE-DESCRIPTION
'A - EMPLOYEE'
-'B - PAST EMPLOYEE'
-'C - CONSULTANT'
-'D - TEMPORARY ASSIGNMENT'.
ELEMENT-HELP '
THIS FIELD DEFINES THE RELATIONSHIP BETWEEN A PERSON'
-'AND AN ORGANIZATION.  VALID CODES ARE:'
-'A - EMPLOYEE'
-'B - PAST EMPLOYEE'
-'C - CONSULTANT'
-'D - TEMPORARY ASSIGNMENT'. .
```

Figure 14-4   Structure Element Example.

resides in a junction record defining the association between organizations and persons. The flag identifies the type of association
(employee, member, etc.) and is set by software rather than by external data (see Figure 14-4).

Generated Elements

Generated elements are those that are originated solely by software
for the purpose of controlling other data. An example would be hash-
totals used to audit the integrity of certain database element occurrences or a counter used to accommodate the total number of transactions processed (see Figure 14-5).

```
ADD ELEMENT NAME IS CTRL-TOTAL VERSION IS 1
ELEMENT DESCRIPTION IS 'NET TOTAL OF TRANSACTIONS'
CATEGORY IS GENERATED-ELEMENT
PICTURE 9(4)
USAGE IS COMP
VALUE IS 0
COMMENTS
'THE FIELD CONTAINS A NET TOTAL OF TRANSACTIONS'
-'EXPECTED LESS THE NUMBER ACTUALLY RECEIVED. IF'
-'THE VALUE OF THIS FIELD IS OTHER THAN ZERO AT'
-'THE END OF THE PROCESSING PERIOD, AN EXCEPTION'
-'REPORT IS PRINTED.  THE FIELD IS MAINTAINED AS'
-'PART OF A QUEUE RECORD.'
```

Figure 14-5   Generated Element Example.

Element Types

While IDMS can handle virtually all types of data elements, we will concentrate our discussion on the three predominant types that generally occur in databases. These are *alphabetic*, *numeric*, and *alphanumeric* (a combination of alphabetic and numeric).

Alphabetic

The alphabetic data element is infrequently seen. It is characterized by the the symbol "A" and limits its data content to alphabetical characters between the letters "A" and "Z." While there are legitimate cases where a data element can contain only letters of the alphabet, most cases allow both letters and numbers. Therefore, the alphabetic data type should be used with care and only where it is unlikely that numbers will ever occur in the field.

Numeric

The numeric data element is identified by the symbol "9" in a data element. Where editing is being performed, the symbols "Z" and "0" define where zero-suppression and zero-filling occur, respectively.

The numeric data type allows only numbers and numeric editing characters (+ - , . $) to be stored in the field.

Alphanumeric

This data type is by far the most popular and used of the data types. It is identified by the symbol "X" and permits all data values to be held within the field.

Element Data Formats

The format used when defining a data element must be reviewed against the intended use of the element. We must also consider where the element may be sent. For example, in these days of downloading data to PCs, data slated for downloading can be handled easier if the conversion to ASCII is taken into account when initially defining the element.

Display

Defining database data as DISPLAY makes it easily compatible with most other uses. It can easily be displayed on a screen, printed, or transmitted. Where conversion to ASCII is anticipated, numeric data should be defined as DISPLAY.

Packed

The packed decimal format is unique to the IBM 370-compatible computer. It is entirely alien to all other makes and models of computer; those that utilize a similar packing method do it differently. Packed decimal *should not be used* for data that will be converted to ASCII. While some up/down loading programs do a credible job of converting packed decimal, physical field length differences make the job harder. Some micro/mainframe packages do not correctly convert packed decimal.

For simplicity's sake, at the least, define numeric data as DIS-PLAY. If database space is a factor, compress the database records; it has the same net effect as defining numerics as packed.

Binary

Binary (COMP) data is always used for database keys (dbkeys) and defined as PIC 9(8). Subscripts are often defined as binary. Floating point binary data frequently has conversion problems because of the difference in the number of bits of precision between computers. Data elements being transferred between computers should avoid floating point definition.

Bit

Bit data definitions provide a highly compacted means of setting flags and switches. Bit-defined data elements must be carefully controlled and *should not be used on data subject to intercomputer* transfer. Frankly, I do not recommend using bit-defined elements in *any* application software.

Element Names

Data element naming conventions are often the inheritance from the first data processing staff in an installation. Depending on when DP arrived there, those conventions may date back to punched card days. The prevailing programming language at the point of original computer installation frequently has had a strong influence on the naming convention. After all, early FORTRAN and assembly languages frequently limited element names to eight or fewer characters.

Today's computer languages are a lot more flexible. Even though COBOL allows 31 characters in an element name, that is no reason to use all of them; names should be descriptive, but the longer the name, the greater the chance of keying error.

Name Length

This leads us to the length of a data element name. For compatibility's sake, let's assume that no element can exceed 31 characters in length. This satisfies COBOL, PL/1, ADS/O, and CULPRIT. The actual basic element name, however, should be shorter to take prefixes and suffixes into consideration. We will discuss prefixes and suffixes shortly.

Name Format

The format of an element name requires careful thought. A commonly used format breaks the element name into three parts, two of which are generally required. Using the element name *MAJOR-AC-COUNT-NUM* as an example, the element parts are:

1. *Qualifier.* The qualifier is used to further specify the subject in order to make the element name unique. *MAJOR* is a qualifier of our example.
2. *Subject.* The principal topic or subject that the element will support is identified. *ACCOUNT* is an example of a subject.
3. *Category.* The category is a specific term that places the element in a grouping of elements of similar content or use. *NUM* identifies the element as a number. If the account number were to include alphabetics, a categorizer such as *ID* could be used to distinguish between an all-numeric and alphanumeric element.

Element Prefix vs Suffix

It is common to append prefixes or suffixes to a basic data element name to further qualify it for additional use. Again, the selection of a prefix or suffix needs to be carefully reviewed. Prefixes and suffixes provide a higher level qualifier of the element, retaining the basic name for cross-referencing while establishing uniqueness in specific situations.

Prefix. Prefixing a data element extends the logical structure of the element as described earlier. The prefix provides a measure of structure control not available with suffixing. It is possible, for example, to locate the start of the basic element by counting the number of positions to the element begin point (where the prefix is always the same length) or by locating the first hyphen. It is then easy to strip off the prefix, if desired, and use the basic element name.

Standard prefixes permit instant understanding of the use of an element by visual or computer scan. The following standard prefixes illustrate my point:

1. *S0000-* The prefix assigned to schema elements. *0000* is the record identifier where the element is used.
2. *W-* This is the prefix assigned to elements used within work records. An alternate, *W000-*, uses numerics to identify the work element as belonging to a specific work record. This extra qualification is useful when the same basic element is used in multiple work records, two or more of which are associated with a particular program.
3. *M-* This prefix is used to identify elements used as part of map work records. Again, the alternate *M000-*, adds an additional measure of uniqueness.
4. *S-* This prefix is used to identify elements used in scratch records. Here an extension of the prefix should be avoided if machine-readable recognition is desired. A test of the second position of the prefix differentiates between schema and scratch elements.
5. *Q-* The *Q* prefix defines those data elements used within queue records.
6. *R-* This prefix identifies elements used within report formats and output records.

Suffix. Cullinet uses a suffix as part of the definition of their network schema record elements. This was a convention that dates back to the original release of IDMS. Many within Cullinet have indicated a preference for prefixing but here is the classic example of being trapped by a convention that was defined years ago. The cost of modifying software to use element prefixes instead of the current suffixing would be far greater than any potential benefit derived.

As you have probably surmised by the preceding discussion, my own preference is for prefixing. I have used it without problem for more than 10 years in IDMS and in flat file systems long before

IDMS came on the scene. Overall, prefixing seems to have fewer negative points and more positive arguments than suffixing.

Element Descriptions

A number of years ago I was asked to assist in an IDMS installation that was having trouble. After being given a general briefing by the DP manager, I asked to look at their data dictionary. The DP manager was apologetic. There had been some turnover in the database administration staff, he told me, and he wasn't sure that the dictionary was up to date. Asked how long the dictionary had been used and for what, he indicated that every application, IDMS and others, had been entered into the dictionary.

My first discovery was a complete lack of dictionary reports. Not even an element report was to be found. A complete set of element, record, program, and module reports were run. The listings were so thin that I thought the wrong reports had been run. The element report was less than 3 inches thick.

Opening the element report, I was scarcely prepared for what I found. This thin report had over 2000 data elements listed *without a single comment or descriptive statement*. Even the ELEMENT DESCRIPTION statement was missing. For analysis purposes (or most any other, for that matter), the report was a useless pile of paper. The other reports were as bad. After looking them over, I could understand why there were no listings around. As reference documents, they had no value.

My initial report to the DP manager was made only a few hours after my arrival. His key control tool, the data dictionary, was useless. My services were a waste of his money; without the dictionary data, I would have to spend weeks learning his environment in order to make any recommendations.

A year later, I met one of the programmers at the annual user conference. The DP manager was gone, IDMS lay virtually unused, and the DP shop was out of control. That programmer had wisely moved to greener pastures.

The story ends well, however. Still later, I encountered a DBA from the same shop. He had glowing stories to tell me about what was happening. A new manager, his priorities in order, had rebuilt the installation. His first act was to rebuild the data dictionary, enforcing full documentation of all entities.

Element descriptions are THE critical documentation of an installation. If we can understand *what* the data is that is being processed, we can always figure out *how* it is being processed. Without that understanding, software logic loses its meaning.

Long Name/Title

The ELEMENT DESCRIPTION clause, as with the other DESCRIPTION clauses, is misnamed. Its length, 40 characters, is too short to be a description. This clause is really intended to be a long name or element title. While an element name like PART-NUM can be readily identified as *part number*, DATE-COMP-MILE could be confusing unless its long name, *date of computed milestone*, was spelled out.

Every element, even if the system name is self-explanatory, should have its nontechnical name spelled out in the DESCRIPTION statement.

Technical Description

Most data elements have some sort of specific processing requirements. The purpose of the element, how it is populated, and how long the data is valid are all valuable keys to how the element should be processed. These kinds of descriptive statements are grouped under the COMMENTS clause in the element description. These comments are aimed at the analyst and programmer and need to be very explicit.

End User Description

The end user, on the other hand, is not interested in many of the technical details. This user, however, IS interested in what is required to enter the element correctly, restrictions on use of the element, and similar information *prepared in non-DP language*. The user-defined-comment ELEMENT-HELP contains this information. This UDC, referred to by a help facility, may be displayed to assist the user in properly maintaining the data.

Dependency Description

Many elements depend on others to justify their data content. They are dependent on external conditions for their value or presence. The UDC *ELEMENT-DEPENDENCY* is used to document these dependencies.

Validation Description

Many elements require specific validation, other than dependencies. If the element is required when a record is stored, this must be documented. Special conditions, such as a check digit at the end of a field, must be considered. The UDC *VALIDATION-CRITERIA* documents these special conditions.

Element Value Ranges

Most fixed format data elements have a limitation on the range of values that can be placed in the element. (By fixed format, I mean those elements whose data *always* fill the available space. A two-character state code is one example.) Variable format data, such as company name, city, or person last name are difficult to assign value ranges.

Single Value

It is a rare element that has a single value; in fact, I cannot think of a single example other than constants. Single value definition is most often a startup definition, the element containing the value when the program begins execution.

It is common to have an element defined with a series of noncontiguous single values, such as **04**, **06**, **09**, and **11** (those months with 30 days).

```
ADD ELEMENT NAME IS DAY VERSION IS 1
ELEMENT DESCRIPTION IS 'THE CALENDAR DAY WITHIN MONTH'
CATEGORY IS COMMON-ELEMENT
PICTURE IS 99
RANGE IS 01 THRU 31
COMMENTS
'A NUMERIC VALUE NORMALLY FOUND IN COMBINATION WITH'
-'YEAR AND MONTH, AS PART OF A DATE.'
ELEMENT-HELP
'THE DAY OF THE MONTH, WITH A VALID RANGE OF 01-31,'
-'DEPENDING ON THE MONTH.'
```

Figure 14-6   RANGE Example.

Inclusive Range Values

Numeric data elements often have valid ranges of values, such as **01-12** as the valid range for months. It is not unusual to find more than one range of valid values for an element. Keeping with our date-oriented examples, months **01, 03, 05, 07-08, 10,** and **12** are valid for 31 days (see Figure 14-6).

Documenting Ranges

The UDC *VALIDATION-CRITERIA* should be used to provide textual documentation to the range values defined for each data element. This documentation provides the basis for coded software and test plans to test the software.

Element Values

The *VALUE IS* clause associated optionally with each data element establishes the *initial* value for the element. This clause is used by the IDMS system to provide the content of the element at the time the element, within its record, *is first loaded to the program's working storage*. Once that value has been overridden by the program, it

```
ADD ELEMENT IS BIRTH-INFORMATION VERSION IS 1
ELEMENT DESCRIPTION IS 'INFO ABOUT BIRTH OF PERSON'
SUBORDINATE ELEMENTS ARE
 CITY-OF-BIRTH
 STATE-OF-BIRTH
 COUNTRY-OF-BIRTH
 BIRTH-DATE
COMMENTS
'THIS GROUP IDENTIFIES THE LOCATION AND DATE OF BIRTH'
-'OF A PERSON.'
```

Figure 14-7   Element Group Example.

is gone unless the program issues (in ADS/O) the INITIALIZE command for the record in which the element participates. INITIALIZE restores the default value to the element.

When To Avoid

Initial element values should be avoided when the element is redefined. COBOL programmers have all experienced the error messages that occur in this situation. Even though many other languages ignore the condition, it is wise to make a practice of not assigning values to redefined elements.

Element Groups

It is desirable, where possible, to separate related elements into groups. This has the effect of ensuring that the use of one element of a group will at least require review of related elements to see if they are also used. Grouping of elements also represents the normalization of data to second and third levels. A common grouping might be BIRTH-INFORMATION that could be composed of PLACE-OF-BIRTH (itself a group of CITY-OF-BIRTH, STATE-OF-BIRTH, AND COUNTRY-OF-BIRTH) AND BIRTH-DATE (see Figure 14-7).

SAME AS Elements

The SAMEAS facility within IDD permits reduction of data entry and common definition consistency across the data dictionary. Common and standard elements described earlier utilize this feature extensively.

Element Synonyms

It is not unusual for two users of the same data element to know it by different names. An account number in the finance department may also be the customer number in the sales department. IDD provides the facility to define an element and associate it with multiple synonym names, a capability that is especially useful when end users are accessing the database through an interactive query facility. Letting the user utilize familiar names increases their acceptance and effectiveness in using the database.

Caution: Strict control must be maintained over the use of synonyms. Where practical, users should be educated to the use of common names so that the data dictionary will not become polluted with synonyms. Too many synonyms may affect the ability of the database designers to assign meaningful names to new elements.

One place where synonyms are very useful is in the assignment of different types of records. IDMS and IDD have built-in protection controls to prevent one dictionary-driven facility from interfering with another. You may not, for example, delete a schema record from the dictionary if it is being used by another facility, such as the mapper (OLM).

This restriction can be overcome by building a basic record, declaring a synonym and prefixing the data elements. Further use of the elements are assigned unique prefixes. To make each element within a work record unique, when compared to a database record element, work record elements are given standard prefixes. These prefixes create element synonyms within the dictionary, separating the work record element from its parent basic element. See the detail section on prefixes earlier in this chapter.

Generic Elements

There are some elements, such as those making up a date, that are always structured the same every time they are used (if not, they should be). The only thing that changes is the qualification of the element to make it unique for a specific use (START-DATE, END-DATE).

Every organization has a number of these generic elements around. Most, for example, have a standard employee number. Everyone uses the standard Social Security number. Part numbers, organization structure codes, and general ledger account numbers are other examples.

It is very important that Data Administration identify and carefully define each generic element within the organization. Done after the fact, this definition process can be very expensive as retrofitting of the standard is performed against software using the element. It is also useful to create a standard callable validatoin routine to verify the element contents each time an add or change is performed.

Within the data dictionary, each generic element should be assigned an element category that clearly identifies its status. Modification of such elements must be rigidly controlled and a clear understanding of the potential costs of change presented to all parties before proceeding.

15

Records

This chapter discusses the most obvious and common participant in a database, the data record. Many have made the mistake of dismissing records as being a common and boring part of database design. There are numerous subtle considerations that should be included when defining the database record.

Converting Logical Data Models To Physical Structures

Even as I write this section, much of what it will contain is being automated through AUTOMATE PLUS/IDMS ARCHITECT. It is still useful, however, to understand the basis for converting the logical data structures into a physical one that IDMS can recognize. Since IDMS now recognizes both network and relational structures, we will provide a set of capsule conversion rules for each.

Converting To Network Data Structures

To translate a logical model to a network structure:

1. *Define a record type for each entity.* We may collapse some of these entities into one physical record at a later time but start off with a one-to-one conversion.
2. *Assign a set for each 1:M relationship* with the arrow pointing toward the multiple-occurring entity.
3. *If the relationship between two entities is 1:1*, then consider these entities for collapse into a single physical record.
4. *Create a junction record* between any two entities that have a many-to-many relationship.
5. *Create a new record type* whenever a dependent entity is identified. The key of the dependent entity becomes the sort key of the set connecting the two entities.

For each individual record type:

1. *Finalize field sizes* to meet the physical requirements of the application.
2. *Organize the fields in the record to maximize data compression.* It is a good idea to do this even if compression is not initially planned. Compression considerations are discussed later in this chapter.
3. *Decide on how the record will be stored* (CALC, VIA, DIRECT). Record modes will be discussed in more detail in the next few pages.
4. *Assign the record to a specific area.* Areas are reviewed in detail in Chapter 17.
5. *Determine the set membership option to be used* (MA, OA, MM, OM). Set membership is discussed in Chapter 16.
6. MBIDefine the pointers required (Next, Prior, Owner). As a general rule, next and prior pointers are always used. Owner pointers are used only when walking backward along the set; access to the member is via another set (see Chapter 16).
7. *Identify the set order. Set order is also covered in Chapter 16.*
8. *Identify any additional relationships that are required* to achieve the logical relationships defined in the logical structure.

Converting to a Relational Structure

To translate a logical model to a relational structure:

```
┌─────────────────────────────┐
│ EVENT                       │
├──────┬───┬────────┬─────────┤
│ 1000 │ F │ 40     │ CALC    │
├──────┴───┴──┬─────┴──┬──────┤
│ EVENT-IDENT │   DN   │      │
├─────────────┴────────┴──────┤
│ PCS-AREA                    │
└─────────────────────────────┘
```

Figure 15-1 Identifying Fixed Record Type On Bachman Block.

1. *Create a relational table for each entity.*
2. *Define a relational table for each binary relationship* that includes data elements.
3. *Define a relational table for each M:M relationship* even if the relationship has no dependent elements.
4. *For dependent entities, define a relational table* whose key is identified as a foreign key in its logical owner.

Record Types

Back in the days of sequential tape files, variable-length records were the sort of thing used by "experts" to improve processing speed and keep the data file within a single reel of tape. Most programmers shied away from variable-length records because of the bad stories heard about this mode of data handling. Today's variable-length records have been treated in much the same way. This section will help to dispell some of the myths.

IDMS supports both fixed and variable-length records. Each has its strong and weak points. Let's compare the two.

Fixed Record Type

The fixed record type is identified by the "F" in the second box on line two of the Bachman block. See Figure 15-1. Based on the schema syntax, IDMS will generate the record as a fixed type. As far as IDMS is concerned, a record is fixed if:

1. *The database procedures IDMSCOMP and IDMSDCOM* are not used.
2. *OCCURS DEPENDING ON clause* does not appear associated with any element within the record.
3. *The ROOT and FRAGMENT clauses* are not present.

EVENT-DESCR-DETL				LABOR-HOURS				FREE-TEXT			
1021	FC	612	VIA	1062	VC	88	VIA	9899	V	612	VIA
EVENT-DESC-LIN				ASSIGN-HOURS			DL	FREE-TXT-LINE			
PCS-AREA				PCS-AREA				PCS-AREA			

Figure 15-2   Identifying Variable Record Types On Bachman Block.

Advantages of fixed records. These are primarily oriented around performance. The fixed length record is read and written in its full-formatted form. It is not modified, massaged, squeezed, or otherwise changed by the DBMS from the form seen by the application program.

Disadvantages of fixed records. These come from the storage space it requires. Most database records have some unused space. The amount of that unused space varies by the type of data present in the record. Binary data, for example, wastes no space while a character string may waste a lot. We allow 40 characters for a company name; only 20 percent, however, actually use up more than 30 characters. If there are a lot of records with company name fields, the wasted space can be considerable.

Variable Record Type

The variable record type presents a clearer tradeoff. If the application requires speed as a primary requirement, variable-length records are *not* used. If the amount of storage space available is at a premium, variable records *are* used.

Variable-length records are identified by "FC," "V," and "VC" in the Bachman block (see Figure 15-2). Yes, the so-called *fixed compressed* record is actually variable in length. Can you imagine anything quite so wasteful in a DBMS as to compress the data within a record while leaving the physical length of the record unchanged? You use all the processing overhead to squeeze the record's data without any of the benefit of using less storage space.

By the same token, the "V" or straight variable-length record (created by the use of OCCURS DEPENDING ON) would probably further benefit if compression were also applied. As a result, most variable-length records are shown as either "FC" or "VC." Most schemas designed by experienced DBAs contain only "F" or "VC" record types. ("FC" and "VC" are frequently used to mean the same thing.)

Advantages of variable-length records. These are oriented around the space savings that can be accomplished by compressing out the unused data space *and* squeezing some letter combinations into a single byte. Unpacked numeric data, in display format, are squeezed into a packed decimal form. (This feature makes use of COMP-3 less desirable when used in combination with compressed records.)

One of the most subtle effects of variable-length records is the flexibility IDMS has to store the record where there is space. IDMS always attempts to put an entire record on the same physical database page; with fixed-length records, it has no choice but to locate a page that will take the complete record. With variable-length records, however, only the *root portion of the record* must be stored intact; the remainder of the record can be stored on one or more adjacent pages. While processing overhead increases, the data density on database pages increases too. More of the available space can be utilized. This is particularly true of large records that may have difficulty finding a home in a database more than 50 percent full.

Variable-length records, usually compressed, *should be used on most records that are more than 200 bytes long.*

The disadvantages of variable-length records. These come primarily from the increased processing time required to support them. This increase is primarily associated with *the use of compression and decompression.* Little additional processing time is required for the classical variable-length environment.

The way data fields are arranged in a variable-length record affects the efficiency of compression. We will discuss these considerations in detail in the section on compression later.

Repeating Data vs Member Records

Back in our flat file programming days it was common for a file to contain repeating groups of data; the OCCURS DEPENDING ON was a common tool to handle multiple occurrences of data. This feature is available under IDMS. When used it *forces the record to be variable-length.*

```
ADD ELEMENT NAME IS LABOR-HOURS VERSION 1.
02   LHRS-KEY.
   03   LHRS-PERIOD                        PIC X.
   03   LHRS-EFFECTIVE-DATE.
      04   LHRS-EFF-CENT-YR.
         05   LHRS-EFF-CENTURY          PIC 99.
         05   LHRS-EFF-YEAR             PIC 99.
      04   LHRS-EFF-MONTH               PIC 99.
      04   LHRS-EFF-DAY                 PIC 99.
   03   LHRS-SEQ                           PIC 9.
02   LHRS-BLOCK.
   03   LHRS-ENTRY   OCCURS 7 TIMES.
      04   LHRS-ENTRY-DATE.
         05   LHRS-ENTRY-CENT-YR.
            06   LHRS-ENTRY-CENTURY PIC 99.
            06   LHRS-ENTRY-YEAR    PIC 99.
         05   LHRS-ENTRY-MONTH        PIC 99.
         05   LHRS-ENTRY-DAY          PIC 99.
      04   LHRS-REG-HRS                 PIC S9(5)V9.
      04   LHRS-OT-HRS                  PIC S9(5)V9.
      04   LHRS-COMP-HRS                PIC S9(5)V9.
```

Figure 15-3   Repeating Group Data Example.

Should we use multiple-occurring data groups in a record or define it as separate member records? As a general rule, break out the data and place it in an associated member record (if your database is relational, this is required). As many of us found out the hard way, the maximum number of repeating occurrences will be reached by some user regardless of how large a repeating allowance you make.

Repeating groups within a record are advantageous only when I/O performance is critical and the repeating occurrences can be controlled to prevent overflows. Since variable-length processing is involved, this is a questionable tradeoff. It is sometimes desirable to put a number of occurrences of a small variable data group in a member record (see Figure 15-3). As a member, this data group can be repeated as often as necessary. The number of occurrences should be determined by the size and number of expected uses.

Record Modes

IDMS supports four, yes four, different modes of record storage. Many have not heard of sequential mode; it is infrequently used. Each mode has its useful features; no one mode is good for all types of processing. In this section, we will explore where each mode contributes best to the database design.

CALC Record Mode

CALC is the best known of the storage modes. It is synonomous with the old ISAM (indexed sequential access method) way of storing data. The physical location of data is dependent on the value of a *storage key,* one or more of the fields within the record that is used to *uniquely* identify a record.

IDMS relates a CALC record with a physical database key (dbkey) through an algorithm that computes the dbkey from the value of the key field within the record. Of particular interest to database purists is the ability of such an algorithm to effectively distribute the data across the database area without too much clustering (with its accompanying overflows). The IDMS CALC routine has been proved to be very effective in its ability to overcome clustering. CALC clustering occurs when a number of data items are directed to the same database page because their key value is translated by the CALC algorithm to that page.

Even the best algorithms sometimes fail when faced with a certain combination of data. During the development of an early database, we encountered a heavy clustering of data. Investigation of the data showed that the contents of the key field had a pattern that offset the CALC algorithm's anti-clustering feature. The problem was solved by increasing the length of the CALC key by one byte, in the high order position, and inserting the letter *A* in that position. This changed the computation pattern of the algorithm sufficiently to smooth out the data placement. (The use of *A* was accidental. We started there, planning to progress through the alphabet as required. *A* did the job so no further effort was applied to check out other letters.)

You can tell quickly if your database is placing data in its most efficient way by looking at the IDMS area reports from IDMSDUMP.

0000–0099	2
0100–0199	3
0200–0299	12
0300–0399	30
0400–0499	62
0500–0599	101
0600–0699	131
0700–0799	98
0800–0899	80
0900–0999	32
1000–1099	11
1100–1199	6
1200–1299	1
1300–1399	0
1400–1499	3

Figure 15-4   IDMSDUMP Area Fill Report.

If the data fill is a "bell curve," regardless of where it peaks, therefore the CALC algorithm is doing its job (see Figure 15-4).

VIA Record Mode

The VIA record is *usually* stored adjacent to its owner. I say usually because there are notable exceptions that we must cover. First, however, the rule.

The purpose of the VIA record is to reduce the number of physical I/Os that occur when accessing the related member occurrences of an owner record. Performance of the database application is directly related to how frequently physical I/Os occur. The VIA record, therefore, is a strong weapon in control of system performance.

VIA records *can* degrade performance if they are stacked on top of each other (one VIA owns another VIA that in turns owns another). This creates a hierarchical structure that must be entered at a CALC record or index and walked successively down each level of VIA structure. *Do not stack VIA structures more than three deep!* Two-deep should be the normal maximum.

Multilevel VIA structures *should use sorted sets* to quickly move through the processing to the target record at the lowest level.

Earlier we mentioned that VIA records were *usually* stored close to their owners. In the chapter on areas, Chapter 17, we will talk about cluster effects, page offsets, and special areas that are used to increase the performance of applications by moving the VIA records away from the vicinity of their owner.

Direct Record Mode

Before getting into a description of this mode, it is only fair to warn you that I am vigorously opposed to the use of DIRECT storage mode in *any* database design. My presentation of this mode, therefore, will be biased. Hopefully, my explanation of this mode will bias you, too.

DIRECT mode *requires* that the programmer and the program define where IDMS will store its data. This presents two major drawbacks to its use:

1. *The data organization abilities of IDMS are bypassed*, requiring the application software to place each record. If overflows occur, the program must handle them.
2. *The complexity of the application software is increased* by an order of magnitude, making its long-term maintenance more difficult.

The only places where I have seen DIRECT mode used effectively is when the record needs to be directly accessed, but lacks a key field that will uniquely identify the record occurrence. This kind of record, by its nature, is difficult to process. The dbkey, however, must be kept somewhere. Without it, the only way to access the record would be by area sweep. Again, the application software must control the situation.

DIRECT mode has been used for a record that is a *manual* member of several sets.

Sequential Record Mode

Sequential mode is a special addition to IDMS that was created to support a few users who required that their data be store in physical sequential order. The intent of this mode is to dramatically accelerate I/O activity by allowing the data to be stored and read sequentially. The original purpose of SPF was to provide a secondary indexing capability for the users of physical sequential mode records so they could access the records in an order other than the physical sequence.

Record Names

Within the IDMS environment there are two basic types of record names: schema record names and work record names. This section describes each type and the naming requirements for them.

Schema Record Names

Schema record names have traditionally been assigned with titles describing the purpose of the record. PERSON is the record containing basic information about persons in the database while ORGANIZATION describes organizations relating to the database.

ORGANIZATION is a *composite name,* covering a collection of organization types, such as VENDOR, COMPANY, DEPARTMENT, SUPPLIER, TRAINER-COMPANY, etc. It is frequently necessary to identify such data with a generic name that can be applied to several different and distinct types of data. Synonyms may be used to make each of the preceding titles for specific organizations match the generic title.

Work Record Names

Work records are internal temporary occurrences that are created for a specific technical purpose. Many applications will have work records; it is critical that the dictionary not have duplicates. With multiple development projects underway, each feeding into a single production dictionary, there must be a standard naming convention present to prevent the creation of duplicate work records.

Utilizing the standard naming convention described in Chapter 2, the various work record forms are uniquely assigned to their respective projects. Recapping, the work records are named using the format *ABCDE000*. The work record types are defined using characters D ($=$ R for record) and E (see Figure 15-5).

WORK RECORD EXAMPLE
```
ADD REC SCARW000 V 1.
02  W-SUBA                        PIC S9(8) COMP VALUE +1.
02  W-SUBB                        PIC S9(8) COMP VALUE +1.
02  W-SUBC                        PIC S9(8) COMP VALUE +1.
02  W-SUBD                        PIC S9(8) COMP VALUE +1.
```

MAP RECORD EXAMPLE
```
ADD REC SY1RM001 V 1.
02  M-SUB10                       PIC S9999 COMP.
02  M-PFKEY-LINE.
   03  M-PFKEY-GROUP OCCURS 5.
      04  M-PFKEY-INDICATOR       PIC XXX.
      04  M-PFKEY-TEXT            PIC X(8).
```

SCRATCH WORK RECORD EXAMPLE
```
ADD REC SZGRS001 V 1.
02  S-SUB1                        PIC S9999 COMP.
02  S-DIALOG-IDENT                PIC X(8).
02  S-DIALOG-VERS                 PIC S9999 COMP.
02  S-DIALOG-TITLE                PIC X(40).
```

QUEUE WORK RECORD EXAMPLE
```
ADD REC SZGRQ001 V 1.
02  Q-SUB1                        PIC S9999 COMP.
02  Q-DIALOG-IDENT                PIC X(8).
02  Q-DIALOG-VERS                 PIC S9999 COMP.
02  Q-DIALOG-TITLE                PIC X(40).
```

Figure 15-5   Work Record Examples.

W. *General work record.* This category is used for all temporary records used by the application programs.

M. *Map work record.* This work record is used to associate data with a map. Its numeric portion of the record name is normally identical to that of the map that it supports.

Q. *Queue work record.* This is the record format of a queue record used by the application.

S. *Scratch work record.* This record supports a scratch record used by the application.

In each of the preceding cases, the remainder of the record name corresponds to the standard naming convention for applications. This ensures that no two work records from different applications will be named alike.

Record Descriptions

Record descriptions are one of the most overlooked parts of system documentation. For this reason, records are frequently duplicated by follow-on developers who do not understand what is already available for them to use.

Record descriptions can be broken into several groups:

1. Descriptive title. IDD provides the *RECORD DESCRIPTION IS* ... clause to permit an expanded descriptive title. Entry of this title should be mandatory for each record defined, particularly work records.
2. Purpose. Within the general descriptive COMMENTS section, the purpose of the record should be clearly provided. For example, the record ORGANIZATION is intended to serve multiple purposes. Each of these is to be defined. Where multiple purposes requires different specific data, such as a control key, the value for each purpose must be defined.
3. Relationship to other records. Each record within a schema has a unique relationship to other schema records. This relationship may not necessarily be defined by a set between the records.

    For example, the PERSON and the ORGANIZATION records have multiple relationships with each other, depending on which type of organization is involved. These records are indirectly connected, having a junction record between. The junction record must provide the means to differentiate between the kinds of relationships.
4. Test plan. Each schema record and some of the other work record types will have to be tested. A test plan, using the *TEST-PLAN* UDC, must be prepared.

Compressing Records

Compression can have a major impact on the physical size of a database. For example, a 600-byte text record (consisting of ten 60-

character lines) will normally be compressed a minimum of 20 percent and frequently savings will reach 50 percent. The effects of the compression technique, however, will vary depending on how the data fields are arranged in the record.

When To Use Compresssion

Data compression should be used primarily when sufficient disk space can be saved to justify the increased CPU overhead associated with the compression and decompression process. This overhead averages 10 to 15 percent.

When Not To Use Compression

Avoid compression when:

1. *Performance is a major requirement of the system.* Compression will slow down processing.
2. *The record type does not stay in the database* for any amount of time. Short-lived records seldom justify the use of compression.
3. *The record is small.* The minimum overhead for compression is 8 bytes per record. If the record is not at least 30 bytes in length (the 30-byte figure is a general rule of thumb that I use; Cullinet uses 16), the compression can't really be enough to justify its use.
4. *The record data is randomly organized or contains large numbers of packed decimal fields.* Under these conditions, the compression routine will not operate efficiently. See the way to organize data for compression following.

Compression Performed

The IDMSCOMP routine supplied by Cullinet performs several types of compression functions:

1. *Spaces within the record* are eliminated and converted to a 2-byte code.
2. *Display numeric data* is compressed into a form of COMP-3.

3. *Binary numeric data* is compressed only if it contains a long string of zeros. The zeros are converted to a 2-byte code.
4. *Common character pairs* are compressed into a single byte.

The data compression routine operates against the *record* while most other data activities operate against the data field. What this means is the compression routine ignores field boundaries. *It is compressing the whole record, not its individual fields.* The way the data fields are organized, therefore, affects the efficiency of the compression routine. *Changing compression routines after databases have been designed to enhance one technique can actually result in database growth rather than reduction.*

Organizing Data Records For Compression

Considering the way the standard IDMS compression routine works, the fields within a database record should be organized (beginning of the record to the end) as follows:

1. *Key fields.* IDMS does not compress fields used as CALC, index, or sorted set keys. Compressing these fields would affect the computation of the CALC key or the sorting order of data.
2. *Binary elements.* Since binary elements are not usually compressed, they should be placed close to the beginning of the record.
3. *Required numeric fields.* Numeric data fields that must be populated minimize compression.
4. *Optional numeric fields.* Maximum compression occurs when numeric data, defaulting to zeros, is packed.
5. *Fixed required alpha fields.* A fixed alpha field is one where the field length and the data length are constant, e.g., a state code of two characters, always filled by a two-character code.
6. *Variable required alpha fields.* These fields, where the data length is set to the *maximum* needed to hold a piece of data, such as a company name. They usually have 20 to 40 percent empty space in the field.
7. *Fixed optional alpha fields.* Space elimination is most efficient when the fields most likely to be blank are adjacent.
8. *Variable optional alpha fields.* Again, space compression is a factor.

16

Sets

Within IDMS (and other CODASYL DBMS implementations), a set is the thread that associates one record type with another. *Every* set must have a purpose. Otherwise it should not exist.

Sets provide one of the navigational paths through the database. They do not, however, provide all of the navigation routes that may be employed. An index, for example, provides another route for the user to access data. The CALC record provides a point of access; the area sweep provides another means of access.

Pointer Arrays

Pointer array is the term that has been given to a different type of record linking activity. Figure 16-1 illustrates the difference between chain mode, an IDMS feature since its inception, and pointer arrays. System developers now have the ability to use either or both techniques within any schema.

The principal difference between the two forms is that, with pointer arrays, IDMS does not physically walk the set from member record to member record. Instead, it walks the table within the SR8 record. If retrieval of the member record is desired, its dbkey is in the table.

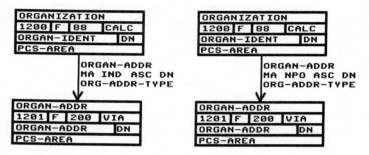

Figure 16-1   Chain And Pointer Array Mode Example.

For this reason, pointer arrays are the most beneficial when used in sorted sets. NEXT, PRIOR, FIRST, and LAST sets have to retrieve the member records anyhow (the SR8 doesn't have any key data to make a determination as to which members to physically read). It is possible, just as it was in SPF, to read only the pointer array without physically moving the record data to working storage.

This is accomplished by issuing a FIND command in the set. If the desired record is located, currency is established. Moving the record to working storage is then accomplished with a GET command. Where set population is quite high, this technique can dramatically improve performance.

Depending on the number of member occurrences in the pointer array set, IDMS can build layers of SR8 records to maintain set balance and performance. The application developer, however, does not see this array or have access to it. It is all performed automatically by IDMS.

Using Pointer Arrays

As mentioned earlier, the pointer array set is best used when the relationship between two records is to be sorted. Figure 16-2 illustrates the same set structure for both chained and pointer array sets. The principal difference is that the MODE statement identifies the set as indexed. Within the schema, a single pointer position is included in the member record. This pointer contains the dbkey of the SR8 record so that walking of the set from the member is possible.

```
SET  NAME  IS  ORGAN-ADDR
ORDER  SORTED
MODE  IS  CHAIN  LINKED  TO  PRIOR
OWNER  IS  ORGANIZATION
NEXT  DBKEY  POSITION  IS  1
PRIOR  DBKEY  POSITION  IS  2.
MEMBER  IS  ORGAN-ADDR
MANDATORY  AUTOMATIC
ASCENDING  KEY  IS  ORG-ADDR-TYPE  DUPLICATES  NOT  ALLOWED
NEXT  DBKEY  POSITION  IS  1
PRIOR  DBKEY  POSITION  IS  2
LINKED  TO  OWNER  OWNER  DBKEY  POSITION  IS  3.


SET  NAME  IS  ORGAN-ADDR
ORDER  IS  SORTED
MODE  IS  INDEX  BLOCK  CONTAINS  5  KEYS
OWNER  IS  ORGANIZATION
NEXT  DBKEY  POSITION  IS  1
PRIOR  DBKEY  POSITION  IS  2
MEMBER  IS  ORGAN-ADDR
MANDATORY  AUTOMATIC
ASCENDING  KEY  IS  ORG-ADDR-TYPE  DUPLICATES  NOT  ALLOWED
INDEX  DBKEY  POSITION  IS  1.
```

Figure 16-2   Chain And Pointer Array Set Descriptions.

CALC-to-CALC sorted sets, the bane of system performance, can be effectively utilized with pointer arrays. In the chain mode, *performance geometrically degrades* as the number of occurrences of the member record increases. Not a real problem with set loading of 25 or fewer records, the CALC-to-CALC chain set becomes a disaster as the number of occurrences climbs past 100.

Pointer array sets, on the other hand, walk only the SR8 record (assuming you use the format-6 OBTAIN) before retrieving the desired record occurrence. I/O activity is consistently small and performance degradation as the set population increases is largely avoided.

Pointer array sets should be considered for most non-VIA sets (where an I/O is required for each read of a member record). Connecting a new record into the set avoids having to physically read

```
┌─────────────────────────┐
│EVENT-OOAK               │
├──────┬──┬────┬──────────┤
│900   │F │48  │CALC      │
├──────┴──┴────┴────┬─────┤
│EOOAK-IDENT        │DN   │
├───────────────────┴─────┤
│OOAK-AREA                │
└─────────────────────────┘
```

Figure 16-3a   Basic Single-Record IDMS Set Structure.

the adjacent member occurrences in order to connect the chain pointers.

NOTE: Since much of the steps and considerations associated with the use of integrated indexing for sets is identical to that for use of an integrated index as as a secondary index, the technical details related to integrated set indexes will be found in Chapter 18, Indexing.

Set Types

The CODASYL specification defines seven different set types. Six of these are implemented within IDMS. The seventh set type recursively links a record to itself. In this section, we will discuss each and identify where they should be used.

Standalone

This is a set that is not a set. The standalone record is a record that is not physically connected to any other record by a defined set. Access to the record is either by key or through a sweep of the area in which the record resides. Figure 16-3a illustrates this structure.

A standalone record is frequently used when it is necessary to maintain control information associated with an application. One or more occurrences may be stored, depending on the type and nature of the control information. For example, control information for each year would be stored in separate occurrences and the year used as the CALC key for the record.

Owner-Member

This is the simplest of all physical sets. The set connects an owner record type to a single member record type. Access to the owner may

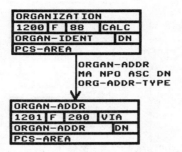

Figure 16-3b   Owner-Member Set Example.

be from the member and principal access to the member is through the set from the owner. Figure 16-3b shows an example of this structure.

The owner-member set structure is used for a majority of IDMS sets. It is the easiest to implement and understand. There are no ambiguities of which member record will be retrieved when an obtain is issued.

Forked Set

The forked set is so named because its structure has the appearance of a fork. Illustrated in Figure 16-3c, the forked set may have any number of member records. The forked set is also known as a *multi-member set.*

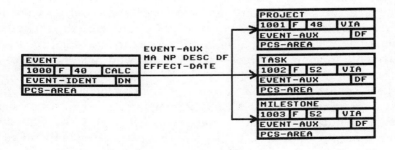

Figure 16-3c   Forked Set Example.

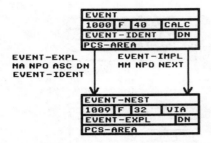

Figure 16-3d   Nest Structure Example.

Forked sets are very useful when an owner has many member record types, each of that has very few occurrences. This permits us to conserve pointer space in the owner record while maintaining performance during obtains. Forked sets are most often used when two or more member types are mutually exclusive (one does not occur when another is present).

Forked sets should not be used when the population of one or more of the record types in the set grows beyond approximately 100 records. Even though your program does not request an occurrence of each record type in the set, IDMS must still read through the record occurrences of all record types in the set.

Nests

The nest structure, otherwise known as the bill-of-material (BOM) structure, permits associating occurrences of the same record type with each other. Figure 16-3d illustrates this structure.

Nest structures have many uses. They are very versatile. They are also very inefficient from an I/O standpoint. The company organization chart is a good example of a nest structure; sections report to departments, that in turn report to divisions, who report to the company president.

A nest structure also permits the associating of similar but different data groups together with a minimum number of sets. Looking at a manufacturing bill of materials, Figure 16-4, we find that there are multiple levels of "parts" that must be associated with each other. As shown in Figure 16-4, linking all of these types to each other creates a spider web of sets. Of significant importance is the

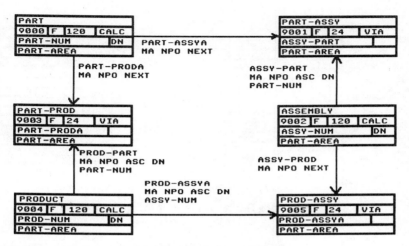

Figure 16-4   Many-To-Many Of Similar Type Structure.

consideration of what happens if another record type is added to the structure. This is an example of design that does not allow for change and growth.

Using a nest structure with a stub owner, such as shown in Figure 16-5a, permits the easy linking of each of the components in a manufacturing process. The forked set members shown each represent a specific type of "part." For any one occurrence of the stub, only one of the several member records will occur. For example, a part is the combination of the stub and the PART member. An assembly is the combination of the stub and the ASSEMBLY record.

Of significance here is the ability to respond to change and growth. In Figure 16-5a, the company was limited to three levels of assembly. If a fourth level became necessary, the entire database structure (and all of the software) would have to be modified. With the structure in Figure 16-5a, an unlimited number of assembly levels can be added dynamically.

Significant to future enhancements to the database structure and possible increases in the types of data that may become part of a bill of materials, lets look at Figure 16-5b. Here an additional member has been added to the forked set, a PROCESS record type. *This new record type was added to the set without affecting the current data or the programs supporting that data.*

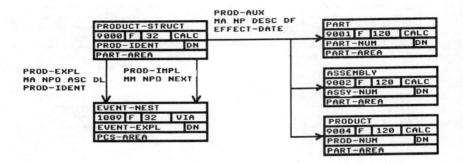

Figure 16-5a   Nest Structure Replacement For Many-To-Many.

Many-to-Many

The many-to-many relationship is also very common in business. A company has many employees; a person may be associated with many companies.

This structure is used whenever *there is a chance* of a many-to-many relationship between two entities. It is far safer to create a many-to-many structure at the outset of a design than have to restructure to insert one later.

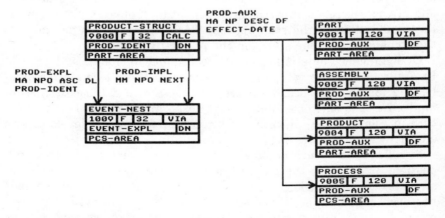

Figure 16-5b   Expanding the Nest/Auxiliary Structure.

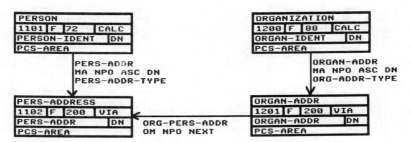

Figure 16-6   Many-To-Many Structure Example.

The record in the middle is called a junction record. It may serve several purposes other than to logically join its two owners (Figure 16-6 illustrates the process):

1. *It may contain a flag* that describes the relationship between the two owners. For example, the ORGAN-ADDR record between ORGAN and PERSON may contain a code that identifies if the person is a current employee, past employee, dependent of an employee, or a contractor.
2. *The key value of the non-VIA owner* record type may be kept in the record. This improves performance by permitting a possible selection before having to expend an I/O crossing to the non-VIA owner.
3. *The record may contain data that is unique* to the association of the two owners. In the ORGAN-ADDR record, for example, the address is uniquely that of the person associated with that organization.

Multilevel Hierarchy

IDMS permits a record to be owned by another record and, at the same time, own another record. This is a multilevel hierarchy and can be structured to any desired depth. Practically, however, such structuring should not go below three levels (owner and two owner-members). Processing overhead increases as access to succeeding levels is required.

Figure 16-7 illustrates a practical example of this structure. ORGAN and PERSON own JOB-ASSIGN that in turn owns JOB-

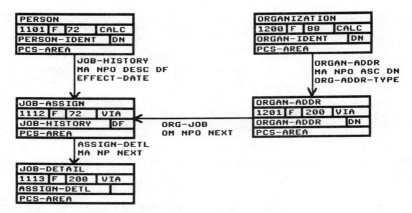

Figure 16-7   Two Level Database Structure.

DETAIL. Access to JOB-DETAIL is simple and straight-forward, using a key value on the sorted set ASSIGN-DETAIL. If an additional record were to be made a member of JOB-DETAIL, an additional layer of processing would be required. Navigating from PERSON to the record following JOB-DETAIL, while simple, would involve considerable DBMS activity.

Multiple Set Relationships

Figure 16-8 illustrates a multiple set. This set is quite different from a nest structure. Where the purpose of a nest structure is to associate occurrences of multiple levels of the same data, the multiple relationship is intended to provide multiple paths between two dissimilar record types.

In our illustration the leftmost set between the organization and person records identifies *any person* who is associated with the organization in the past or current time. The rightmost set, on the other hand, identifies those persons *who are current employees* of the organization.

The usefulness of this set structure is primarily during retrieval. Where there are large numbers of member occurrences (persons associated with organizations, in this case), it may be more efficient to provide a special set to handle a common retrieval requirement.

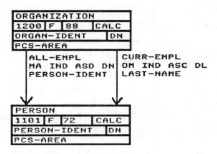

Figure 16-8   Multiple Set Relationships.

This approach is a clear tradeoff between update and retrieval. It will obviously require more time and resources to maintain the sets (as well as more program logic). If frequent requests for current employees are expected, the extra set may pay for itself.

Set Names

There are a variety of set naming conventions; however, the one that this section describes is by far the most commonly used. See Chapter 12 for a detailed discussion of set naming contentions.

Set Pointers

Set pointers provide the navigation facility with which IDMS moves from record occurrence to record occurrence along a defined set path. There are three types of pointers within IDMS: next, prior, and owner. Each has a specific purpose and provides navigating capability to the database structure.

Pointer Position

Every pointer occupies physical space within an IDMS record. Each pointer requires 4 bytes of space; that space contains a binary number that identifies another record occurrence within the set. (In

IDMS, an empty set is identified by a zero value in the owner positions and a -1 in the member positions.

The set pointers are clustered at the physical beginning of each record occurrence. The order of the pointer positions is determined by the schema developer. Pointers for a set are normally placed adjacent to each other for convenience and ease of tracking them if manual review of the sets are required.

In the early days of IDMS, a guideline known as the *Clock Rule* was recommended by Cullinet. This procedure assigned set pointers around a record type beginning at the top, or 12 o'clock, and proceeding clockwise until all pointers had been assigned. This process has largely fallen into disuse. It was useful for initial definition but became confusing if database restructuring was required at a later date.

CALC records have two additional set pointers that are automatically placed in the first two physical positions in the record. This is the CALC set and we will deal with it in more detail later in this chapter. The developer still assigns pointer positions one and two to sets; in a CALC record these positions begin after the CALC set pointers.

Next Pointers

The next pointer within a record, owner or member, contains the dbkey of the next physical record occurrence within the set. This pointer is *required in all sets*. It is necessary in order to walk the set in a forward direction. When assigning pointer positions the next pointer is normally the first position assigned for any set.

Prior Pointers

The prior pointer provides the ability to navigate a set backwards. It is *required* when the DML commands FIND/OBTAIN LAST/PRIOR are used as these commands walk the prior pointer exclusively.

The prior pointer is *optional, but strongly recommended* on all sorted sets. The reason for this is the manner in which IDMS locates the proper position to insert a record in a sorted set. IDMS walks the set, looking for a record whose key value is higher (lower on DES-

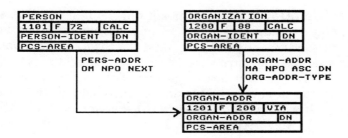

Figure 16-9   Owner Pointer On Many-To-Many Sets.

CENDING sets) than the key value of the record to be inserted. Once
it locates that record, it places the new record in the set in front of
the higher (lower) record. If only next pointers are available, IDMS
cannot walk backward to the previous record in the set (the record
that must be changed to contain the dbkey of the new occurrence); it
is forced to walk the set a second time to locate the prior record. Performance suffers accordingly.

Owner Pointers

Owner pointers occur only in member records. The pointer contains
the dbkey of the record occurrence of the owner of the set.

Why They Are Useful. The owner pointer provides a direct path
from a set member occurrence to the owner occurrence bypassing all
other member occurrences between it and its owner. This improves
processing considerably when walking a many-to-many structure.
Using Figure 16-9 as an example, if we wish to locate a person associated with an organization, it is necessary to retrieve the ORGAN
record, walk the ORGAN-ADDR set to the ORGAN-ADDR record,
and retrieve the owner off the PERSON-ADDR set.

   If the PERSON-ORGADDR set does not have owner pointers,
IDMS must walk through each occurrence of ORGAN-ADDR associated with the specific PERSON before reaching the PERSON
record itself. This can be very time-consuming if there are many
ORGAN-ADDR records in the chain. The owner pointer allows us to
go directly to the owning PERSON record occurrence.

When To Use. Owner pointers should **not** be used on all sets. Each owner pointer occupies 4 bytes of physical space in its member record and sometimes there is no need for them. For example, in a simple owner-member structure, there is no need to issue an OBTAIN OWNER when currency is at one of the member occurrences. The owner had to have been previously retrieved and should still be in memory. If a reread of the owner is necessary, an OBTAIN CURRENT of the owner record type will accomplish the job quicker and faster.

Owner pointers, therefore, should be reserved exclusively for those sets where *backward navigation* is required. This applies to all many-to-many structures, nest structures, and hierarchical structures where entry will be effected at a lower level of the hierarchy.

The rule, therefore, is: Owner pointers are used whenever entry into a member record will commonly occur from a source other than the set whose owner is to be read.

Set Membership

The membership criteria associated with a member record must be carefully evaluated. Assigning the wrong membership category can cause database software developers to go to much extra work to use the database and can adversely impact performance. There are two types of membership in a set: mandatory and optional. We will go into each in depth below. Remember that set membership is by individual member record. Where a forked set exists, each member record can have a different membership criteria.

Mandatory

Mandatory is the term applied when the relationship must exist in order for a member record to be stored in the database. For practical purposes, a member record cannot be disconnected from a mandatory set; it must be erased.

Mandatory relationships should be used in many-to-many and nest structure situations. In these cases, the member record exists primarily for the purpose of linking two owner occurrences together. If the linkage is to be broken, it is natural to assume that the mem-

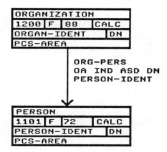

Figure 16-10   One-To-Many Structure.

ber record would be deleted as its purpose in life has been fulfilled and is no longer required.

Mandatory relationships *should not* be used where it is possible that a member record occurrence could be disconnected from one owner and moved to another. For example, in the Bachman chart in Figure 16-10, we assume that a person can only be associated with one organization at a time. If we wish to move that person from the finance department to the accounting department, it will be necessary to disconnect the PERSON record from the finance department ORGAN record and connect it to the accounting department ORGAN record.

If the set is MANDATORY, the PERSON would have to be erased and restored under its new owner. An OPTIONAL set permits the program to *disconnect* the PERSON from its current owner and connect it to the new owner.

Optional

The OPTIONAL membership relationship permits the application software to alter the association of specific member record occurrences with owners. The DML verb DISCONNECT may *only be used with an OPTIONAL set.*

The CONNECT verb can be used *only with either an OPTIONAL set or a MANUAL set where the member has not yet be connected into the set.*

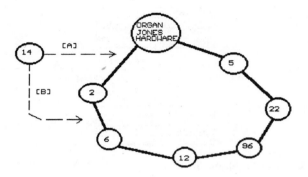

Figure 16-11   Record Placement.

Set Positioning

The set positioning options identify where IDMS is to position the set currency before performing the desired database function. Proper selection of the set positioning option can be very critical to the effective and accurate operation of the database. This section describes the four principal unsorted positioning options: NEXT, PRIOR, FIRST, and LAST. Sorted sets are reviewed in a separate section.

NEXT

The NEXT option places a new record occurrence logically into the set immediately following the record that is CURRENT OF SET. Figure 16-11 illustrates the two most common situations for next membership: (a) When the CURRENT OF SET is the owner record and (b) when the CURRENT OF SET is a member somewhere in the chain.

In Figure 16-11, record 14 will be stored between the owner and record 2 (a) when the CURRENT OF SET is the owner record. It will be stored between records 2 and 6 (b) when record 2 is CURRENT OF SET.

NEXT is the most efficient of the set options (for storing data), because IDMS does not have to establish any other currencies before storing a new record (assuming currency to the owner has already

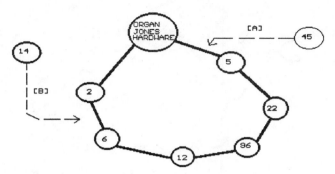

Figure 16-12 NEXT/PRIOR Record Placement.

been established). When the CURRENT OF SET is also the owner record, NEXT and FIRST are functionally equivalent.

PRIOR

The PRIOR option is the reverse of NEXT. Instead of walking the chain forward, each PRIOR retrieval walks from the end of the set toward the beginning. Storing a new record in a prior set is illustrated by Figure 16-12. Here again two conditions can occur: (a) The CURRENT OF SET is the owner record; and (b) the CURRENT OF SET is one of the members. In each case, the new record is stored in front of the CURRENT OF SET. When the owner record is CURRENT OF SET, PRIOR and LAST options are functionally equivalent. The PRIOR option requires that PRIOR set pointers be present in the set or an error will occur. As a general rule, however, all sets should be defined with PRIOR pointers.

FIRST

The FIRST set option forces a new member record to be placed as the first record in the set, immediately following the owner. This option is less efficient than the NEXT option because IDMS must always reestablish the owner record as the CURRENT OF SET before storing a new record. FIRST is equivalent to the last-in, first-out

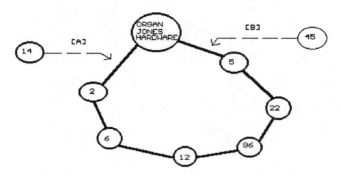

Figure 16-13   FIRST/LAST Record Placement.

(LIFO) queuing technique. Figure 16-13 illustrates the placement of new records in both FIRST and LAST environments. Record 14 will be placed as shown if the set order is FIRST and record 45 will be inserted as shown if the set order is LAST.

LAST

The LAST set option stores a new member record immediately preceding the owner record on the end of the set. Again, currency must be established for the owner record before the new member can be stored. LAST is equivalent to the first-in, first-out (FIFO) queuing technique. *Prior pointers are required for the LA⊔T option.*

Retrieving Data

The major point to be remembered when retrieving data from un-sorted sets is that a loop must be programmed to scan the entire set. Whether the full set is actually scanned depends on the location of the desired record in the chain. Unfortunately, the only way to be sure the desired data is *not* present is to scan the entire set.

The four unsorted set options take on a different perspective when retrieving data:

1. FIRST and LAST are used only to establish currency to the beginning and end of the set, respectively.

```
WHILE DB-STATUS-OK
 REPEAT.
   OBTAIN NEXT PCS-DESCR-DETL WITHIN DESCRHDR-DETL.
   IF DB-ANY-ERROR
     EXIT.
   [process the record]
 END.
```

Figure 16-14   Source Code To Retrieve Data From Unsorted Set.

2. NEXT and PRIOR are used to "walk" the set from the beginning and end, respectively.

If the CURRENT OF SET is the owner record, as it usually is when the scan process begins, FIRST and NEXT are functionally equivalent (the next member record in the set is also the first one). LAST and PRIOR are also functionally equivalent for beginning the set walk at the end of the set.

Figure 16-14 illustrates typical ADSO source code that will retrieve data from an unsorted set. Remember that it is possible to retrieve the data from the set in any of the four orders regardless of the order in which it was stored, even if it was sorted.

Sorted

Storing. Of all of the set options, the sorted option is the least efficient when storing new member records. That lack of efficiency in storing data is frequently offset by the improved efficiency when modifying, deleting, or retrieving the data. The placement of data within a sorted set depends on the value of the key field of the new record and the suboptions that have been selected. Figure 16-15 illustrates all of the variables:

1. *Key value 3 is stored when ASCENDING order is used.*
2. *Key value 6 is stored when ASCENDING, DUPLICATES FIRST order is used.*
3. *Key value 6 is stored when ASCENDING, DUPLICATES LAST order is used.*

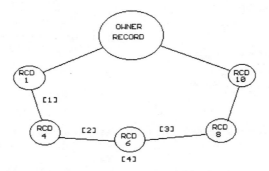

Figure 16-15   Sorted Set Data Positioning Ascending.

4. *Key value 6 is rejected when ASCENDING, DUPLICATES NOT ALLOWED* order is used.

Figure 16-16 illustrates the use of descending sort orders.

1. *Key value 3 is stored when DESCENDING* order is used.
2. *Key value 10 is stored when DESCENDING, DUPLICATES FIRST* order is used.
3. *Key value 10 is stored when DESCENDING, DUPLICATES LAST* order is used.
4. *Key value 10 is rejected when DESCENDING, DUPLICATES NOT ALLOWED* order is used.

Figure 16-17 illustrates typical source code used to store a record within a simple owner-member sorted set.

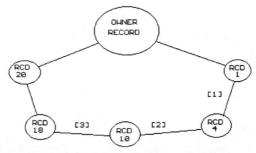

Figure 16-16   Sorted Set Data Positioning Descending.

```
!
!   ESTABLISH CURRENCY TO THE SET OWNER
!

  MOVE [key data] TO S1200-ORGAN-IDENT.
  OBTAIN CALC ORGANIZATION.
  IF DB-ANY-ERROR
     DO.
        CALL ERRORX.
        DISPLAY MESSAGE CODE 900326
           PARMS = (ORGAN-IDENT).
     END.
!
!   THE ORGANIZATION OWNER HAS BEEN FOUND
!  LOAD THE DATA OF THE ORGAN-DESCR RECORD
!
  MOVE [data fields] TO [organ-descr fields].
!
!   LOAD THE SORTED SET KEY FIELD
!
  MOVE SEQUENCE-NO TO S1208-ORGAN-DESC-SEQ.
!
!   STORE THE RECORD
!
  STORE ORGAN-DESCR-HDR.
  IF DB-ANY-ERROR
     DO.
        CALL ERRORX.
        DISPLAY MESSAGE CODE 901299
           PARMS = ('ORGAN DESCRIPTION').
     END.
```

Figure 16-17 Sorted Set Store Record Example.

Modifying. Modifying a member occurrence within a simple sorted set illustrates how advantageous sorted sets can be for database maintenance. Compare the source code in Figures 16-18 and 16-19. The first section scans the set as if it were unsorted; the second section illustrates sorted set source logic.

```
!
!   ESTABLISH CURRENCY TO THE SET OWNER
!
MOVE [key data] TO S1200-ORGAN-IDENT.
OBTAIN CALC ORGANIZATION.
IF DB-ANY-ERROR
   DO.
     CALL ERRORX.
     DISPLAY MESSAGE CODE 900326
        PARMS = (ORGAN-IDENT).
   END.
!
!   THE ORGANIZATION OWENR HAS BEEN FOUND
!   LOCATE THE RECORD TO BE MODIFIED
!
WHILE DB-STATUS-OK
   REPEAT.
     OBTAIN NEXT ORGAN-DESCR-HDR WITHIN ORGAN-DESC.
     IF DB-ANY-ERROR
        EXIT.
     IF S1208-ORGAN-DESC-SEQ EQ SEQUENCE-NO
        DO.
!
!   LOAD THE CHANGES
!
         MOVE [change fields] TO [descr rcd chg fields].
!
!   MODIFY THE RECORD
!
         MODIFY ORGAN-DESCR-HDR.
         IF DB-ANY-ERROR
            DO.
              CALL ERRORX.
              DISPLAY MESSAGE CODE 900899
                 PARMS = ('ORGAN DESCRIPTION').
            END.
       END.
    END.
```

Figure 16-18   Modify Unsorted Set Record Source Example.

```
!
!   ESTABLISH CURRENCY TO THE SET OWNER
!
MOVE [key data] TO S1200-ORGAN-IDENT.
OBTAIN CALC ORGANIZATION.
IF DB-ANY-ERROR
   DO.
      CALL ERRORX.
      DISPLAY MESSAGE CODE 900326
         PARMS = (ORGAN-IDENT).
   END.
!
!   THE ORGANIZATION OWENR HAS BEEN FOUND
!   LOCATE THE RECORD TO BE MODIFIED
!
OBTAIN ORGAN-DESCR-HDR WITHIN ORGAN-DESC
   USING S1209-ORGAN-DESC-ID.
IF DB-ANY-ERROR
   EXIT.
IF S1208-ORGAN-DESC-SEQ EQ SEQUENCE-NO
   DO.
!
!   LOAD THE CHANGES
!
      MOVE [change fields] TO [descr rcd chg fields].
!
!   MODIFY THE RECORD
!
      MODIFY ORGAN-DESCR-HDR.
        IF DB-ANY-ERROR
           DO.
              CALL ERRORX.
              DISPLAY MESSAGE CODE 900899
                 PARMS = ('ORGAN DESCRIPTION').
           END.
      END.
```

Figure 16-19 Modify Sorted Set Source Code Example.

Deleting. Deleting a member occurrence within a simple sorted set is accomplished with nearly the same logic as was used in Figure 16-19 to modify a record. The only difference is that fields are not changed and the MODIFY statement is changed to ERASE.

Retrieving The retrieval of member records in sorted sets was the first step in modifying or deleting the record. As can be seen from Figure 16-22, sorted sets have a distinct advantage during retrieval. Only a single DML statement is required; only one DBMS action is taken.

Some special conditions occur when retrieving members of a sorted set, particularly if the selected member occurrence is not present. Using Figure 16-22, a request for record 3 is made. It is not found. NEXT currency points to record 4; PRIOR currency points to record 1. Set currency remains at whatever record was successfully retrieved in the set *on the last read even though a 0326 ERROR-STATUS is indicated.*

Sorted vs Unsorted Sets

Sorted sets are one of the most powerful, yet least understood, features of IDMS. They are much maligned as being expensive to use. Under the right circumstances, however, the sorted set can enhance the usefulness of your database immensely.

Pros And Cons Of Sorted Sets

Sorted sets require much more analysis than the other set orders. There are several subtle considerations that can make or break an application. The complexity of the tradeoffs associated with sorted sets is such that instructors frequently advise against their use.

Let's look at the major considerations for using sorted sets:

1. *Retrieval is faster than the other set orders* when looking for a specific record occurrence. A single DML command causes IDMS to scan a member chain, regardless of length, until the target record is located. The application program must initiate *every* read within *unsorted* set orders.

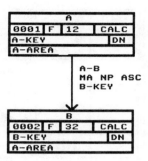

Figure 16-20a CALC-CALC Record Structure.

2. *Where database updating is mostly modifications or deletions* from the database, the locating ability of the sorted order will improve update performance.
3. *Applications running under CV (vs. local mode batch)* require the use of a SVC for each DBMS access. Sorted order records require fewer DBMS accesses and reduce system overhead.
4. *Some data editing can be automatically accomplished* through the use of the DUPLICATES NOT ALLOWED clause, permitting the DBMS to ensure that duplicate items do not exist.
5. *Retrieval of the data on-line is frequently done* in a specific order. Sorting on-line is undesirable because of the time consumed. Having the data already in the most often desired order improves on-line performance.

On the other hand, there are some situations in which sorted sets are not desirable:

1. *A sorted set should not be used* when associating two CALC records. Figure 16-20a shows a CALC to CALC structure; figure 16-20b illustrates how record occurrences stored in the CALC mode can occur in the database. Connecting such records is very common. However, a sorted set requires that the chain be walked for each store or access. Many I/Os result and performance rapidly degrades. See the uses of index sets in Chapter 18 for an alternate approach that reduces the hazards of CALC-to-CALC sorted sets.

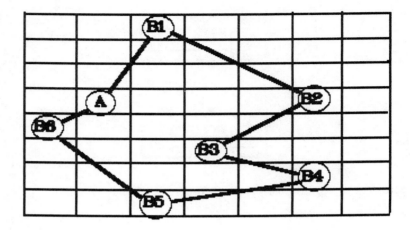

Figure 16-20b   CALC Record Distribution In An Area.

2. *Both sets of a many-to-many record relationship in* that the
   owners are CALC should not be sorted. The effect is the same
   as placing a sorted set between CALC records (Figure 16-21).
3. *The non-VIA set of a many-to-many record relationship in that*
   the junction record is stored should not be sorted. This also
   has the effect of placing a sorted set between CALC records.
   Even if the owners are not CALC, it is much better to place the
   member record via the sorted set. This will reduce paging I/O
   during access on the sorted set.

Sorted sets provide a number of additional options that, properly
used, can make a significant difference in performance. The first of
these is the ASCENDING/DESCENDING clause:

1. *ASCENDING is the most commonly used set order.* It should be
   specified when:

   a. *Addition of data within the set is to occur randomly* across
      the entire set.
   b. *New data records being added* will, a majority of the time,
      fall within the first half of the range of the sort key.
   c. *On-line retrieval* requires the data to be in ascending order.

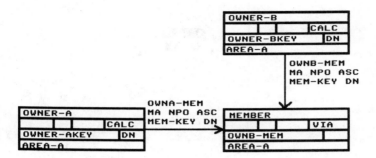

Figure 16-21   Undesirable Sorted Set Structures.

2. *DESCENDING order is frequently overlooked.* However, it is very useful when new data being added to the set will be placed in the second half of the set range. This is particularly true of chronologically organized sets. Figures 16-22 and 16-23 illustrate the placing of new record occurrences within ascending and descending sets. In these illustrations, a specified new record with a sort key of 4 is being stored. In Figure 16-22 the record is stored after walking most of the set, while in Figure 16-23 it is the second record in the set.

3. *The next major option of the sorted set* is the DUPLICATES clause. The three versions of this clause are:

   a. *DUPLICATES FIRST.* New record occurrences with duplicate sort keys are stored ahead of their duplicates already resident in the set. This has the effect of a last-in, first-out sequence when retrieval starts from the front of the chain.

   b. *DUPLICATES LAST.* Sets sorted in ascending order that permit duplicates use this option more frequently than the FIRST option. It just seems natural that the duplicate, arriving second, is placed behind the first occurrence of the key value.

      Figures 16-22 and 16-23 illustrate the positioning of a new record in both ascending and descending mode using these options.

   c. *DUPLICATES NOT ALLOWED.* This option, briefly mentioned earlier, has the effect of verifying the sort key data as being unique. Eliminating duplicate key data has the

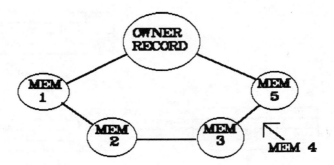

Figure 16-22   Ascending Sorted Set Occurrence.

advantage of reducing the complexity of the application software logic. When duplicates are allowed, it is not possible to issue a single DML OBTAIN command and assume that all relevant data will be retrieved. A second OBTAIN must *always* be issued to be sure that duplicates are not overlooked.

Recommendation: When using sorted sets, try to organize the data so that the DUPLICATES NOT ALLOWED feature may be selected.

Caution: Prior pointers MUST be used in sorted sets.

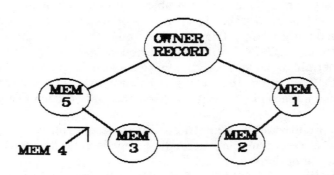

Figure 16-23   Descending Sorted Set Occurrence.

The CALC Set

The CALC set is a "system" set. It is used only by IDMS and serves to connect those record occurrences defined as *CALC* that should be physically stored in a certain database page.

IDMS provides random access to database records by computing the physical page where a record is to be stored from the value of its CALC key field(s). Every CALC record is assigned to a specific physical page within its area.

As a record is stored on the page, it is connected to the CALC set for that page (every page has its own) in ascending sorted order. Once placed on a page, the physical record never moves from that page. It does frequently move around within the page as IDMS closes up free space after another record was deleted.

It is possible, of course, for more records to CALC to a certain page than there is space on the page. When this happens, a condition known as page overflow occurs. IDMS solves the problem by physically storing the record on the nearest higher numbered available page. The record, however, is placed in the CALC set of the page where it should have gone. This allows IDMS to travel all over the area, if necessary, to locate a physical record even though it logically should be located on one particular page.

This process permits us to modify the key value of a CALC record at will without major consequences. IDMS simply disconnects the record from the CALC set of one page and inserts it into the CALC set of the page to which it now logically belongs.

Modifying the key value of a CALC record is not recommended procedure because it increases the physical I/O overhead of processing. One I/O is required to retrieve the page where the record should be and a second to retrieve the page where it actually resides. Performance will degrade if this is done too often; this is why there is a general rule against modifying database record key values.

Page overflow is also the reason why we do not let databases fill to more than 70 percent. Statistically, page overflows increase in number dramatically when a database reaches this level of loading. If a database accidentally reaches a higher level of fill, overall performance will gradually decrease. Performance *will not improve* by simply expanding the page size. Since the physical records do not move from their page of residence, the overflow condition remains. The only thing we have accomplished is to make more space avail-

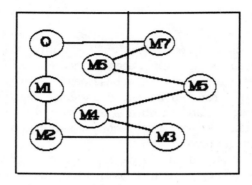

Figure 16-24   Adverse Effect Of Page Expansion.

able on each page for new records. This may, in fact, degrade performance further.

Let's look at Figure 16-24. By expanding the page size of an area, we permit more records to CALC to a page and be stored there. The CALC set has been extended to records stored on a subsequent page by overflow. Now, suddenly, it can use its own page again. It pointers now come back to its page for the new records being stored. Walking the CALC set takes us from its own page to an overflow page and back, *potentially creating additional I/O activity*.

The only way to clean up the ensuing mess is to unload and reload the database.

Cross-Area Sets

Cross-area sets are those whose owner record resides in one area and the member in another. There are valid reasons for using this technique but it should be used with caution.

Looking at Figure 16-25, we see that the ORGAN owner record is located in the A-AREA, the ORGAN-ADDR member record is located in the B-AREA, and the PERSON owner record is located in the C-AREA. There are several considerations to be made when evaluating this structure:

1. *Storing an ORGAN-ADDR record **always*** requires a physical I/O because the member is in a different area from its owner.

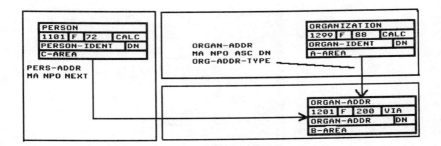

Figure 16-25   Database Structure With Cross Area Sets.

2. *The member record is stored in B-AREA* in approximately the same location within the area as its ORGAN owner. Let's look closer at this condition. If A-AREA is 100 pages and B-AREA is 100 pages and the ORGAN record owner occurrence is stored on page 55, IDMS will attempt to store the ORGAN-ADDR member record occurrence on page 55 of B-AREA.

3. *A failure or recovery requirement* that occurs in any of the three areas will require all of the areas to be recovered. This domino effect is the major drawback to cross-area sets.

4. *If a member record is to contain sensitive data* that you wish to secure, a cross area set may be a good approach. Figure 16-26 illustrates such a situation. Here the PERSON-DATA1 record will contain sensitive information about job and salary. By placing it in its own area, the subschema can include or exclude the area and control access to the record type. When creating a dependent area such as shown here, define both primary and dependent areas in the same physical data set to simplify recovery.

Recovery

As we discussed earlier, recovery of cross-area sets can be very sticky. The recovery of one area, C-AREA above, requires the recovery of B-AREA because it is possible that set connections were made between database backups. Where such connections had been made, broken chains would be present.

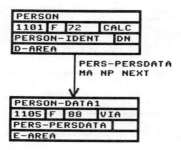

Figure 16-26   Cross Area Set To Enhance Security.

The domino effect continues because the same conditions could exist between B-AREA and A-AREA. A-AREA would also have to be recovered.

Depending on the level of integration within the total database, the recovery of one area could require a majority of the database areas to be recovered. Not only is this a time-consuming task, many users would be out of service who were not affected by the original problem.

Tie-Point Technique

The tie-point structure technique involves planned redundancy of key values. Figure 16-27 illustrates tie-point design. We will use the Bachman chart of Figure 16-25 as our base for this example. As you see in Figure 16-27, the B-AREA now has two additional records, ORGAN-T and PERSON-T. These are known as *tie-point* records. They contain only the key value of the corresponding record in the A-AREA and C-AREA.

No set crosses the area boundaries. If a database recovery is required in any one area, the other area pointers are not affected. A subtle side benefit also occurs. The B-AREA is now logically complete. It does not have to rely on the other two areas to be tested.

Access to the ORGAN-ADDR from the ORGAN record is accomplished by obtaining the ORGAN-T record (using the ORGAN record occurrence CALC key value) and then reading the address record. There is no increase in physical I/Os; reading the address

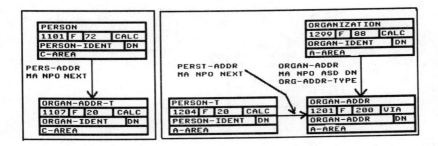

Figure 16-27   Cross Area Communication Via Tie Points.

record cross-area would have required an I/O anyhow. One addition-al logical I/O is required.

Access to the ORGAN-ADDR from the PERSON record is ac-complished in much the same way. Here, however, a second physical I/O is required because the address record is via ORGAN-T and is probably stored on a separate page.

Access to either the ORGAN or PERSON record occurrences from the address record is accomplished by obtaining the desired record through its CALC key value that is stored in the tie-point record.

Database maintenance is more complicated because you must remember to update the tie-point record occurrence if the key value is changed on the corresponding owner occurrence. This is not as bad as it may seem initally, however, since good database design mini-mizes key value changes. Deleting one of the two owners in their own area must result in the deletion of the corresponding tie-point record, the address member, *and the other tie-point record occur-rence.* We must remember, in this example, that the three records in B-AREA are equivalent to the junction of a many-to-many relation-ship.

Is That Set Really Necessary?

The purist of network database design connects all related record types with sets. In general, this ensures the physical association of related data. There may be reasons why, however, we do not estab-lish a set; our previous discussion of cross-area sets is one example.

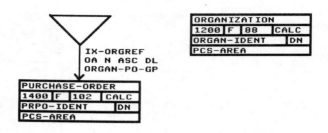

Figure 16-28   Using An Index To Cross Areas.

The case for set elimination is primarily one of performance. Offsetting the improvement in performance is an increase in storage requirements because the elimination of a set invariably means that planned data redundancy, of at least the key field, is necessary. Planned redundancy isn't all that bad, *if you have really planned for it.*

Let's look at one example of set elimination. Figure 16-28 illustrates a situation where the purchase orders associated with an organization are separated from the ORGAN record. The processing frequently accesses a specific purchase order. Purchase order numbers may be duplicated across organizations.

Since the organization identifier is required to establish a unique occurrence of the PURCHASE ORDER, we have two options for accessing a specific purchase order. We can enter the database at the ORGAN record and walk a set to the PURCHASE ORDER desired or we can enter the PURCHASE ORDER record directly (making it CALC also). When the users will frequently desire to review a specific purchase order, the latter approach is faster and more efficient.

It is still possible to read all of the purchase orders associated with a specific organization by walking the index after scanning the index on the organization identifier with a blank purchase order. This will place the index pointer just before the first purchase order for the organization.

This is a particularly good example of the best use of planned redundancy. Since the organization identifier is one key value that changes infrequently, the maintenance of redundant data is minimized. *Consideration for such a change, however, must be made as part of the software design unless changing that key is prohibited.* Planned redundancy should be avoided when the redundant data field values are subject to frequent modification. Such a situation increases system overhead and software complexity.

17

Areas

While most programmers think of the database area as specifying the physical location of data, *it actually identifies the logical grouping of data within the IDMS database.* Database areas are used primarily to group data for specific purposes, such as security.

The physical mapping of an area to an operating system file is performed by the DMCL. In this chapter, we will probe the uses of areas and how they can be used to enhance the operation of a database application.

Why Have Areas?

Why, the novice asks, if it makes database design more difficult, should we have areas in the first place? There are times that even the more experienced ask the same question as well. There *may* be cases where too many areas are designed into a database. More often, however, there are too few.

Let's look at some of the better reasons for multiple database areas:

1. Serial processing, the sweeping of an area to locate and process data, requires fairly small areas. The record size is usually

small, too. The physical requirements are critical to the system performance.
2. Different processing requirements may dictate separating some data from others. Sensitive information can be placed in a separate area that can be more effectively protected.
3. Indexes may be placed in a separate area to optimize their physical use of storage space.
4. Backup and recovery is enhanced when areas are smaller. The larger the area, the longer backup and recover time required.

Sizing Areas

Database areas are sized by the number of *pages* that are included within each area definition. The number of pages selected depends on the amount of occurrences of the record types assigned to the area. The anticipated size of the page also directly affects the number of pages required. An area page is a physical fixed block of DASD storage, normally sized so that a maximum number of pages can fit on the physical track of the storage device used.

Each area is defined as a contiguous range of pages, each of the same size. Each logical page of the area maps directly to a block within a physical direct access file.

A Little History

In the early days of IDMS, the sizing of areas was limited to a few specific values, oriented to the track size of the disk device on which the database would reside. Practical page size maximums were in the 6000 to 9000-byte range and the exact page size was an evenly divisible fraction of a disk track.

Prime Number Page Sizing

In early versions of IDMS the user was encouraged to select the number of pages in an area using a prime number nearest to the number of pages required. While I am sure that this technique improved performance in some instances, I was never able to prove (or disprove) the benefit. The use of odd numbers of pages in an area actually caused some management problems when numerous applications ran on the same central version; overlapping page numbers or unusual gaps between number assignments occurred if the DBA was not very careful.

Small Size Pages

Whether small or large, there are advantages to sizing pages. Here are some of the advantages of making database pages small:

1. It takes less time in the I/O channel to read a database page, reducing the time a program idles while waiting for data to be read. Partially offsetting this advantage is the need for more pages in the database.
2. Because a smaller page size means more pages for the same total space, CALC record occurrences are better distributed over the area and the chance that CALC records will map to the same page is reduced. The CALC set path on each page is shorter.

Large Page Size

On the other hand, large pages have their advantages, too:

1. Area sweeps can be run faster. This may prove to be an advantage only if there is a large amount of batch processing performed on a daily basis.
2. More data is transferred to and from DASD with each page because the page can hold more records. I/O transfer time increases, however, and may degrade performance in very high-volume applications.
3. Overflow of records onto an adjacent page is reduced since more space is available on each page.
4. Larger VIA clusters can be handled on a single page. We will discuss clustering further on in this chapter.

As you can see, there are several considerations, most offset by others, to the page sizing decision. We will discuss the most important in detail as we progress through this chapter.

Storage Device Optimization

The large-capacity disk drives of today, as well as the dramatically reduced cost per megabyte, has made us less careful about optimizing the page size to the storage device. Cullinet provides an excellent set of tables identifying the optimum number of pages per disk track for all of the common IBM-based disk drives. There is no excuse for wasting track space.

Storage Device Contention

The very large storage device, of which the 3380 is a good example, does create a different type of problem. High database activity rates across several databases (or the same database) can cause contention for the device. Optimum operation of a high-volume database may dictate the spreading of the areas across multiple physical devices. Unless handled carefully, this can cause some devices to be badly underutilized.

Record Sizes

Database record sizes have a direct impact on the size of a page. The page must be *at least* large enough to store an occurrence of the largest record type assigned to an area plus the page overhead. Obviously, sizing the page to just hold one record occurrence would be ridiculous. In the next section, we will discuss the *cluster effect* and how it can assist in determining the practical *minimum* page size.

If the size of a fixed-length record or the root portion of a variable-length record will occupy more than 30 percent of a page, space management problems are likely. Depending on the mix of CALC to VIA records, area size should be four to 10 times the size of the largest record in the area. There are tradeoffs, however, some of which are discussed elsewhere in this chapter.

Computing Area Page Size

The following formula computes the physical number of pages required for a page. Two computations should be run, one identifying the current needs and a second to define the anticipated needs *two years from now*. Figure 17-1 illustrates the formula. The steps in the formula are:

1. *Calculate the number of record bytes to be stored* in the area. Record bytes consist of the data bytes necessary to contain the area's data and the associated with each data record.
2. *Compute the number of base pages* by dividing the total record bytes by the proposed page size -32. (This takes the page header and footer into consideration.)
3. *Divide the number of base pages* by the space utilization percentage. 70 percent is the standard factor; this figure should be lowered as the turnover rate for data increases.
4. *Compute the number of space management pages*. Subtract 32 from the page size and divide by two. Divide the quotient into the number of base pages and round up.
5. *Calculate the total number of pages* by adding the number of base pages and space management pages together.
6. *Compute the number of tracks required* by dividing the number of pages by the number of pages that can be placed on a track of the DASD device being used.

Maximum Page Size

Release 10 of IDMS provided the DBA with a new database management tool. The dbkey, instead of the fixed format of old, can be adjusted to increase the number of record occurrences that can be stored on a page. This finally permits efficient use of page sizes greater than 10,000 bytes.

Even with this option, we must be careful not to make a page too large. Why? Let's look at an example. If our page size is 19,000 bytes, we have about 18,900 available for storage of record occurrences. If our average record length is 50 bytes and we are limited to 255 occurrences on the page, only 12,750 bytes would be used by the time we had stored our 255 record limit. *7000 bytes would be wasted.*

1. $D + P = Rs$ $Rs \times Rv = Rb$

where

D = the number of data bytes in the record	[44]
P = the number of pointer bytes in the record	[8]
Rs = the length of the total record [52]	
Rv = the number of record occurrences	[1000]
Rb = the number of record bytes in the area	[52000]

2. $Pt = Rb / (Ps - 32)$

where

Ps = the proposed page size   [3000]
Pt = number of pages at proposed size, rounded [18]

3. $Pg = Pt / Su$

where

Su = the space reserve percentage   [70%]
Pg = gross number of pages, rounded   [26]

4. $Sm = Pt / ((Ps - 32) / 2)$

where

Sm = number of space management pages   [1]

5. $Pt = Pg + Sm$

where

Pt = total number of pages   [27]

6. $Tr = Pt / Tp$

where

Tp = number of pages on a track of device [6]
Tr = number of tracks   [5]

Figure 17-1   Area Page Size Computation.

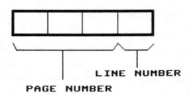

LINE NUMBER

PAGE NUMBER

Figure 17-2   Default Dbkey Format.

Worse yet, the database statistics would show the database to have lots of available space when, in fact, it was full.

Dbkey Format

The database key, or dbkey, is the root of all IDMS storage activity. Every record in the database has a unique dbkey assigned. Each of these records is stored *logically* on a page within the database based on the dbkey value. The word *logically* is emphasized because, as we have seen, it is possible for a database record to be assigned to a specific page and have to *physically reside elsewhere* because the target page was full.

The IDMS dbkey is a 4-byte binary field. It is composed of two sub-fields: the page number and the "line" number.

Default

Prior to Release 10, IDMS permitted the user to identify up to eight million pages, each of which could contain up to 255 lines (records). The first three bytes of the dbkey contained the page number and the fourth byte contained the line number. Figure 17-2 illustrates this format.

This format is still the one most commonly used and is the default assigned by IDMS unless requested otherwise by the developer.

When To Alter

The dbkey format can be altered to increase the number of pages in the area, by adding bits to the page definition portion of the dbkey. Up to 1,073,741,824 pages may be defined. When this is done, the number of records that can be stored on the page decreases. Each additional bit added to the page definition doubles the number of pages and, at the same time, cuts the number of records per page in half.

Given today's increasing disk capacity, the most likely alteration of the dbkey would go in the other direction. The number of available pages is reduced and the number of records that can be stored on the page is increased. This permits us to store more records on a larger page that is optimized to the increase physical track size of a disk device. Up to 2727 records can be stored on a page if the dbkey is optimized in this direction.

There is, however, a very good performance rationale for increasing the number of pages and reducing the number of records per page. Let's assume that our database is very large, i.e., millions of records. A very high percentage of the database record occurrences are CALC records. Your analysis has shown that few of these records will CALC to the same physical page if the number of pages is set at 32 million or more.

Altering the dbkey format to provide a database page capacity of 32 million will ensure that little, if any, page overflow will occur. Most pages will contain only a single occurrence of the CALC record, reducing the walking of the CALC set. Assuming that the page size is designed to accommodate the cluster effect, overflows should be virtually nonexistant. System performance is enhanced because via I/O is largely reduced to moves within the page buffers.

Cluster Effect

This brings us to the *cluster effect*. The term defines the natural clustering of VIA records around their CALC owners. Each CALC record with VIA members has its own unique clustering factor. To minimize page overflow, this clustering must be considered.

Average Cluster

During database design, we should have identified the minimum, average, and maximum number of occurrences of each database record type. For VIA member records, we identify the number of occurrences per owner record occurrence. The aggregate total of the CALC record and the average number of ALL of its VIA occurrences is the *average cluster size.*

When an area has several CALC records, each with a different cluster size, the most populous should be used as the basis for the average cluster. Be sure, however, to consider a less frequent cluster if its size is quite large. Of course, if you only expect a large cluster to occur less than 1 percent of the time, overflow degredation is not worth considering.

Overflow

When the page size is less than the average cluster size, overflows occur regularly. Since every page overflow causes I/O activity, minimizing overflows is important to high system performance.

Experiments conducted over the years have shown that a page size of two and one-half times the average cluster size minimizes page overflow. The page size can be increased beyond this point but it should not be reduced to less than the two and one-half times size. Increasing page size beyond this baseline will improve performance only when the number of CALC occurrences (cluster bases) as a percentage of the total database increases.

Space Management

IDMS creates a *space management page* every so often within an area. The first page of an area is always a space management page. The purpose of the space management facility is to minimize the number of I/Os that will occur when IDMS tries to find space for a new record *in a nearly full database.*

IDMS, in fact, only updates the space management fields when a page reaches the 70 percent full level. Below that, it assumes that a page has plenty of room for new records. The space management facility, therefore, *is only useful when an area is operating near its capacity.*

No database should be operated beyond the 70 percent full level. Once the 70 percent level is reached, CALC and cluster overflows increase quickly. Once stored as an overflow record, *every access of a CALC record requires at least two page accesses.* The only way to clean up the database is to unload and reload the entire area, a tedious task.

Reserving Space

IDMS permits you to reserve space in every page for future activity. PAGE RESERVE can limit the amount of space used on each page before overflows occur. It is common to reserve up to 50 percent of a page when initially batch loading the database. The default is 80 percent.

The effect of page reserving space during the initial load is to spread the data more evenly across the pages, leaving room for the natural growth of the database; overflows occur less often during normal updating.

An undesired side effect of reserving too much space on the page is excessive overflows. A reasonable balance must be met. It is also important to initially load data from the end of the database downward to prevent cascading overflows, the most expensive kind of overflow.

Variable-length records that are expected to grow over time need special handling. An increased page reserve should be established to permit the records to grow without fragmenting.

Cascading Overflow

This is a good time to discuss cascading overflow. Not much is said about this overflow condition but it is a major contributor to performance degradation in database applications where large clusters are common. Figure 17-3a illustrates this problem.

As we see, the CALC owner is stored on the first page along with several members. This page, now full, overflows to the next available

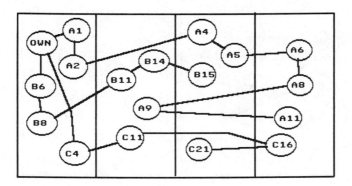

Figure 17-3a   Cascading Overflow Example.

page (higher in sequence) as two more members are added. Note that
the set path runs back and forth because the new members are inserted in the set in their sorted order. As the set membership continues to grow over time, the next available pages are used. As illustrated, walking the set will require reading data from four physical pages, traversing back and forth to follow the set path.

The subtlety that makes this condition dangerous is the activity
that goes on with other data in the same area. Records may be
added and deleted from any of the pages illustrated. Record *A9,* for
example, is placed on the second page instead of the fourth because
some records were deleted from the second page, freeing enough
space to hold record *A9.*

There is no ironclad way to avoid cascading overflow. It can be
minimized through larger page sizes, placing member records in a
separate area (we'll talk about that next), and the use of PAGE OF-
FSET to scatter members when an owner has multiple member sets.
All of these processes have tradeoffs in performance.

PAGE OFFSET

Figure 17-3b illustrates the effect of using PAGE OFFSET to scatter
the members in such a way that they do not interfere with each
other. In this illustration, the *A* group of records are offset from the
owner by three pages, as are the *C* group of records. The *B* group of

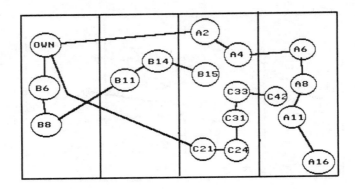

Figure 17-3b   PAGE OFFSET Example.

records are permitted to locate themselves on the same page as the owner.

Let's look first a the *A* group. While a physical I/O is now required to walk from the owner to the first *A* record, *A2,* only one I/O is required to walk the remainder of the set's members. Previously, four I/Os were necessary to walk the entire set; offsetting the records cut the number of I/Os in half.

Our illustration does not show any improvement for the *B* group, the assumption being that other data still forced the data to be written on advancing pages. The *C* group, on the other hand, reduced its physical I/Os from three to two while increasing the number of record occurrences in the set by offsetting the members by three pages.

It is likely that both the *A* and *C* groups would have improved their I/O efficiency even more if they had been offset to different pages. It would appear that all of the *A* group records (assuming their length to be approximately that of the *C* group records) could have been placed on the third page if the *C* group were offset to page five. All of the *C* group, offset to page five, would probably have been located on the same page.

The PAGE OFFSET option, therefore, will nearly always improve the performance of a database where an owner has multiple VIA sets, each with several member occurrences. The number of pages to offset each member record is determined by calculating the space requirements for the member record closer to the owner. An extra page or two of space over the calculated requirement should be allowed to

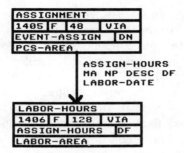

Figure 17-4   PCS Labor Hour Data Structure.

account for growth and the use of one of the pages by other records outside of the cluster.

Members In Separate Area

Where a particular set will contain very high volumes of data, it may be desirable to dedicate an area to that set's members. Figure 17-4 is a Bachman chart of such a relationship in PCS. The data volume is such that it is practical to place all member occurrences in their own area.

By sizing the pages of the special member area to optimally handle multiples of the member record, physical I/O can be minimized and performance improved. Page size should be large enough to handle the average member cluster; room for one or two extra records is even better.

This area arrangement contains the same hazards that are present in other cross-area set structures. Since the structure is specialized, the principal consideration is that both areas are backed up at the same time. You can make sure the concurrent backup occurs by placing both areas *in the same OS file.*

SMI

Space Management Interval (SMI) is used ONLY when the pages of the database area have been expanded beyond their original size. An explanation of the space management concept is useful at this time.

IDMS databases contain a certain number of pages (the exact number varies with the number of pages in an area and the page size) that are called space management pages. There is at least one of these pages in every area and it is located at the beginning of the area (page one).

IDMS allocates a block on each space management page for each remaining database page in the area. If the area is large and/or the size of the database page is small, multiple space management pages may be identified. These additional pages are scattered at regular intervals through the area, the interval being determined by how many database page blocks can be placed on a space management page.

When the database page is expanded, IDMS expects the space management page to be located following the standard algorithm that identifies how many page blocks will be on a space management page of a certain size. If IDMS were to use this algorithm to locate the space management page in the expanded area, it would select the wrong page. The SMI clause in the schema is used to signal IDMS that the space management interval is other than normal.

The SMI clause, therefore, contains the *original length* of the area database page. IDMS can locate the space management pages and is happy. The expanded space management page has some wasted space since it still contains only the page blocks in its original assignment.

Physical Characteristics Of A Page

Each page can be considered as a mini-database since each normally stores several records and contains its own control areas. The IDMS database page is broken into four distinct sections, illustrated by Figure 17-5:

1. The header is 16 bytes long, consisting of the page number (4 bytes), the next pointer for the CALC set (4 bytes), the prior pointer for the CALC set (4 bytes), the space available count (2 bytes), and a 2-byte unused space. The latter four fields are also known as the SR1 system record (the CALC record).
2. The page body that contains all of the object data records being stored on the page. This space varies in size based on the size of the total page within the area. The data stored in the page

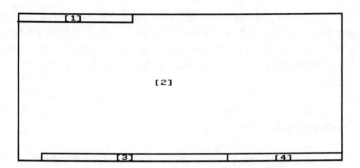

Figure 17-5   Database Page Structure.

body *is always concentrated at the front of the page body.* This feature, that continuously optimizes the available space on the page, reduces unusable space to a minimum and makes it easy to expand the size of a page. Like some of today's jet airliners, a page can be made larger by opening it up in the middle and inserting more space.

3. The page index contains a variable number of line indexes and the page number. Note that the page number occurs as the first and last four bytes of each page. This is added protection against undetected database damage. IDMS actually checks both values each time a page is read; an unequal value causes immediately alarm within the DBMS.

The line index group contains one or more *line index pointers,* one for each record stored on the page. The indexes move from the end of the page backward into the page body as more records are placed on the page. One thing to keep in mind is that *once a line index has been established, it remains on the page as long as the page exists.* For example, we store six records on a page; subsequently we delete three of these records. While the data is no longer present, the empty line indexes remain, waiting patiently for more records to be stored.

The line index itself is 8 bytes in length, broken into four 2-byte fields: the record identifier (this is that four-digit number that we assign to every record type defined); the displacement of the beginning of the record from the start of the page; the length of the record, and the length of the record prefix (the pointers).

4. The page footer consists of 16 bytes, broken into a line index for the SR1 record (8 bytes), the line space count (2 bytes), the page update count (2 bytes), and the page number (4 bytes). Line index zero always points to the CALC record for the page.

Area Processing Modes

Database areas may be processed in one of two modes: update and retrieval. Within each, three *submodes* are provided: shared, protected, and exclusive. This section will identify the most effective use of each option.

Update Modes

Every time you wish to change the database, your program must open the database in update mode. By default, a database opened in update mode is also opened in retrieval mode. (It would be a bit difficult to modify or delete a record you could not retrieve.)

Shared. Any number of other processing programs may access the area in either update or retrieval mode. This is the normal update mode for on-line processing; it permits multiple terminals to concurrently access the area.

Protected. Only one processing program may *update* the area at a time. Any other update programs must wait until the current one is done. Any number of *retrieval* programs can access the area concurrently while the single updating program is operating. Protected mode is used only when it is critical that a complex update process be completed in an area before any other user can update that area. Retrieval programs, however, may access the area concurrently.

For example, a database area contains a universally accessed control record group. Every user's software looks at the contents of this group and modifies its activity based on the group content. To prevent erroneous results (if the control group was changed while another user was working in the database), protected update will prevent other update activity until the control group is updated.

Exclusive. The single processing program that has requested exclusive update is the *only* program that can access the area. Other updating *and retrieval* is locked out until the requesting program completes. This mode is prohibited by most installations for normal processing that includes on-line access. It single-threads the database area and forces *all* other users to wait.

The only rationale for using exclusive mode is to perform a critical update to the database that could adversely affect *all other users* if they were using the database at the same time as the update.

Retrieval Mode

Retrieval mode is used when access to the database is for the purpose of retrieval only. Retrieval mode makes more efficient use of IDMS, minimizing the journalling activity.

Shared. As with shared update, this mode allows other users of the database to share the area without restriction. This mode is the preferred and most commonly used on-line retrieval mode.

Protected. This mode permits a retrieval program to gain access to the database and, while it is executing, prohibit any other program from updating the area. If this mode is used during active on-line transaction usage of the system, all updating users will be locked out. Protected retrieval is useful for taking backups of the database, and for producing reports that make wide use of many records in the database.

Exclusive. Exclusive retrieval locks out *all other users* while the program is actively accessing the database. Its use must be heavily restricted. Many installations prohibit its use entirely. Little justification exists for use of this mode.

Adding A New Area To The Database

As the database grows or changes to meet business requirements, it is often necessary to add new areas to the database. The following outlines those IDMS facilities that must be executed in order to made a new area available for use:

1. *On-line schema compiler.* Add the new area, its records, and sets to the schema definition. Generate the revised schema.
2. *DMCL.* Recompile all DMCLs that include the revised schema or any part of it after including the new area into the DMCL source.
3. *Subschemas.* Modify those subschemas that require the new area and generate. Generate the subschema loads modules and load them to the OS load library.
4. *Initialize the area* using IDMSINIT. The area is then ready for use.

18

Indexing

Indexing is a process used to provide an alternate path to data within the database. In IDMS, indexing has been available since introduction of the Sequential Processing Facility (SPF) with Release 4.0. This original indexing capability had so many idiosyncracies that it was not used to the extent it deserved.

SPF was an add-on to IDMS, not a part of the main DBMS software. As a result, it did its indexing job in unusual and often mysterious ways, frequently to the frustration of the developer.

With Release 10.0, SPF has been replaced by a fully integrated indexing facility. In this chapter, we will deal with this new capability in depth because its power can open the door to structuring techniques that previously were prohibitively hard on performance.

Integrated indexing provides two facilities, separate yet similiar in many ways. Each fulfills a badly needed capability. **Secondary indexing** replaces the Sequential Processing Facility (SPF) that has been with us since Release 4.0. **The pointer array (index) sets** is a new facility, long awaited, that provides an alternate record association capability to the standard chaining method.

Much of what we will discuss in this chapter applies equally to secondary indexes and index sets. The principal difference between these facilities is the owner of the index (SR8) record. Secondary indexes are owned by another system record, the SR7; index sets are owned by the application owner record type.

Pointer Array (Index) Sets

A pointer array is a means to relate two records within the database without physically chaining them together. The approach builds a list of member records of a particular owner occurrence and and stores the list adjacent to the owner. The list contains a pointer (dbkey) to each member. The term *pointer array* stems from this array of dbkeys. Usually the member also contains a pointer to the list record.

When comparing index sets to the conventional chain sets, three performance points stand out:

1. Index sets normally require fewer I/Os to retrieve member records than are necessary with chained sets. I/O processing during database updating is improved by index sets.
2. Chain sets require less CPU time to support member processing.
3. Chain sets use disk storage space more efficiently.

This summarizes to mean that high volume, I/O intensive applications can get a performance boost from judicious use of index sets, sacrificing some storage space and CPU time to gain improvement through reduced I/O.

Secondary Indexing

A secondary index is frequently so named because it provides a secondary path to data. Within IDMS, we look at the secondary index as providing the second direct path to data. The remainder of the chapter will concentrate on the details of secondary indexing, called *integrated indexing*

The integrated index is identified as a SYSTEM set. This simply means that its owner is the DBMS system itself. Integrated indexing has an owner record but it is invisible to the schema in IDMS/R.

When To Use Indexes

There are numerous uses for secondary indexes, many of them subtle. Nearly all secondary indexes are used to speed retrieval. Here are a few examples of index use:

1. *CALC record locating.* CALC records that are not members of any set can be located quickly by their symbolic key. If the key value is not known, however, an area sweep is required to find a specific record of all of the record occurrences. A secondary index whose member is the CALC record can be walked, quickly locating each record occurrence. Sorting the index will present the records in the desired order.
2. *Sorted retrieval.* All member records within the index set can be retrieved in a specified order.
3. *Random retrieval.* Using a sorted index, it is possible to locate a specific occurrence of a record on other than its primary key. This is particularly useful when the target record type contains *foreign* key values used to locate other records.
4. *Generic search.* A partial key value may be used to locate record occurrences that begin with a specific character string.
5. *Fast area sweep.* A secondary index sorted on dbkey permits retrieving target records in their physical sequence but bypassing those database pages not containing the target record type.
6. *Record clustering.* Records that are located VIA a secondary index are physically clustered together in the database. This technique is useful when there are a small number of occurrences of a record that must be accessed frequently (such as a validation table).
7. *Key data retrieval.* The RETURN verb may be used to supply the symbolic key of an indexed record without retrieving (with the associated I/O) the physical member record.

Integrated Secondary Index Records

A pair of new system-owned records were added to IDMS to implement integrated indexing. The SR7 record is the invisible owner of system-owned (secondary index) index sets. The SR8 record is used by the pointer array set facility that we will discuss shortly.

The SR7 Record

Every time a system-owned index is defined, IDMS creates a SR7 record as the owner of the index set. The SR7 is an OOAK record that owns the index set that has been defined. A separate SR7 is defined for each secondary index. The SR7 is actually treated by IDMS as a CALC record, stored using its name as the CALC key. Figure 18-1 illustrates the database structure of the secondary index using integrated indexing.

You can actually locate SR7 record occurrences by walking the CALC set. If you wish to find a specific occurrence of the SR7, use its set name (padded to 16 bytes) within quotes.

The SR8 Record

The second system record supporting integrated indexing is the SR8. It is created and maintained automatically by IDMS. It, too, is invisible to the application user. The SR8 contains a table of entries, each one corresponding to an application record that is the member of the index set. Figure 18-2 shows the structure of the SR8 record. Note that the record contains next, prior, and owner pointers. These support the set in which the SR8 resides, the SR7 (for secondary indexes) or the application owner record (for pointer array sets).

Let's look at the fixed data block in more detail. The components of this block are:

1. *Approximate dbkey of uplevel node.* This field will contain HIGH-VALUES if the index is unsorted. When the index is sorted, the dbkey of the SR8 at the next higher level of the index is stored here.

2. *Count of orphaned entries.* It is possible for orphaned entries to occur at any time in the index. If the dbkey of any member of the index is not present in its index record, the record is considered an orphan. Graphically, Figure 18-3 shows four database records whose set pointer points to an SR8 while the SR8 contains only three of the records. Record C is an orphan.

   If SR8 has been lost from its higher level SR8 in a sorted index, the orphan count of the higher level SR8 would be set to one.

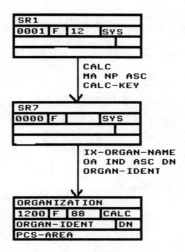

Figure 18-1   Secondary Index Database Structure.

3. *Cushion size in bytes.* Every SR8 (except orphan only SR8s) has a cushion that is used to insert new index entries. The cushion ensures that there is adequate space in the SR8 to accept a new index entry. Once a new entry is added, the cushion is expanded. When the SR8 can no longer be expanded, a split will occur.

4. *Level.* The level of the SR8 within the index. If unsorted, the level number is always zero. Sorted index SR8s contain a level number representative of how many splits have occurred earlier in the SR8. The top level of a sorted SR8 is set to zero.

5. *Total key length.* This field contains the total length of the symbolic keys in the index.

6. *Flag byte.* This byte indicates the status and type of SR8 record. The flag values are:

X'80' — sorted index
X'40' — sorted on symbolic key
X'20' — compressed keys
X'10' — descending key sequence
X'00' — bottom-level SR8

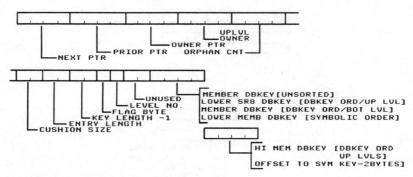

Figure 18-2 SR8 Record Structure.

Two reserved bytes make up the remainder of the fixed portion of the SR8 record.

The arrangement of the key pointers and symbolic keys is somewhat complicated if the index is sorted; unsorted indexes are simple. Let's take the simple unsorted index first. The dbkeys to the member records are strung in the order of the records within the set.

The sorted key arrangement includes the dbkey of the member record and a 2-byte field containing the offset to the beginning of the symbolic key. The symbolic key itself is broken into three sections: a prefix, length-1 of the key, and the actual key. If the key is uncompressed, the actual key is the entire symbolic key (with the final character possibly a repeating pad character). If the key is compressed, the complete key can be composed of several key segments.

SR8 records are physically stored VIA their owner in the same area as the owner (another departure from SPF that normally kept the indexes in a separate area). IDMS will usually attempt to store the SR8 on the same page as its owner; it can be offset a defined number of pages if desired.

NOTE: Page offset considerations will be discussed in more detail in Chapter 21. For our purposes here, offsetting the SR8 records is done when the number of VIA members clustering around an owner causes frequent page overflows. Offsetting the SR8 may make it possible for all SR8 occurrences for a particular set owner to reside on the same page, reducing physical I/Os and improving performance.

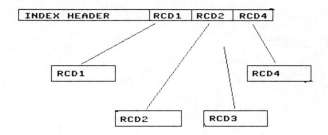

Figure 18-3 Orphan Index Record Example.

Compressed Keys

A new feature of IDMS, with release 10.0, is the ability to process sorted sets on a compressed key. Previous releases required that all sort key fields be uncompressed. This forced the record designer to place the keys at the beginning of the record. While this was usually no problem, it precluded adding an additional index or set at a later date if the key was a compressed field. It is now possible to add additional indexes to a record without having to redefine the compressed area.

Index Definition

The index set must be defined with as much, if not more, care than any other set in the schema. Parameter selection has a direct impact on system performance.

Computing The SR8 Population

The number of SR8 record occurrences is not as important as the number of levels that will occur when the index is sorted. Since unsorted indexes are always at the same (zero) level, the number of SR8 occurrences will equal the number of members of the index divided by the SR8 entries (the number identified in the set INDEX BLOCK CONTAINS clause).

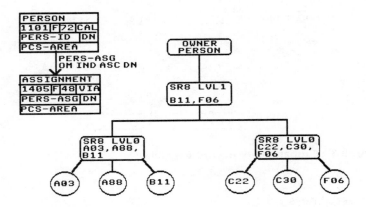

Figure 18-4   Single Level SR8 Index Split.

Sorted indexes will split when the number of SR8 entries is not adequate to handle the number of set occurrences. The number of times
this split occurs has direct bearing on the number of levels that will
exist. Since it is desirable to keep index levels to two or less (below
the root), the SR8 entries value becomes critical.

Before we go much further, let's be sure that we are together on
what constitutes a level split. Figure 18-4 illustrates an index root
that has been split twice. Even though two new SR8 records have
been spawned, the number of levels have been increased by only one.
Both spawned SR8s are at the same level with each other.

The double split occurs when the system attempts to add a new
index entry between two existing entries after the index has been
filled. The detail index entry is pushed to the next level and the first
level has been created. The index entry now points to the lower level
SR8 and the symbolic key identifies the *highest key value* in the lower
level SR8.

Once the root has spawned a lower level index, its level number is
incremented. This indicates to IDMS that the root is no longer a
detail index but points to lower levels.

Later, the system attempts to insert another entry in the filled root.
The spawn process repeats, creating another lower level SR8. As this
level fills, it too spawns another SR8, making the second level. Figure
18-5 illustrates the spawning of the second level.

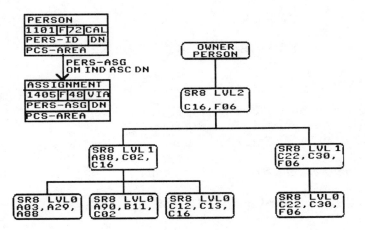

Figure 18-5   Second Level Index Creation.

Computing The Number Of Levels

There are two ways of computing the number of levels that will occur in sorted indexes: a repetitive computation of each level beginning with the root based on a fixed number of index entries in an SR8, or assuming that the number of levels will be two and computing the number of SR8 entries appropriate to achieve two levels with a given number of index members.

The first approach can be done manually with ease; the second requires a computer. Figure 18-6 illustrates the first; The IDMS User Association Contributed Micro Library contains a BASIC program to accomplish the second technique.

The number of iterations of the formula identifies the number of levels that can be anticipated. Since our goal is two, however, the number of entries in an SR8 must be varied until the right number of levels is found. This can be a time-consuming job. The program in Appendix A increments the number of entries in the SR8 one by one until the ideal value is found. It is recommended that you add one entry to the result of this program as a pad.

The program computes the number of SR8 entries that are required for the optimum two- or three-level index. The number of members or the symbolic key lengths may make the length of the SR8 too long to

Bottom Level Computation

1. **SQ0 = (EQ + IBC - 1) / IBC**

where

SQ0 = Number of SR8 records at bottom level
EQ = Total number of record entries
IBC = Index Block Contains count

Intermediate and Top Level Computation

2. **SQn = (SQn-1 + IBC -1) / IBC**

where

SQn = Number of SR8 records at that level
SQn-1 = Number of SR8 records from previous level

3. **Repeat 2 until SQn = 1**

Figure 18-6   Manual Computation of SR8 Levels.

fit on the database page. When this occurs, two basic options are available:

1. *Allow more index levels.* Given the page size, the system will automatically spawn more index levels when the SR8 will no longer fit on a database page. Since index records are not fragmented across pages, it is possible for a SR8 to spawn another level sooner if other record occurrences reduce the available space on a page.
2. *Expand the page size.* Page size may be expanded to accommodate larger index records. Keep in mind that, once spawned, a new index level remains unless all member records linked to the new SR8 have been deleted.

Optimally, the page size should be sufficient to accommodate three SR8 records. This will minimize fill and overflow problems. The BASIC program provides a length for the desirable *minimum* page size, taking header, footer, and page reserve into consideration. Page reserve is assumed to be 15 percent.

Performance Considerations

Performance is directly affected by the size of the SR8 record. Optimum performance occurs when the lowest index level is full or nearly full. For static databases this is relatively easy to achieve; dynamic databases may have to be resized and rebuilt periodically to maintain peak performance.

Locks

An implicit exclusive lock is placed on an SR8 when an entry is either added or deleted. If this action changes the space available on the page, the page is also locked. Other run-units are prevented from using the locked SR8 until it is released. The splitting of an SR8 due to index update will exclusively lock the SR8s immediately preceding and below the split.

This locking condition may impact high-volume multiuser updating of an area. The larger the SR8, the more likely that lockout will occur. Therefore, it is important that update transactions accessing indexed sets or secondary indexes complete their database access as quickly as possible.

The SR8 is *not* locked during modification of a database record associated with the SR8 as long as the modification does not change the index key. Retrieval activity elsewhere in the set is not affected.

The SR8 *is* locked if modification of an index member changes the index key or if a member is inserted or removed from the index. One or more SR8s will be affected and exclusively locked.

All exclusive locks are held until the end of the run-unit occurs as the result of a FINISH, COMMIT, or ROLLBACK verb execution. On long-running transactions, frequent COMMITs should be performed to minimize lockout of other transactions.

Index Loading

Index loading **must** be a part of the database design process if the most effective and efficient use of the facility is to be made. This section points out the major factors that must be considered during design and implementation of applications using integrated indexing.

Area Considerations

While small set indexes can readily coexist with their owner records, large or high-volume environments can lead to clashes between the index and database records. Application record activity can force index records to be paged out of the buffer prematurely. Index activity can have the same effect on the application record. Both situations increase I/O activity and degrade performance.

Where this conflict can be predicted, it is a good idea to separate the index set member record in a different area from its owner. *Because of the nature of pointer arrays, this approach will avoid the usual problems associated with cross-area sets.* Performance advantages are realized when each area has a separate set of page buffers.

DMCL Considerations

As with other DBMS activities, the number of buffer pages has a direct impact on index performance. At least eight buffer pages should be assigned to *every* area; areas may share buffers but the performance improvements gained by eight pages versus four is nearly 100 percent (12 pages achieve an additional 80 + percent improvement).

Index sets are governed by the buffer configuration associated with the owner's area. Integrated (secondary) indexes are frequently placed in their own areas and the buffering may be tailored to the indexing function.

A three-level index should have a minimum of nine index pages. This is based on:

1. Three pages for the SMP, index owner, and top level of the index.
2. Three pages for each level of the index below the top level.

Future Requirements

Few databases are static; the only real consideration is how fast it will grow and where. Index performance is dependent on accurately gauging that growth and allowing adequate space to prevent excessive SR8 splitting. Oh, sure, you say! Get out the turban and crystal ball and off we go again, flying again by the seat of our pants!

There *are* ways to put some order into the process. The PAGE RESERVE option will set aside space during the index loading process so that there is room for index expansion as growth occurs. In this case the area containing the index owner is reserved up to 30 percent to allow for the anticipated growth. The actual amount reserved should be adequate to accommodate a full-size SR8 record in most cases.

If your calculations indicate that more than 30 percent is needed for reserve, it is better to set PAGE RESERVE at zero and expand the page with IDMSXPAG after the index has been loaded.

PAGE RESERVE is removed from the DMCL after loading is completed. This now permits the system to use the reserved space. The index set definition in the schema is then changed to increase the maximum number of entries in the SR8 to allow for the anticipated growth. Be sure to regenerate each of the schema's subschemas.

Loading Order

Sorted indexes should be loaded so that additions occur either before the beginning of the index or after the end of the index. If the size of the index record is small (less than 20 to 30 entries), loading so that additions occur before the beginning of the index will usually be more efficient.

The difference lies in the place within the index where most of the work takes place. Loading before the beginning causes adjustment within the bottom-level index record itself. Overhead increases as the number of entries in the index record goes up.

Loading after the end of the index causes extra activity within the intermediate levels of the index as those index records carry the key value of the *highest* entry in the next lower level.

In any event, if duplicates are allowed, the index should be loaded in the same direction as the duplicate option. For example, an index with entries in ascending order and DUPLICATES LAST, is best loaded in ascending order.

Loading Methods

Index performance is at its best when all additions to the index occur at the end of the index. The index structure, in this mode, is optimum because all SR8 records are filled, splits will occur only at the last SR8, and splits will occur into either the free space next to the last SR8 on the page or on the next page.

Displacing Index Records

The displacement of the bottom level of an index from its owner is frequently desirable to avoid a conflict for space by the SR8 records. Since top and intermediate level SR8 records are often longer than those in the bottom level, there may not be enough room for the bottom level SR8 or inadequate space for the upper level SR8s (causing extra splitting).

When both index owner and member reside in the same area, the index member record should be displaced from the owner to provide room for the index records. If the number of member records is such that displacement will simply impact some other owner's index space, the page range should be expanded. The problem can be avoided by placing the set member in a different area. This option should be carefully reviewed, however, as creating too many areas can have its own impact on system performance.

Index Updating

The same conditions that bear upon the loading of an index also affect the updating of indexes. System performance can be severely impacted if the database updating patterns are not considered when designing index processing.

DMCL Considerations

Index areas, for secondary indexes, should be assigned a separate DMCL buffer pool. Where activity is heavy, the buffer pool should be large enough so the index will remain in memory during area processing. Unfortunately, available memory often does not allow for a buffer of such size. *Too large a buffer* (more than 30 pages in some cases) *may actually cause performance to degrade.*

Locks

Database locking can be the downfall of an on-line system unless the database design considers the patterns of data use. Indexes are particularly vulnerable to deadlocks because a single SR8 record services many database records. The larger the number of index entries in an SR8, the greater the deadlock risk. Efficient index sizing, therefore, must be compared against usage patterns. While the number of SR8 records and levels will increase as the number of entries is reduced, databases with very high activity rates from many concurrent users may suffer badly from deadlocks unless the entry count is kept low.

SR8 records are locked during updating when:

1. *Modification of an index member alters the index key.* This results in an exclusive lock on the SR8 as the old key is removed and the new key inserted. More than one SR8 may be affected.
2. *A member record is inserted into the index.* If the insertion results in an index split, several SR8s may be affected.
3. *A member record is removed from the index.* This normally affects a single SR8 unless the removed entry is at the end of the SR8; the high value key of the next higher level SR8 would have to be modified, locking that SR8 too.
4. *A member record is added after the end of the SR8 and a split results.* This locks the index owner in addition to the SR8 affected. When the index owner is exclusively locked, *no other run-unit will be able to access any record in the index from the top of the index.*

All locks remain in force until the completion of the run-unit. Application programs using indexed database areas, therefore, should be designed to minimize the amount of time that the database is accessed.

19

Database Procedures

Database procedures are one of the more significant tools for the DBA provided within IDMS. Unfortunately, they are also one of the least understood. As a consequence, they are rarely used. This chapter attempts to resolve many of the questions that currently inhibit effective use of database procedures.

Purpose Of Database Procedures

Database procedures are extensions of the IDMS system. They are treated by IDMS as if they were part of the system software. For this reason they must be treated with great care. Most database procedures are written in assembly language.

The database procedure provides IDMS users with the ability to modify the system's processing of specific areas, sets, and records in a manner invisible to the application program. This is quite different from the use of exits in the DBMS itself; exits affect *all* database processing while procedures affect *only* those entities to which they are related.

Pros And Cons Of Database Procedures

Like many other features supplied within IDMS, database procedures have two faces, one promoting and the other questioning their use. Each use of procedures must be carefully evaluated to be sure the weight of decision is positive.

The Advantages

The principal advantages of database procedures are:

1. *Installation of common processing code* across many entities of an application or all applications. The common data compression and decompression routines are a good example of this advantage.
2. *Special control logic* that the DBA does not want the application programmer to see or be able to modify. The database procedure is an excellent tool for enhancing the security of the application or system. The procedure's execution is transparent to the application program and the programmer.

The Disadvantages

Database procedures have only two real disadvantages: performance degradation and maintenance.

Performance Degradation. The seriousness of this problem depends on where the procedure is called and how much work it has to do.

Area procedures affect all records associated with them and must be carefully checked to ensure maximum processing efficiency. These procedures probably should be written in assembly language to maximize performance. In turn, they should have few, if any, file activities of their own.

Record procedures, while focused on a particular record type, can severely affect performance if that record type has very highvolume.

The bottom line on database procedures, therefore, is to carefully consider how much traffic will flow through the procedure in comparison to the work it does.

Procedure Maintenance. Once implemented, *database procedures have very long lifetimes.* Since most database procedures are central to the overall processing of the organization's data, it is unlikely that they will disappear without major impacts on the application and its data. Removing the compression and decompression routines, for example, would require updating every compressed record in the database prior to discontinuing the procedures.

The effect of this dependence is to require long-term maintenance support. The persons supporting procedures must be highly qualified. The damage that can be caused by an error in procedure processing is so great that only the most capable system programmers should be permitted to work on procedures.

Database Procedure Characteristics

Database procedures may be either resident or nonresident. If the procedure is used frequently, test performance by running the procedure in both resident and nonresident forms. Very heavy use of a procedure may keep it in memory long enough so that, for practical purposes, it is resident.

Most procedures are written in assembly language to make their processing more efficient. Assembler programs are also easier to make reentrant, a very desirable condition for procedures. This is especially true for a resident procedure. IDMS will load another copy of the procedure if the resident copy is busy.

The IDMSPROC Statement

The IDMS systen includes a statement to describe a database procedure to IDMS. While not required, IDMS assumes that any dynamically called procedure:

1. *Has an entry-point name identical to the procedure name.* The procedure program must have the same name as the procedure itself.
2. *The procedure is quasi-reentrant.* This means that, while multiple programs can use the procedure, they must do so one after another in a controlled fashion.
3. *The procedure is not resident.*

4. *The procedure is written in assembly language.*

Types Of Database Procedures

There are two types of database procedures: area and record. Each serves specific purposes. Within this section we will review the basic functions performed by each procedure type and identify some of the common uses of each.

Area Procedures

The area procedure acts against a DML statement pointed to a specific database area. It provides the ability to perform actions across an entire database area as compared to a single record for a record procedure.

Area procedures can be used to open files at the same time the area is readied, set up access control for an area containing sensitive data, gather statistics at COMMIT or FINISH time, and control use of OB-TAIN .... WITHIN AREA statements. Figure 19-1 illustrates the COBOL program data statements that are required to support an area procedure.

Record Procedures

The most common record procedures are the IDMSCOMP and IDMSDCOM routines that compress and decompress variable length records. These database procedures are supplied by Cullinet.

Record procedures may be used to apply security to a record that is transparent to the programmer or user. Some of these security techniques are described in Chapter 7. Figure 19-2 illustrates the COBOL data statements required to support a record procedure.

```
LINKAGE SECTION.
01 COPY  PROCEDURE-CONTROL-BLOCK.
01 COPY  APPLICATION-CONTROL-BLOCK.
01 COPY  APPLICATION-PROGRAM-INFORMATION-BLOCK.
01 COPY  AREA-CONTROL-BLOCK.
01 COPY  IDMS-STATISTICS-BLOCK.

PROCEDURE DIVISION USING
   PROCEDURE-CONTROL-BLOCK,
   APPLICATION-CONTROL-BLOCK,
   APPLICATION-PROGRAM-INFORMATION-BLOCK,
   AREA-CONTROL-BLOCK,
   IDMS-STATISTICS-BLOCK.
```

Figure 19-1   Area Database Procedure COBOL Statements.

```
LINKAGE SECTION.
01   COPY PROCEDURE-CONTROL-BLOCK.
01   COPY APPLICATION-CONTROL-BLOCK.
01   COPY APPLICATION-PROGRAM-INFORMATION-BLOCK.
01   COPY RECORD-CONTROL-BLOCK.
01   COPY IDMS <record name>.

PROCEDURE DIVISION USING
   PROCEDURE-CONTROL-BLOCK,
   APPLICATION-CONTROL-BLOCK,
   APPLICATION-PROGRAM-INFORMATION-BLOCK,
   RECORD-CONTROL-BLOCK,    <record name>.
```

Figure 19-2   Record Database Procedure COBOL Statements.

20

Buffers

DBMSs live and die on their buffers and IDMS is no exception. The proper sizing, populating, and use of the various buffer areas within IDMS are critical to the efficient operation of those applications using the DBMS. This chapter will discuss page and storage buffers and how they can be tuned to improve system performance.

Page Buffers

The DMCL page buffer is the intermediate storage area for data between the DBMS and the application. It is, in this role, the potential choke point of the system. Poor page buffer utilization can ruin an otherwise outstanding application.

Buffer Size

Page buffers may be sized to the desire of the DBA. Practical use of memory matches buffer size to that of the database area pages that will be served by the buffer. The page buffer must be at least large enough to contain the largest database page using the buffer.

Page buffers, in a number of installations, are all sized identically regardless of the page sizing within the database. This approach makes it possible to expand the page size of database areas without reconfiguring the page buffer. *It also wastes large amounts of precious region space.* There is no reason I can think of, other than laziness, for this approach.

Page buffer pools need not be all of the same size nor is their assignment to a particular application system sacrosanct. As the databases served by IDMS change, the supporting environment should change too. In fact, it is desirable to move systems around within the buffers to tune the system's performance. We obviously do not wish to concentrate all of the high usage applications in one or two page buffers while placing the low usage applications elsewhere.

Buffer Sharing

Properly organized, a single page buffer can support multiple applications. A mixture of low-, medium-, and high-volume systems will complement each other; however, buffer sharing creates a responsibility for the DBA. The activity of the buffer's applications must be continuously watched. Changes in activity patterns may dictate a reevaluation of the buffer-sharing arrangement.

Applications sharing buffer space *must be complementary*. Let's look at the types of systems that work well together:

1. *High- and low-volume systems.* Low-volume systems generally can work unimpeded alongside the high-volume user. Low-volume applications generally have relaxed response time requirements and a few extra seconds will not disrupt their user's operation. The low-volume transaction rate seldom interferes with the larger user.
2. *Medium-volume users.* Multiple medium-volume users can often be placed together. No one application is operating at sufficient volume to have more than occasional impact on the others.
3. *Offset schedule users.* An application whose peak operation is in the morning can coexist with one where peak hours are in the afternoon. Evening peak operation complements another whose peak is during the day. Beware, however, of changes in operating patterns.

Conversely, there are certain types of applications and situations where sharing a DMCL buffer is just asking for trouble:

1. *Two high-volume applications whose peak hours overlap.* There is no way to avoid paging conflicts, even when the buffers are assigned large numbers of pages.
2. *Medium- to high-volume application and a batch-oriented system. Batch systems occupy more buffer pages unless the data is presorted to load in dbkey order, something that is seldom done. On-line systems request large numbers of random pages while the batch program will systematically gather and use pages.*

The on-line transaction is usually the first to suffer because of the time passing between uses of the page. The batch system, running continuously in a single run-unit, will force the on-line page out of the buffer. This makes IDMS reread the page for the on-line application each time the operator presses the enter key.

3. *Systems using secondary indexing.* Secondary indexing requires more pages to operate efficiently than other database activity. The most efficient operation of a system with secondary indexes is to provide enough pages to keep a majority of the index in memory at all times. Obviously, two systems with indexes will either require an unreasonable number of pages or they will flail the page buffer if operating at the same time.
4. *High-volume systems and secondary indexes.* As with 3 above, both high-volume and indexed systems require a higher number of buffer pages to operate efficiently. The index, however, will attempt to overpower the remaining operations in order to remain in memory. Since index activity in update mode frequently affects many index records, the indexes and their buffer pages are the likely winners.

Sharing of buffer pools, therefore, must be done with care and planning. It is wise to consider separating large multiarea applications into separate buffer pools in order to reduce contention. Indexing, particularly secondary indexing, should be separated from its supported area pools whenever possible.

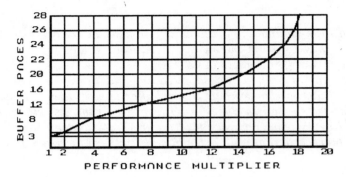

Figure 20-1 System Performance Varying Buffer Pages.

Number Of Pages

IDMS *requires* at least three pages in each buffer pool, one for the current space management page, one for a database page, and one for a new space management page if the next requested database page is outside the range of the current space management page. Obviously, operating with one database page at a time is ridiculous.

Many users, however, operate low volume applications with only four pages in the buffer pool. This is quite a bit better than three (see Figure 20-1), but is nowhere near the performance potential available.

As Figure 20-1 illustrates, performance dramatically improves as the number of pages in the buffer increases from 4 to 8 and from 8 to 12. As the number of pages increases beyond 12, performance improvements begin to taper off. This is because IDMS is spending more time tracking what is happening with each buffer page, including what database page is there and when it was last used.

It is possible to increase the number of pages in the buffer to the point where performance will actually *decrease*. When the buffer management activities exceed the I/O activities, DBMS performance will degrade. This doesn't happen often in high-volume applications but performance improvements may become so small that the additional region overhead is not worth the effort.

Also worthy of note is the effect large DMCL page buffers may have on the operating system paging rate. If the *working set* of the region is increased by large DMCL page buffers, the number of operating system page faults will increase as the computer's load goes up. IDMS can continue to do other work while it calls for I/O to read a database page *but no overlap of processing occurs while the operating system services a page fault.* It is not unusual to see IDMS performance *improve* by *reducing the number of DMCL pages in a buffer.*

Page buffers supporting a local mode batch loading program can be increased without impact. A large batch load *should* be given 30 to 50 pages in the DMCL page buffer. This obviously requires a separate DMCL for the batch loads, but it is worth the trouble.

A Practical Buffer Arrangement

Bringing all of the above points together, the most practical DMCL buffering arrangement for on-line applications is:

1. *No more than two high-volume applications to a buffer.*
2. *Mix low-volume applications with high- and medium-volume systems.*
3. *Separate secondary indexes from their respective applications.*
4. *Provide each buffer pool with page sized to support the database pages assigned to them.* Do not oversize the buffer page; it simply wastes space.
5. *Assign at least 8 pages to each buffer pool;* 12 is ideal.
6. *Do not assign more than 24 pages to any buffer pool* unless it supports secondary indexes; add up to eight more for secondary indexes.

Storage Buffers

The storage pool supporting IDMS/CV provides working space for every application and *IDMS itself.* The manner in which IDMS manages the storage pool changes from release to release but the way we use the pool should be consistent.

The first thing to understand is that the storage pool is separated into a series of storage "pages," each 4096 bytes in length. Pages are assigned to applications as a whole, even if the application only needs 100 bytes.

Further, the storage pool is broken into two classes of pages: short-term and long-term. Short-term usage is generally IDMS system oriented while long-term pages are normally supporting applications. There are some exceptions to this rule, but these are not worthy of our spending time on them. Short-term storage pages are clustered together at the front of the storage pool, while long-term pages are assigned from the rear of the pool.

Primary Buffers

Every application using the DBMS requires some space to hold its working storage, records used by the application, and control data. When a transaction begins execution, IDMS assigns a *primary buffer* to the transaction. This buffer is sized according to the parameter in the system generation for primary buffers. This primary buffer *remains with the transaction for its lifetime.*

Since the storage pool page size is 4096 bytes, it is logical to build the primary buffer in approximate multiples of 4096. It would be wasteful to define the primary buffer as 2048 bytes, for example, because a full 4096-byte storage page will be assigned anyway.

Since each application page buffer has a 12-byte control record, the buffer itself should be 4084 bytes long. Assigning a 4096-byte buffer will result in a 5008-byte allocation, forcing the DBMS to assign *two* storage pages to the primary buffer.

Actually there is no practical limit to the size of a primary buffer. However, keep in mind that a primary storage buffer is assigned and kept for every transaction in the DBMS. The buffer is not released until the operator exits back to the system prompt. Making the primary buffer too large can cause storage shortages when the number of system users increases.

The best approach, therefore, is to make the primary storage buffer as small as practical. In this case, a 4084-byte primary buffer is the best compromise.

Secondary Buffers

Many transactions cannot get by on a single 4084-byte buffer. This is particularly true of transactions that call others, cascading the storage requirements of the transaction.

IDMS provides the ability to dynamically assign an unlimited number of secondary buffers to a transaction. Again, the sizing of these buffers needs to consider the size of the storage pool page.

Secondary buffers, unlike their primary counterpart, are held by the application only as long as needed. When all of the working space assigned to a secondary buffer has been released, the buffer is returned to the DBMS for reassignment.

The maximum size of the secondary buffer must consider the size of the largest database record *anywhere in the applications supported.* Since IDMS does not allow a record work area to overlap between buffers, no database record can be larger than the size of either the primary or secondary buffers. (Why anyone would build a database record or even a work record bigger than 4000 bytes is beyond me, but it happens.) Installation standards should be defined to prevent any record definition greater than the size of the biggest storage buffer.

Again, 4084 seems like a good number for secondary storage page buffers. Smaller is wasteful and larger makes it more likely that too much space will be set aside for the buffer. IDMS will set aside the entire secondary buffer space even though the program only uses a few bytes. Storage contention is more likely to occur on multipage buffers, too.

Storage Contention

As IDMS assigns and releases storage pool pages, the pool tends to become fragmented. IDMS has a storage management algorithm to minimize this fragmentation, but it can be overloaded. As long as the DBMS only needs a single page, the request can nearly always be satisfied. As the number of pages requested grows, however, the possibility of locating a group of contiguous pages in the pool decreases. Since all original page requests are for contiguous pages (pages immediately adjacent to each other), the larger the space requested the more likely it is that space will not be found.

Transaction performance degrades when this contention for space occurs. IDMS is somewhat forgiving when it cannot find storage space for a transaction; it tries continuously until its resource wait timeout period has been reached. Then the task is aborted. The terminal operator normally sees this as extended response time.

21

Schemas

No discussion of IDMS would be complete without a section on schemas. This chapter will concentrate on some of the techniques for creating effective schemas and avoiding pitfalls rather than delve into the routine mechanics; Cullinet's manuals cover the mechanics quite well.

First, let's define what is meant by a *schema*. While many have used the term interchangeably with a Bachman diagram, they are quite different. The schema is the *physical* database definition, represented by a description in a structured source format. A Bachman diagram is a pictorial representation of the physical database structure as *implemented* by the schema.

Before the days of logical data structure diagrams, the Bachman diagram was used to support both logical and physical data structures. Today it is focused as a representation of the physical database. Throughout this book the Bachman chart will be assumed to represent a physical database structure.

Schemas come in a number of forms. Some installations have implemented several different types of schema to satisfy their particular development methodology. In this chapter, however, we will concentrate on two *levels* of schema, global and area.

Global Schemas

The global schema has become a practical necessity in CV installations where the number of implemented applications has climbed to 10 or more. Some, with very large applications, have implemented the concept even earlier.

Central version requires that a global DMCL be defined, a single unit to support the entire CV. Building a global DMCL with references to many individual schemas has proven to be dangerous. Not only is it an adminstrative nightmare, but it is possible to create some incompatible situations that could destroy your databases. For example:

1. *Overlapping page ranges within two schemas no longer, in theory, are of concern.* However, strange things have happened in a CV environment to systems with overlapping pages. A DMCL compiled from area schemas does not check for or catch a page overlap.
2. *Overlapping record identifiers are not identified when individual schemas are linked to the DMCL.* Again, this should not be a problem in most cases. However, if applications in one schema desire to communicate with applications in another schema, overlapping identifiers may cause problems.
3. *The local schema, referenced by a global DMCL, must be handled carefully. If it is modified or deleted, a recompilation of the DMCL will be required. If these duties are handled by different people, not unusual in a large shop, the DMCL may fail to compile.*

Before proceeding, we need to be clear about the preceding points. IDMS and good procedures render the preceding arguments meaningless. Practical experience, however, has shown that all of the preceding have haunted even the most experienced DBA at one time or another. The global schema puts in place a level of system management that will more nearly prevent these kind of problems from happening.

How does the global schema help? Let's look at the previous three problems again, showing how each is controlled under a global schema:

1. Overlapping page ranges cannot occur within a single schema. The schema compiler enforces that rule.

2. Record identifiers cannot overlap within a schema, nor can record names be the same.
3. A local schema, now independent of the global DMCL, can be altered as desired without impacting the operating environment.

Building A Global Schema

The global schema is created *exclusively* by copying schema descriptions from other schemas. This ensures consistency between operating schemas as well as reduces the amount of keying necessary to create and maintain the schema.

Record descriptions only, without elements, are copied to the global schema. Subschemas will be built from the area schemas, removing the need to include elements within the global schema. (You can certainly include the elements if you desire, but the schema listing will get VERY large over time.)

Area Schemas

The area schema is nothing more than a schema of a particular application. It is built and maintained in the normal fashion that all schemas are supported. When worked in conjunction with a global schema, however, the DBA has the flexibility of being able to update an area schema, at the same version number, without impacting on ongoing production use of the database represented by the schema.

This ability to function on two levels is increasingly important as the size and complexity of the database environment grows. Version numbers, while useful, have caused a great deal of pain when not rigidly controlled. Even when controlled, confusion frequently sets in when the DBA is faced with multiple versions of the same record.

An area schema, therefore, should be kept at a single version number and maintained as a complete entity. Changes to this schema should be reflected in the global schema as soon as possible.

The area schema, not the global, should be used to support batch jobs using the portion of the database covered by the area schema. Wait a minute, you say. If production batch uses the area schema, therefore we can't play around with the schema without affecting batch work. That's true and is the principal reason behind separating the development and production systems into different dictionaries.

The On-Line Schema Compiler

Until Release 10.0, it was necessary to delete the existing copy of a schema in order to recompile it (using the same version number). This had the unfortunate side-effect of discarding all of the sub-schemas too. Even worse, if someone had made the mistake of linking a schema record to a map, the map would also have had to be deleted before the schema record could be released. IDD had a wonderful, and frustrating, way of protecting us from ourselves.

When the on-line schema compiler became available, a whole new way of handling schemas was *required*. The old tried and true techniques could still be used, but didn't take advantage of many of the new capabilities available with the on-line compiler. Unfortunately, many of us learned the hard way about the "features" of the new compiler. Most of these features were again designed to protect us from oursel-ves and, at the same time, ensure the integrity of the schema. Here are a few pitfalls that should be avoided:

1. Deleting an area from the schema will cause the area's records to be deleted, too.
2. If the owner record of a set is deleted, the set will also be deleted. If a set is deleted and the member record(s) have no other owners, the member records disappear, too.
3. Deleting the only member record in a set will cause the set to be deleted, too.

One of the new features of the schema compiler allows the compiler to assign the pointer numbers. This is a nice touch *when preparing a schema for the first time*. Once generated, however, the compiler chan-ges all of the variable source statements to the actual pointers. I com-plained about this to Cullinet because it made early development schema work even more confusing. Again, the compiler designers are protecting us from our own potential for creating a disaster.

Once a schema has been compiled, it must be assumed that it will be used. Leaving the pointer number floating would make it possible for the schema designer to insert another set into the schema in such a way that the pointer assignments would change. You can imagine the results if your database records were linked together with a particular pointer arrangement and, all of a sudden, that arrangement changed. The garbage that was your database would be almost impossible to recover.

The most dangerous part of the on-line schema compiler is the ease with which we can compile a schema at any time. Since the schema compiler *is single threaded to the dictionary,* each time the compiler generates a schema all other use of the dictionary ceases until the compile is completed. A schema compile at the peak programming time of the day can bring the entire programming staff to a long coffee break, usually with numerous task abends at the end. *Schema compiles should be run only during off-hours.*

22

DMCL

DMCL stands for Device-Media Control Language. The language is used to define the interface between the logical world of the schema and subschema with the physical world of the DASD device and tape drive.

Purpose Of A DMCL

The purpose of the DMCL module is to map the database areas and their pages to physical DASD blocks in data sets. The DMCL also identifies the number of page buffers to support each area, the number and name of the journal files to be used by the DBMS.

SMI

The Space Management Interval (SMI) identifies the frequency of space management pages within the area. SMI is automatically computed by IDMS based on the size of the database page. IDMS places page management fields on a space management page and spaces the pages appropriately through the database.

SMI must be specified in the DMCL when the size of the page for any area is expanded. Unless an SMI value is provided, specifying the original page size, IDMS will try to locate the space management pages based on the new page size and a fatal system error will result.

SMI, therefore, tells IDMS to use the space management distribution of the smaller original page size rather than the distribution that would normally occur with the large page size.

Page Reserve

IDMS permits the DBA to reserve space for future expansion within each page of an area. This feature is appropriately named PAGE RESERVE. The basic purpose of reserving space is to leave some space on every page for future additions of new records and expansion of existing records.

Placing a page reserve of 25 percent on an area during initial data loading will spread the data more evenly, preventing early page overflows during future updates. This reserve is reduced to 5 or 10 percent after the initial load (some users eliminate the reserve altogether if variable length records are not used in the area).

Under no circumstances should the page reserve be set at move than *30 percent*. The space management feature of IDMS updates the space management pages only after a page has filled to the 70 percent level. A space reserve of 30 percent or more will make the space management facility indicate that pages have available space when, in fact, they have no room to store additional records. The result is a repetitive area sweep each time a new record is to be added, dramatically reducing performance.

Chapter

23

Subschemas

The subschema is one of the least understood pieces in the IDMS puzzle. It provides a wide variety of options for performance tuning and, at the same time, has the potential to cause a severe degradation of system performance. This chapter will address a number of the more important aspects of subschemas and identify the tradeoffs associated with its features.

Purpose Of Subschemas

The subschema can be consisdered a window into the database. The size and shape of the window are defined by the use we will make of the database. While a subschema can expose the entire database structure, it can also limit the window to a single database record.

In reality, the subschema represents a physical run-time view of that portion of the database that is to be made available. It also maintains the tables of dbkeys that support run-time currency during the execution of the application. From the computer's standpoint, the subschema represents a program consisting of fixed and variable parts.

Chapter

241

Composition Of A Subschema

The subschema is compiled just like other programs. With Release 10.0, an on-line subschema compiler became available that simplifies the process. Two object modules actually result from the compilation, the fixed portion and the variable portion. We will look at each shortly.

The subschema is broken into fixed and variable portions to permit it to serve multiple transactions concurrently. The fixed portion is stored in the *program pool* while the variable portion is placed in the *storage pool*. Only one copy of the fixed portion of the subschema is required whether one or many concurrent users are present. The variable portion, however, is copied for each user.

The fixed portion of the subschema identifies the areas, records, and sets that make up the subschema structure. The set relationships between these entities are identified; *the subschema structure is actually a network database.*

The variable portion contains all of the varying information that changes as the database is accessed; the dbkeys of records, sets, and areas maintain currency as well as the key value variables necessary to control database processing. Since each transaction operates independently, there must be a variable portion to keep the currencies separate for each run-unit.

The Fixed Portion

The fixed portion of a subschema consists of a set of area, record, set, and key field tables that are structured in the same way as an IDMS database. The IDMS system software actually treats this module as if it were a database. Since the early days of IDMS the way that these tables are structured has followed a consistent pattern. Understanding the pattern and taking advantage of the process can have significant effects on system performance.

Since IDMS must search the subschema tables each time a database access is performed (it must locate currencies for run-unit, area, set, and record), the organization of the table can speed up or slow down processing. The three principal tables, area, set, and record, are ordered differently:

1. *Area tables*. Area tables are ordered in the sequence in which they appear in the subschema source. This means that you can place the most often used area at the beginning of the source and reduce search time. Since most subschemas have a limited number of areas, this feature has little affect on overall performance.

2. *Set tables*. Set tables are ordered in alphabetical sequence by the set name. Don't ask why; I did and no one seems to really know. Since most installations name sets after a concatenation of owner and member names, taking advantage of this feature to tune system performance would appear to be the luck of the draw.

   You can, however, make a visible difference in system performance when the names of a large subchema's sets are changed (by adding a prefix) to force the high-use sets to the front of the table. In times past, I have improved batch program performance by 25 to 50 percent by making this change. Of course, you have to modify the programs too to reflect the set name change.

3. *Record tables*. Record tables use still another ordering approach. Records are ordered by their *record id*. That's right! Record 1000 gets found quicker than 1001. Now here is a place where you can make the system work for you without causing havoc with naming standards. Figure 23-1 illustrates a technique for numbering record types that gives priority to the key records of any cluster.

As you can see, the CALC record of the cluster has a record identifier ending in zero. This gives that record the highest priority and, at the same time, makes the record immediately recognizable as a key record in a cluster.

The nest record, if present, is a number ending in one to give it a higher priority that the other members. Since nest record processing is already the least efficient of all structure processing, every little bit helps.

Many-to-many records, the next most frequently processed, are given the next priority. Dependent members are at the bottom of the list.

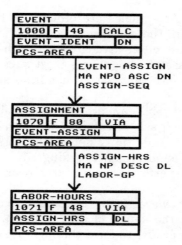

Figure 23-1   Number A Cluster Of Record Types.

The Variable Portion

The variable portion of the subschema is a large variable table generated by the subschema compiler and loaded to the storage pool during execution. Each table entry is located by using an *offset from the table beginning.* The offset is stored in the fixed portion of the subschema and needs only the reference point of the start of the variable portion to located each table entry.

Tuning the Subschema

We have already discussed one subtle way to tune subschemas. In large systems, the opportunities for performance improvements are much greater than in small systems. (That is also a clue to tuning.) Let's look at some of the major tuning techniques as they apply to subschemas:

1. *Break up the subschema.* Large subschemas are performance killers. They:

    a. *Have larger and longer internal tables to walk.*

b. *Take up more program pool space*, reducing available space for other programs.

c. *Take up more storage pool space*, increasing the likelihood that they will be rolled out to make room for other data requirements.

d. *Are used by more programs*, requiring more copies of the larger variable portion in memory, further impacting on available space.

2. *Eliminate subschema segmenting.* Segmenting the records within a subschema is great for enhancing security. It permits limiting the record view of a program to just specific elements; it also requires each element group to be moved individually from the subschema buffer to the record buffer in the program. If the record is not segmented, the data can be moved directly from the page buffer to the program record buffer.

   If the record is compressed, however, the move from page buffer to subschema buffer occurs anyhow. The decompressing is performed in the subschema buffer. The return trip also stops for recompressing.

3. *Avoid variable-length records.* There is a definite tradeoff here. While fixed length records (that are not segmented) avoid the overhead of a stop-over in the subschema buffer, the extra disk space saved by compression may be worth the cost.

4. *Avoid logical records.* Here is another tradeoff! Logical records provide an improved measure of friendliness to the database structure. Programming is simplified somewhat and ad hoc queries are easier to define. But the logical record facility utilizes the subschema buffer to bring individual database records together to form a logical record. This increases the system overhead and may impact performance sufficiently in high-volume situations to make it impractical.

An overall point to remember: The subschema buffer will be large enough to contain the largest record defined to the subschema. A subschema buffer is not generated at all if the subschema records are not segmented, of variable length, or use logical records. Depending on the size of that biggest record and the number of concurrent uses of the subschema, significant storage savings could be realized.

The tuning approaches mentioned earlier *should not be interpreted as condemning the use of segmentation, variable-length records, and logical records.* Each of these features has its place and should be used when the situation dictates. The database designed must simply keep in mind that *tradeoffs in flexibility and performance must be considered in each case.*

Subschema Access

How big should a subschema be? How many programs should a subschema support? What are the risks of many subschemas? Of a few? This section will discuss how a subschema should fit in the overall picture of your database and some of the considerations that must be reviewed when designing subschemas.

Subschema Size

Before Release 10.0, most installations kept the number of subschemas to a minimum because IDMS threw away all of the subschemas every time their schemas were regenerated. The time required to recompile a large number of subschemas was considerable and many avoided the pain by having a few very large subschemas.

Early users of IDMS were heavily batch-oriented. Batch environments were not as concerned about size and performance (and still aren't) as on-line users. Today, however, the emphasis is on on-line use of database and size and performance are very much at the forefront of our concerns.

Release 10.0 allows us to update schemas, eliminating much of the time and effort of reloading subschemas. We can create as many subschemas as we want. However, how many should that be?

Except in rare situations, a subschema should support a *single functional requirement* of an application. This may mean that a subschema could have one area, one record, and no sets; it may also have several of each. Update subschemas must often be larger than retrieval subschemas because all sets (and associated records) must be present for any record type being updated. This can have a domino effect if not carefully managed.

Subschema design, therefore, should not be an afterthought; *it must be a part of the initial physical database design.* The effectiveness of subschema design can be lost if the database structure is such that all updates must be done with a subshema that maps the entire database.

Retrieval subschemas *may be focused* more closely than updates because you need include only those records and sets required to accomplish the retrieval. The smaller subschema will also speed up the program's performance.

Assuming that you maintain the subschema source in a separate library, the risks associated with having many subschemas are minimal. Regeneration today is quick and easy. I would err, therefore, in favor of too many subschemas rather than too few.

Program Coverage

It is often expedient to have a few large subschemas designed exclusively to support batch processing for those programs that operate *in local mode*. Remember that a batch program operating under central version can have significant impacts on the overall functioning of CV, especially if a very large subschema is involved. *CV should never be used for batch report programs.*

For the on-line environment, our greatest area of concern, many small subschemas are encouraged. Where heavy overlapping of the data structure occurs on high-volume transactions, a single subschema made resident may be more desirable than several dynamic ones.

The processing threads of a transaction and the proper time for checkpoints (COMMITS) becomes an important consideration when laying out subschemas. For example: A single update transaction dialog calls several other dialogs, both mapped and mapless, in order to complete a logical data update. At any point during this calling process, one of the subordinate dialogs may detect a data error that would require purging the update. In order that a ROLLBACK can accomplish the purge, it is important that no COMMITs occur during the processing.

The *extended run-unit* feature allows us to call as many other dialogs as we want *without a COMMIT* as long as the same subschema is used. Changing subschemas, however, starts a new run-unit, terminating the current one, and preventing a purge of any data stored or updated prior to the begin of the new run-unit. Obviously, *the definition of a subschema is integral to program design.* Just as obviously, most development staffs have never thought of it that way.

Defining A Subschema Plan

From what we have discussed thus far, a subschema plan becomes a necessary part of the overall system design. The scope and features of each subschema *MUST* be considered as part of the tuning of an application. To ignore one of the most critical parts of a system and leave it to last minute consideration is asking for trouble. And trouble will surely arrive, usually at a time when the system is experiencing its heaviest use.

Using Automate to define the data required for each transaction, it is fairly easy to structure the subschemas. The data stores associated with each DFD process (and the associated functions and events) clearly identify the data that must be present. Once the subschemas are laid out, create a subset of the schema Bachman for each subschema. Be sure to include a clear description of the purpose and use of each individual subschema.

24

Logical Records

The Logical Record Facility (LRF) is one of those controversial features that is either loved or hated. Early IDMS users have often avoided use of LRF because of its initial restrictions and the processing overhead. Newer users, inexperienced at currency and set walking, have embraced LRF as the tool to make database navigation easier.

This chapter will not go into the depths of coding LRF structures, path-groups, and access logic. A whole book would be required to do the subject justice. Our concentration will be to introduce the concept and provide an overview so that you can make some value judgments on where and when to use LRF.

In the chapter on subschemas, we pointed out that subschema design should be considered during the early physical design stage of the application. The use of logical records must also be considered early. LRF is of little practical use, except for retrieval optimizing, when it is implemented after the application has been coded. In most cases, LRF must either be included in the initial physical design planning or not considered at all.

This chapter will look at both ends of the LRF spectrum and attempt to clarify its use and identify the best way to approach logical records. No definitive recommendation about LRF will be made; as with other IDMS features, LRF has its tradeoffs that must be evaluated for each application.

Logical Record Background

LRF had its debut with Release 5.7 of IDMS. It was Cullinet's answer to user requests for a way to make end user query preparation easier, eliminating much of the need for end users to understand sets and currency.

Unfortunately, the initial release of LRF had some significant restrictions, the most serious of which was the inability to handle nest structures. Since a nest structure is, conceptually, the most difficult of all structures to understand, this omission seriously limited LRF usage in one of the places where it would do the most good.

Currency was also a problem. Addressing a logical record composed of two physical records could meet with serious trouble if the individual physical records were being accessed directly in the same subschema. Loss of currency sometimes caused hard-to-trace system malfunctions. Ultimately, LRF records were placed in separate subschemas.

With Release 10.0, LRF became an integral part of ASF. The logical record capability came into its own and began to enjoy a following. Most of its earlier problems and restrictions had been solved at the time of this writing.

LRF Pros and Cons

As mentioned earlier, LFR has its tradeoffs. This section will generally list the advantages and disadvantages of the facility. Each should be carefully considered when deciding if and where to use LRF.

Advantages Of LRF

1. *The application developer doesn't have to understand the database structure.* Addressing records by logical function can reduce the experience level normally required by IDMS programmers.

2. *A database environment with both relational and network capabilities is available.* Closely coupled physical records can be viewed as a single logical record while high-volume process-

ing of individual physical records is possible in the same structure.

3. *Database access efficiency is improved by reducing the number of program calls to IDMS. A logical record composed of two physical records is addressed by one DML statement. Inside the subschema, numerous database calls may occur, but the program calls only once.*
4. *Redundant logic in the application programs for a system can be eliminated, concentrating the logic within the subschema. Where a particular database path is used frequently, significant code can be eliminated and processing improved.*
5. Privacy of data can be improved by selecting only those fields in each physical record that are required to support the application.
6. *Database structure changes can become transparent to the application program by modifying the logical record path logic in the subschema.*

Disadvantages of LRF

1. *A heavier burden is placed on the DBA staff* to develop and test subschemas containing LRF paths. Most of the logical record definition process becomes a DBA task. In some shops, this could be a bottleneck to the development process.
2. *LRF requires data to be moved from the page buffer to the application working storage through the subschema buffer.* This extra step is time-consuming for large logical records. Extra buffer space is also required.
3. *Mixing currencies with direct record accessing is still a potential problem and must be carefully managed. Separate subschemas for LRF and non-LRF records can cause confusion and increase processing logic complexity.*

Logical Record Paths

Logical records are created by defining a path between the physical records that will comprise the logical record. The DML logic required to read the physical records resides in the subschema.

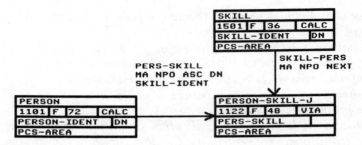

Figure 24-1   Person/Skill Database Structure.

Let's look at a logical record structure using the PCS database structure. Figure 24-1 shows the skills inventory part of the database. Our desire is to create a logical record that consists of the person's name, skill, and skill level.

Figure 24-2 details the physical data definitions of each of the three records to be used in the logical structure. For our logical structure, we will select certain data elements as shown in Figure 24-3.

In the preceding example, we have created a single logical record from parts of three physical records. To retrieve this information from the physical database, we would have had to write program logic such as that shown in Figure 24-4.

Contrasting with the preceding example is the logical record DML statement to accomplish the same thing:

OBTAIN PERSON-SKILLS WHERE PERSON-IDENT = yvalue
ON NO-RECORD-FOUND GOBACK.

The preceding directly corresponds to the logic in Figure 24-4. Additional logic must be defined if we were to want to read the next skill for the same person. But LRF does have a big advantage as far as the program logic is concerned. Figure 24-5 illustrates the LRF path logic in the subschema that accomplishes the desired database access.

```
ADD RECORD NAME IS PERSON VERSION 1.
02 PERSON-IDENT                    PIC X(12).
02 PERS-NAME.
   03  PERS-LAST-NAME              PIC X(15).
   03  PERS-FIRST-NAME             PIC X(15).
   03  PERS-MIDDLE-NI              PIC X(10).
02 PERS-STATUS                     PIC X.
02 PERS-EXPER                      PIC 99V99.
02 PERS-LOCATION.
   03 PERS-BLDG                    PIC X(10).
   03 PERS-ROOM                    PIC X(10).
   03 PERS-MAIL-STOP               PIC X(10).
   03 PERS-PHONE                   PIC X(12).


ADD RECORD NAME IS SKILL VERSION 1
02  SKILL-IDENT                    PIC X(10).
02  SKILL-TITLE                    PIC X(40).
ADD RECORD NAME IS PERSON-SKILL-J VERSION 1.
02  EFFECTIVE-DATE.
   03  EFFECT-CENT-YR.
      04   EFFECT-CENTURY          PIC 99.
      04   EFFECT-YEAR             PIC 99.
   03  EFFECT-MONTH                PIC 99.
   03  EFFECT-DAY                  PIC 99.
02  SKILL-TIME                     PIC 999V9.
```

Figure 24-2   Person/Skill Physical Record Structure.


```
ADD LOGICAL RECORD NAME IS PERSON VERSION 1.
ELEMENTS ARE
                 PERSON
                 PERSON-SKILL-J
                 SKILL.
```

Figure 24-3   Person/Skill Logical Record Structure.

```
MOVE <key value> TO PERSON-IDENT.
OBTAIN CALC PCS-PERSON.
IF DB-ANY-ERROR
   DO.
      PERFORM ERROR.
      GOBACK.
   END.
OBTAIN NEXT PERS-SKILL WITHIN PERSON-SKILL.
IF DB-STATUS=OK
   OBTAIN OWNER WITHIN SKILL-PERSON.
GOBACK.
```

Figure 24-4   Conventional Person/Skill Access Logic.

Roles

It is often necessary, particularly with nest structures, to define a physical record more than once within a single logical record. The second, and subsequent, definition is identified as a *role*. An example makes it easier to understand. In the PCS system, the ORGANIZA-TION record identifies multiple levels of an organization with a nest structure (see Figure 24-6). For the purpose of our example, we can assume that every organization is to be accessed by a logical record to three levels: company, division, and department. Figure 24-7 illustrates the definition of a logical record with three occurrences of the organization record, two of them with defined roles.

It is not necessary to use a role name with the first use of the ORGAN record, although you can if you wish (in this case, the role would be COMPANY). When you use a role name, the path syntax must use the role name instead of the record's element name.

```
ADD PATH-GROUP OBTAIN PERSON-SKILLS
   SELECT FOR FIELDNAME-EQ PERSON-IDENT
      OBTAIN PERSON WHERE CALCKEY EQ PERSON-IDENT
         OF REQUEST
         ON 0326 CLEAR RETURN NO-RECORD-FOUND
      OBTAIN EACH PERS-SKILL WITHIN PERSON-SKILL
      OBTAIN OWNER WITHIN SKILL-PERSON.
```

Figure 24-5   LRF Path Logic.

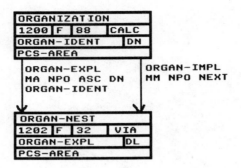

Figure 24-6   PCS Organization Nest Structure.

While you can use a 32-character role name for IDD records, the subschema compiler will only accept a role name of 16 characters; for consistency, therefore, keep all role names to 16 characters or less.

Figure 24-8 illustrates coding for the path group to support the preceding logical record.

```
ADD LOGICAL RECORD ORGAN-TOP-LVL
ELEMENTS ARE ORGAN
              ORGAN ROLE IS DIVISION
              ORGAN ROLE IS DEPARTMENT
              ORGAN-NEST.
```

Figure 24-7   Organization Nest Logical Record Definition.

```
ADD PATH-GROUP OBTAIN ORGAN-TOP-LVL
   SELECT FOR FIELDNAME-EQ ORGAN-IDENT
      OBTAIN ORGAN WHERE CALCKEY EQ ORGAN-IDENT OF REQUEST.
         FIND EACH ORGAN-NEST WITHIN ORGAN-EXPL.
      IF ORGAN-IMPL MEMBER
         OBTAIN OWNER DIVISION WITHIN ORGAN-IMPL.
         FIND EACH ORGAN-NEST WITHIN ORGAN-EXPL.
         IF ORGAN-IMPL MEMBER
            OBTAIN OWNER DEPARTMENT WITHIN ORGAN-IMPL.
```

Figure 24-8   Multilevel LRF Path Logic.

25

IDD

A data dictionary is an essential tool during the process of defining and developing database applications. The dictionary is based around a software package that permits database designers to store descriptive information about an application in a formal and machine-readable form. For IDMS, this dictionary software is the Integrated Data Dictionary (IDD).

The formality of the dictionary format forces designers to carefully follow a design and development methodology, improving application quality. The use of dictionary definition statements to describe the complete scope and detail of the applications reduces the probability of overlooking significant features. If these features were added later, they would greatly increase the cost of the overall application life cycle.

Machine-readable dictionary data increases the flexibility of the design personnel. The application information can be displayed in a number of different forms to improve its usefulness. This feature is of particular importance when the application under development interfaces with another planned or operational application. When the dictionary contains all organizational systems, the process of comparing the contents of a new application to those already existing can be greatly simplified.

Background Of IDD

IDMS has always had a data dictionary. In its early days, it was known as a data directory and was used to compile the schemas, sub-schemas, and DMCLs. Responding to requests from the user community, Cullinet (then Cullinane Software) began the development of IDD in 1976. IDD has continuously evolved to reach today's capabilities. IDD is a prime example of the responsiveness of Cullinet to user requests and suggestions. A majority of IDDs end-user features came from the user community.

The Active Dictionary Concept

Data dictionaries are either *passive* (no dynamic reference to the continuing operation of the DBMS) or *active* (the dictionary takes an active part in the operation of the DBMS). Most DBMS products on the market today have no data dictionary product or the product is passive. IDD took the lead in the development of an active dictionary; most other DBMS vendors are now following suit. (One of the largest criticisms of DB2 has been its lack of a data dictionary.)

In 1976 I had breakfast with Bob Goldman, then a senior analyst. Bob described his concept of an active data dictionary that would control the operation of the DBMS dynamically. He felt it would be practical if some performance hurdles could be overcome. Today we see the fruits of that concept; IDD provides the IDMS user community with a central dictionary facility that dramatically enhances the flexiblity of IDMS.

What Is An Active Dictionary?

An active dictionary is used by the DBMS to control its operation. The DBMS refers regularly to the dictionary to verify such things as the list of authorized users, terminals, and active on-line dialogs. In turn it posts activity to the dictionary. Users can change the operating configuration of the DBMS by updating the dictionary "on the fly."

Figure 25-1   Dictionary Arrangement For Loading Non-IDMS Systems.

Dictionary Scope

Many DP professionals assume that a data dictionary actively associated with a DBMS like IDMS cannot be used to support independent applications that do not use the DBMS. This is a false assumption. In fact, *using IDD to document non-IDMS systems is a major feature* that should be used extensively. Documenting existing non-IDMS systems in IDD provides an insight into the structure and function of the application and an excellent lead-in to future conversion of the application.

Loading Non-IDMS Applications

It is advantageous for every installation to load its existing non-IDMS applications to the data dictionary. *Up front, understand that this is a time-consuming and frequently frustrating job.* While there are some utilities available to assist in loading the dictionary, it is best to look carefully at how the utility handles the load before actually doing it.

DO NOT LOAD NON-IDMS APPLICATIONS TO THE SAME DICTIONARY AS IDMS APPLICATIONS. Use a secondary dictionary. This will prevent the old application data from polluting the main dictionary. And pollute is the right term. Few existing applications were developed with the controls and conventions enforced by a data dictionary. I suggest a further step: Load each application into an empty secondary dictionary. Clean up the data there and then merge it with the dictionary being used to hold all non-IDMS applications. This dictionary arrangement is illustrated in Figure 25-1.

Pitfalls Of Loading Existing Applications

Unless it was written entirely by the same programmer (and sometimes not even then), existing batch applications often had different names for the same data element. *This condition must be resolved* in order to effectively document the application in IDD. It can be resolved in one of two basic ways:

1. *Assign synonym names* to all multiple names for the same data element or record. This is the easiest solution and requires the least amount of extra effort. It does, however, perpetuate some of the confusion caused by multiple synonomous names for the same element.
2. *Change the element names to be consistent.* This will require recompiling the programs of the application after changing the element names throughout the programs. This alternative is seldom used because of the costs involved. Few managers can justify updating existing software just for the sake of making data element names consistent.

Probably the most frustrating part of loading existing system descriptions into the dictionary is the lack of up-to-date documentation. It is very difficult to explain the use of a data element if there is no documentation and the programmer who developed the application is no longer around. In this case, it may be possible to reconstruct the element purpose and use from looking at the source programs. *Caution: It is not unusual for a data element to be used for a purpose other than its original intent in older systems.* This condition occurred frequently when the intended purpose of a field was never utilized and, rather than change the system files, programmers used the space for other purposes.

Dictionary Entities

This section discusses many of the dictionary entities. We will concentrate on the uses of these entities, leaving much of the mechanics to Cullinet manuals.

```
ADD CLASS NAME IS APPLICATION
    PREPARED BY TOWNER
    CLASS TYPE IS CLASS
    ATTRIBUTES ARE MANUAL PLURAL
    DELETION LOCK IS ON
    COMMENTS
    'Application identifies all of the system applications'
   -'represented within the data dictionary.  A separate '
   -'attribute is assigned for each application.'
```

Figure 25-2   Class Definition Syntax Example.

Class/Attributes

The Class. This is a major category of cross-references that populate the dictionary. Classes, and their associated attributes, can be linked to most of the principal entities within the dictionary. This capability provides the data administrator with a very powerful tool to scan the dictionary in an unlimited number of ways.

Classes are used to identify a major reference, such as *APPLICATION*. This class, described more fully in Chapter 10, permits us to assign each dictionary entity occurrence to one or more application projects. Figure 25-2 illustrates the APPLICATION class as a general example of class definition.

The class can also be used as a user-defined entity. This facility permits us to define our own dictionary entities. Figure 25-3 shows the use of the entity definition to create the entity TEST-PLAN in which the test plans for each of the programs in the application are documented.

We need to look back at the two previous figures and briefly discuss a few of the statements within the class definition:

1. *CLASS TYPE IS type.* While the default, if the statement is omitted, is the CLASS type, it is good documentation to be overt about entering the class type. It serves to remind you that is what we are defining. Identifying a class as an entity really only makes it possible to use syntactical shortcuts when accessing the entity.

```
ADD CLASS NAME IS TEST-PLAN
     PREPARED BY TOWNER
     CLASS TYPE IS ENTITY
     ATTRIBUTES ARE AUTOMATIC PLURAL
     DELETION LOCK IS ON
     COMMENTS
     'Each software module within the application system must'
    -'include a test plan supporting the functions performed'
    -'by the module. Test plans will be created at the multiple'
    -'levels of an application system:'
    -' '
    -'System:  The system test plan will describe those tests'
    -'that can be performed only when all components of the '
    -'system have been developed and tested.'
    -' '
    -'Subsystem: The subsystem test plan is similar to that of'
    -'a system but focused on a subset of the system.'
    -' '
    -'Program: The program test plan tests the entire program,'
    -'including all options and paths. Out of bounds tests are'
    -'also performed. Tests will encompass the results of module'
    -'tests.'
    -' '
    -'Module: Each individual program module, self-contained
code,'
    -'must be tested to validate each of the functions
performed'
    -'by the individual module. Ideally, the module test plans
come'
    -'together to form the bulk of a program test plan.'
```

Figure 25-3   User-Defined Entity Example.

2. *ATTRIBUTES ARE AUTOMATIC PLURAL.* While you also
    have the option to indicate that attributes are manual (you
    must overtly define the attribute through IDD before using it)
    and/or singular (there can be only one occurrence of an at-
    tribute), many users permit the entry of a previously undefined

```
ADD ATTRIBUTE PCS WITHIN CLASS APPLICATION
DELETE-LOCK IS ON
PUBLIC ACCESS IS ALLOWED FOR DISPLAY
INCLUDE USER IS TOWNER REGISTERED FOR ALL
COMMENTS
'THE PROJECT CONTROL SYSTEM.'.
```

Figure 25-4   An IDD ATTRIBUTE Example.

attribute in an IDD statement. AUTOMATIC will insert the new attribute into the class if it is not there already.

You will note that the example for defining an entity allows automatic attributes while the definition for class does not. There is no correlation. Some classes should be restrictive; we found that allowing automatic attributes in the APPLICATION class quickly cluttered up the system with multiple versions of the same application name.

3. *DELETION LOCK IS ON.* This feature requires that deletes of dictionary data be done in two steps. As long as the deletion lock is turned on, the entity cannot be deleted. To actually delete the entity, you must first *turn off the deletion lock.* Then, on a second access of the data, the data itself may be deleted. I recommend that this feature be implemented across the board on all IDD entities. It will be frustrating on some occasions but will save your life on others.

The Attribute. This is a subset of class. Using our APPLICATION example again, the statement APPLICATION IS PCS identifies the class as APPLICATION and its ATTRIBUTE as PCS. A different attribute is assigned for each new application supported by the dictionary. Figure 25-4 provides an example of the PCS attribute associated with the APPLICATION class.

Let's look at two of the statements in this figure:

1. *PUBLIC ACCESS IS ALLOWED FOR DISPLAY.* IDD permits us to restrict the usage of individual dictionary entities. With this example, anyone can retrieve the description of the PCS attribute but updating is restricted.
2. *INCLUDE USER IS TOWNER REGISTERED FOR ALL.* This statement identifies me as authorized to perform all of the

maintenance and retrieval options against the attribute. If this statement were not included, only a person with high level data administration authority would be able to update the attribute.

There are a number of other options associated with classes and attributes, particularly attributes. They permit associating with other classes and attributes and keys.

System

Each time a system generation is performed, an IDD SYSTEM record is created. The sysgen itself adds statements that do not appear in the IDD manual. While a system can be created using IDD, it is not recommended because the sysgen performs some functions that are hidden from IDD.

We can, however, enhance the sysgen with additional information. Comments can be added describing the system, its function and purpose. Special conditions and considerations are added to the comments. Appropriate class/attribute information may be inserted, such as APPLICATION IS. Using the APPLICATION IS class/attributes, we can document all of the applications that are supported by this specific system. A system title (the SYSTEM DESCRIPTION statement) should be added. Users of the system can be registered.

Terminals

As with any teleprocessing monitor, IDMS/DC requires a table of terminals, both logical and physical.

Logical Terminals. These are those terminals generated by the sysgen. The number of logical terminals defines the limit in the number of concurrent physical terminals that may be active in the system at one time. A logical terminal may be assigned to a specific physical terminal where desired. This assignment occurs frequently to associate master terminals, always available, to the system.

The logical terminal permits users to link to CV without having to supply physical device identifiers. This permits dynamic run-time assignment of a user to any available logical terminal.

Using the DC OPTION statement, the system definer can:

1. *Hard link the logical terminal with a physical one.* The PHYSI-CAL TERMINAL IS statement ensures that a specific physical terminal always has access to the system.
2. *Force a special task to be executed at startup* whenever the logical terminal is assigned. This is useful to implement a menu system or electronic mail facility. For master terminals, the startup might initial the display of system statistics.
3. *Enable or disable the terminal.* A terminal can be disabled at system startup, requiring overt enabling process. This feature can be used to enhance system security, requiring a phone call from the potential user before the terminal is allowed on-line.
4. *Set the priority level of the terminal.* Special terminals, usually hard-linked to a physical terminal, may be given higher priority to ensure that any request from that terminal is serviced ahead of the general terminal population.
5. *Set upper or lower case input.* Using the UPPER key word causes all text input to be translated to upper case. The LOWER key word permit entry of both upper and lower case text.

Physical Terminals. Physical terminals should be processed through the sysgen compiler. Each definition identifies the characteristics of a physical terminal device.

Messages

The message section of the dictionary physically resides as a separate area and data set. This makes it possible for a common message area to serve multiple central versions. There are both advantages and disadvantages (as usual) to this approach (see Figure 25-5). The major advantage is consistency of messages across all systems. The major disadvantage is possible contention. If a large number of messages are generated by application programs, performance can suffer because of device contention.

Except in the most unusual situations, I still recommend that a single message area be established and shared by all systems and CVs.

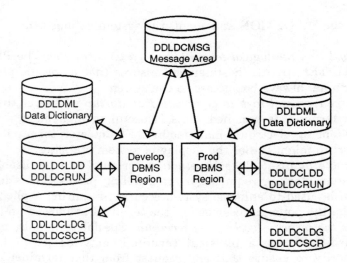

Figure 25-5   Message Area Sharing Across CVs.

Users

The heart of the IDMS security system is the user. Particularly in development CVs, user identification is the key to accessing the various system components. There is a good deal of controversy in the user community as to how much data about a user should be kept in the dictionary.

Some installations keep a complete record of the current user status, including job assignments, date of birth, and date of hire. Physical location by building, mail stop, and room are normally kept as is the person's telephone number. Other installations keep only a minimum amount of user data.

Part of the basis for this controversy is the time and effort required to keep user information current in multiple dictionaries. Unlike the message area, which can serve multiple CVs and dictionaries, the user information is held in each dictionary. Users cannot sign on to a dictionary unless they are registered in that dictionary. Users who have authority to access several dictionaries must be registered in each of them.

One solution to this problem is to place a master copy of user information in one dictionary, usually the primary dictionary of the production system. This information is then copied to other dictionaries as required. Comments in the master dictionary identify where the data has been copied, permitting easier updating if necessary.

Programs

The program record in the dictionary often confuses the novice. It serves *all* types of programs that execute in the IDMS environment. ADS/O dialogs are programs just as are COBOL batch jobs. If program registration is turned on within the dictionary, the program information must be entered before actually compiling a program. While this may prove somewhat painful initially, I recommend using the registration function. The end result is a less cluttered dictionary.

Each program may be thoroughly documented using the dictionary. A number of user-defined-comment types can be set up to cover the categories of document text. Program documentation based on the dictionary is more likely to be maintained than that kept separately.

Modules

Within IDD, modules take on multiple faces. IDD allows us to add modules of source code for a variety of languages and functions using a different entity name. ADS/O processes, for example, are updated using ADD PROCESS instead of ADD MODULE. We can use ADD MODULE LANGUAGE IS PROCESS, but it is certainly easier to use ADD PROCESS. The same technique is used to store tables.

One overlooked use of modules is to store JCL and control data. The module can be used to hold any number of source-type data that may be needed in the future. Again, the dictionary makes an excellent repository for this type of unusual data, avoiding the need to store it in separate files.

Updating The Dictionary

We can look at the data dictionary as the recipe book for all of the corporate data. As such, it is more valuable than any of the

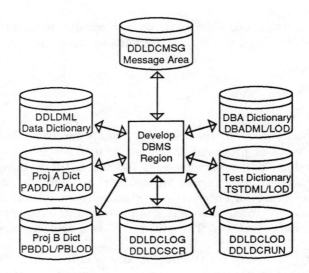

Figure 25-6   Secondary Dictionary Use For Development.

databases it supports. Loss or corruption of the dictionary can bring disaster to the company who depends on large-scale integrated databases. Update control of the dictionary, therefore, is a critical responsibility of the Data Administrator.

With the availability of secondary dictionaries, it became possible to isolate the development efforts from production. A master data dictionary, accessible by many but updatable by only a few, provides the baseline of data definition for the installation. Secondary dictionaries are assigned to each development project, effectively isolating potential problems. Figure 25-6 illustrates this arrangement.

The second effect of separating dictionaries by project is to prevent contention between the projects. Contention may take the form of physical device contention, particularly with large projects employing many developers. Data element contention must also be considered, each project potentially using the same element.

Single vs Multiple Primary Dictionaries

For several years I supported the use of a single primary dictionary across both development and production regions. The primary dictionary could be read in development and updated only in production.

There are a number of advantages to this approach, the most significant being the reduction in labor needed to maintain two primary dictionaries and transfer data between them. In a small shop, I still recommend this approach.

In the larger shop, however, the practice can become a bottleneck where several development projects are in progress at any time. The separation between development and production needs to be more complete, with specific and hard-line procedures in place for transferring data from development to production.

Secondary Dictionaries

As we saw in Figure 25-6, assigning secondary dictionaries to multiple development projects effectively isolates those projects from each other and *from the primary dictionary.* This is important to the overall integrity of the system. The primary dictionary must be the mirror image of the production system, available as a reference at any time. Until a new application is ready to migrate to production, it is held separate from the primary dictionary.

How Many Secondary Dictionaries?

I know of one installation that has more than 20 secondary dictionaries in its development region. Most, but not all, are used for individual project development. In addition to project development, secondary dictionaries are used for:

1. *Migration.* As an application reaches the time for transition to production, a migration dictionary is established that *is a mirror copy of the primary dictionary.* The new application is then merged into the migration dictionary and tested. If testing is successful, the resulting composite dictionary is copied to the primary dictionary, replacing the previous copy. The primary dictionary is then copied to the production dictionary to complete the transition of the application to production. Figure 25-7 illustrates this transition.

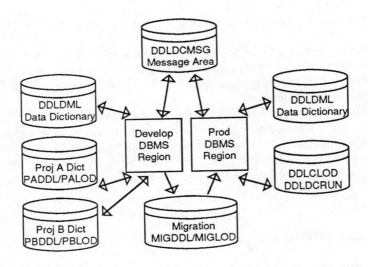

Figure 25-7   Migrating An Application To Production.

2. *Program maintenance.* Bug fixing and other minor maintenance tasks are accomplished by transferring the program's
   dictionary references to a secondary dictionary, correcting the
   problem, testing, and then replacing those altererd entities in
   the primary dictionary.
   It is important that we test the change carefully in the
   development primary dictionary before copying to the production dictionary. In an integrated environment small changes in
   one area may have impacts elsewhere in the system. This is
   particularly true when the change is applied to a mapless
   dialog or other common use item. Figure 25-8 illustrates this
   process.

3. *Major enhancements.* A major enhancement to a production
   system starts with the copying of the entire application's dictionary data to a secondary dictionary. The enhancements are
   therefore developed and tested. The application is then
   migrated back to the production environment in the same manner as any new system, with one exception: *Database structure
   changes, if required, must be performed concurrently with
   migration.*

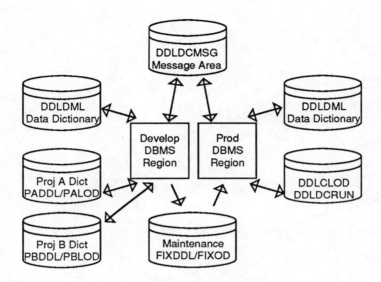

Figure 25-8 Minor Program Fix Dictionary Setup.

26

Restructuring

This short chapter focuses on *not* having to do a restructure. While it is usually necessary to restructure your database at some time during its lifetime, proper design and intelligent guessing can minimize the need.

What Causes A Restructure?

Within IDMS, restructure is necessary for only two reasons:

1. *Altering the database structure.* A schema change modifies one or more records within the database and those records must be unloaded and reloaded in their new format. While this is not a true restructure of the database, it falls in the general category.
2. *Adding new pages to the database.* Once a database fills to a certain point, it begins to operate inefficiently.

Altering the Database Structure

The updating of the database structure, particularly the changing of sets, necessitates the restructure of the database. The physical format of a record is changed and the subschema no longer properly positions the record's reference pointers. Here are the types of database alterations that normally require a restructure:

1. *Adding a new set.* The new set will change the pointer offset for those records affected.
2. *Removing a set.* Again, the pointer offset will be changed.
3. *Adding or removing fields from an existing record.* If the changes occur at the beginning or the middle of the record, the field pointers will be incorrect for all fields to the right of the change.
4. *Moving a record from one area to another.*
5. *Adding a record that requires a new set.* This affects the offset of the set pointers in the existing record.

Alterations That Do Not Require Restructure

There are some database changes that do not require a restructure:

1. *Add a new record to an existing set.* The new record is inserted into a forked set (or creates a forked set). The owner is unaffected because no set changes occur in the owner; existing members are not affected either. Since the new member hasn't previously existed, unloading and reloading are unnecessary.
2. *Add a new CALC record.* The new record has no set ties to be concerned about. If it is to be a member, therefore it can be added to a forked set. If an owner, it starts fresh.
3. *Remove a record from an existing set.* If the record is one of several on a forked set, it can be removed from the schema without affecting the database. The record's occurrences will remain in the database and cannot be accessed.

Adding Pages To The Database

Unless we check the fill rate of a database area regularly, it is possible for the database to fill up. Once an area reaches approximately 70 percent of capacity, performance begins to degrade. First, the space management page is checked and updated with each update of a database page. Second, the frequency of CALC overflows grows.

CALC overflows are very expensive to performance. Once a CALC record overflows to another page, *it remains there for its entire lifetime*. This means a second I/O each time the record is accessed.

Adding pages to the database will affect the computation of the CALC algorithm. The same record key value will compute a different target page when the page boundaries change. Therefore it is a given that adding pages will force a restructure of the area. *If records in other areas directly reference a record in the changed area, these areas will have to be restructured, too*. This is another strong reason for avoiding cross-area sets.

Avoiding A Restructure

Restructure is the bane of database management systems. Some systems require a periodic restructuring to consolidate empty space in the database files. IDMS is among the very few that perform automatic "garbage collection" each time the database is updated, consolidating each page dynamically.

Record Padding

One of the favorite techniques for reducing maintenance of tape file systems was to pad the end of each record so that we could add more fields without having to change all of the programs. This option is still used by many designers. The only problem is the clarity of the designer's crystal ball. My own experience is that we add too many characters to the wrong records and not enough to the right ones.

Padding nest and junction records should be avoided. Since these records are the most populous in the database, a lot of unnecesary empty space ends up in the database.

Page Expansions

Expanding the database page is an excellent option. Cullinet's utility to perform this function operates smoothly and quickly. Little additional effort is required except to recompile the DMCL and insert the SMI statement.

The page expansion process actually opens up the top and bottom of the record and inserts some additional data space in the middle. Records are not moved so dbkey values do not change. It is important, however, to expand the page before the area fills to the point that CALC overflows occur.

27

Physical Design Considerations

This chapter is one of the most important of the book. Here we will go into some of the subtleties of designing a physical database. While we will find CASE tools such as Automate Plus and IDMS/Architect assuming some of the basic activities of the physical design process, the final tuning will still require intelligent human intervention.

Fixed vs. Variable-Length Records

Before we go to the depths of design, it is worthwhile to look at the structure of a record. Many of our physical design decisions can be biased by whether the record is fixed or variable-length.

Variable-Length Records

The variable-length record is very familiar to old-timers. In the flat file days, many systems had variable-length extensions to a record, principally to make it easier to locate the extended data. The advantages of such a capability extend to the IDMS world, too:

1. *One database call retrieves all extensions of the record.* This speeds up processing by reducing the amount of I/O required.

2. *Pointer overhead is reduced by eliminating a set.*

Unfortunately, most of the advantages (except reducing pointer overhead) also have undesirable sideeffects:

1. *The storage space required to hold the extended record is greater.* If the program doesn't need all of the occurrences of the extended data, space and time are wasted.
2. *The potential of record overflow and fragmentation is increased* by the use of variable-length records. Variable-length records tend to be large, requiring either overt fragmentation or larger page size (often both).
3. *System overhead increases* because variable-length records should be compressed to minimize wasted disk space.
4. *The extensions cannot participate in other sets.* This limits the flexibility of the database structure.
5. *There is a maximum number of extension occurrences* that can be held in the record. If the user requires more than the maximum, significant database restructuring and program modification may be required.

Simple Structures

This section will open up the different "simple" data structures that IDMS supports. The quotes around simple are to emphasize that simple is in the eyes of the beholder. The truly simple structure, owner-member, can be expanded and twisted to become a very complex environment.

The CALC Record

The simpliest data structure in IDMS is simply a CALC record without any members, as shown in Figure 27-1. Where would we use such a thing? Let's look at it in detail.

The standalone CALC record may be an OOAK record (see the discussion on OOAK records that follows) when it occurs just once within the database. Some reference records, however, will occur several times over the life of the database.

```
┌─────────────────────────────┐
│EVENT-OOAK                   │
├──────┬────┬────┬────────────┤
│900   │F   │48  │CALC        │
├──────┴────┴────┼────┬───────┤
│EOOAK-IDENT     │DN          │
├────────────────┴────────────┤
│OOAK-AREA                    │
└─────────────────────────────┘
```

Figure 27-1   Standalone CALC Record.

For example, each year the company begins a new sequence of purchase orders. The previous year's data, however, must be retained because not all of those purchase orders have been closed out. The control record contains not only the control sequences but a running audit total of purchase orders written, outstanding, closed, and canceled.

Nest Structures

The nest record is used to provide a special data relationship that occurs when a record occurrence of a type owns another occurrence of the same type. Nest structures, also known as bill-of-material or BOM structures, appear to be one of the simpler structures. After all, there are only two record types and two sets, right?

Wrong! While physically simple, nest structures are logically complex. The relationship between two occurrences of the same record type is abstract and many designers grope in darkness for a long time before they understand how the nest works.

The best way to illustrate the nest structure is with a *bubble* chart. The bubble chart displays the *occurrences* of each record type as circles. It is much easier to relate to the bubble chart than to the Bachman. Figure 27-2 shows the bubble chart that illustrates the occurrences of the records depicted in the organization chart shown in Figure 27-3.

The first myth to dispel about nest structures is that they only apply to manufacturing bill-of-material environments. The opportunities to use nests abound, possibly too much so. Here are a few examples, in the business environment:

1. *An organization structure.* One organization reports to a higher level organization. Both are represented by the same record type (ORGAN). The nest identifies the pecking order. Figure

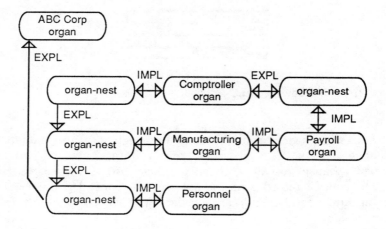

Figure 27-2   Bubble Chart Of Organization Nest.

27-3 illustrates this relationship and the Bachman chart that provides the database.

2. *Persons.* It is frequently desirable to be able to associate a person with another person, such as father and son, husband and wife, teacher and pupil.

3. *Accounts.* A general ledger account may contain subsidiary accounts.

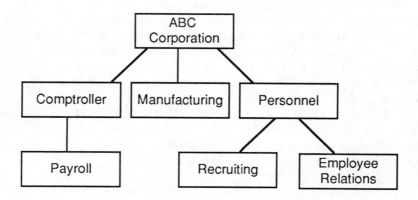

Figure 27-3a   Organization Chart Example.

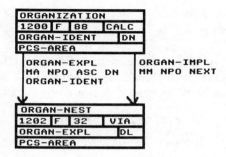

Figure 27-3b   An Organization Chart Nest Structure.

4. *Tasks.* A task may be composed of many subtasks, each of which could have further subtask breakouts.

Currency In Nest Structures

One of the most difficult things about nest structures is the way it handles its currency. Using Figure 27-4 as an example, let's look at how IDMS maintains currency in a nest:

1. *Let's first obtain the Comptroller record* of our organization in Figure 27-3. Once obtained, this record becomes current of:

   a. *The ORGAN record type*
   b. *The PCS area*
   c. *The ORGAN-EXPL set*
   d. *The ORGAN-IMPL set*
   e. *The run-unit*

2. *The first step in obtaining the Payroll ORGAN record* subordinate to the Comptroller, is accomplished by reading the first ORGAN-NEST record. Once obtained, this record becomes current of:

   a. *It own record type*
   b. *The ORGAN-EXPL set*
   c. *The ORGAN-IMPL set (if connected, and it should be).*

    d. *The PCS area*
    e. *The run-unit*

What has happened here is that first the ORGAN record was current of both sets and then the ORGAN-NEST became current of both sets as it was read because it is a member of both sets.

  3. *The owner of the ORGAN-IMPL set is read.* This accesses the Payroll ORGAN record occurrence. This occurrence therefore becomes current of:

    a. *The ORGAN record type*
    b. *The PCS area*
    c. *The ORGAN-EXPL set*
    d. *The ORGAN-IMPL set*
    e. *The run-unit*

What has happened at this point is that the Payroll ORGAN record has replaced the Comptroller ORGAN record as current of the ORGAN record type. Unless we have saved the currency of the Comptroller record occurrence somewhere we will have lost our ability to proceed on to the Personnel ORGAN record that is also subordinate to the Comptroller.

Actually we must save the currency of the next ORGAN-NEST record in the ORGAN-EXPL chain before *retrieving the Payroll ORGAN record through the ORGAN-IMPL set.* This permits us to retrieve the currency (dbkey) of that next ORGAN-NEST record, obtain it, and walk its ORGAN-IMPL set to the Personnel ORGAN record. This process is repeated until all subordinate organizations of the Comptroller have been retrieved.

Spend some time walking through this exercise using the Bachman chart in Figure 27-4, the organization chart in Figure 27-3, and the bubble chart in Figure 27-2. Be sure you are thoroughly familiar with how the nest structure actually works within IDMS before going further.

Software Logic for Nest Structures

Two routines are illustrated in Figures 27-5 and 27-6 that walk a single-level nest and a multilevel nest respectively. (A single-level

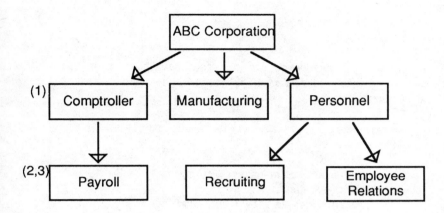

Figure 27-4   Currency In Nest Structures.

nest is one in which only the first layer of subordinate occurrences is processed.)

Data History Tracking Structures

Frequently, for audit or other reasons, it is desirable to maintain the history of specific data updating on-line. There are several approaches to this requirement. One of the most effective is described in this section.

```
WHILE DB-STATUS-OK
 REPEAT.
  OBTAIN NEXT EVENT-NEST WITHIN EVENT-EXPL.
  IF DB-ANY-ERROR
    EXIT.
  OBTAIN OWNER WITHIN EVENT-IMPL.
  CALL PROCESS.
 END.
```

Figure 27-5   Single-Level Nest Processing Logic.

```
MOVE 1 TO W-SUB1.
  WHILE W-SUB1 GT 0
    REPEAT.
!
!  WALK DOWN THE EXPLOSION SET OF SUCCESSIVE LEVELS OF THE
!  NEST.  RECORD THE POSITION OF THE NEST RECORD ITSELF
!  AS A RETURN POINT.
!
       OBTAIN NEXT EVENT-NEST WITHIN EVENT-EXPL.
       IF DB-STATUS-OK
         DO.
           MOVE DBKEY TO W-DBKEY1 (W-SUB1).
           ADD 1 TO W-SUB1.
           OBTAIN OWNER WITHIN EVENT-IMPL.
         END.
!
!  WHEN THE BOTTOM OF A NEST HAS BEEN REACHED, BACK UP ONE
!  LEVEL AND SEE IF THERE ARE MORE NESTS TO BE WALKED FROM
!  THAT LEVEL.  AS EACH SUCCESSIVE LEVEL IS EXHAUSTED,
!  DECREMENT THE STACK POINTER TO THE PREVIOUS LEVEL
!
       ELSE
         DO.
           FIND CURRENT EVENT-NEST.
           FIND OWNER WITHIN EVENT-EXPL.
           IF DB-ANY-ERROR
             NEXT.
           CALL PROCESS.
           SUBTRACT 1 FROM W-SUB1.
           FIND EVENT-NEST DB-KEY W-DBKEY1 (W-SUB1).
         END.
     END.
GOBACK.
```

Figure 27-6   Multiple-Level Nest Processing Logic.

In this scenario, we are interested in maintaining a complete history of job assignments for all persons within a company. It is necessary that we be able to quickly retrieve the current assignment as

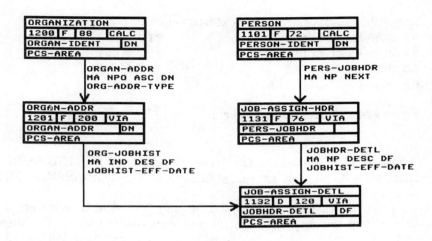

Figure 27-7   Data Structure Maintaining History On-line.

well as list all assignments in chronological order. Figure 27-7 illustrates the Bachman chart for this function.

This database structure provides these features:

1. *A person may be associated* with one or more organizations.
2. *An organization may have one or more persons associated with it.*
3. *The job assignments of a person,* and the organizations associated with each assignment, are maintained chronologically
   with the most recent at the front of the set between JOB-AS-
   SIGN-HDR and JOB-ASSIGN-DETL.
4. *The number of history records,* the oldest history record date,
   the latest history record date, and the identifier of the updater
   is maintained in the JOB-ASSIGN-HDR record.

Let's take a moment to look closely at this structure.   Prior to
Release 10.0, this structure would have been an invitation to disaster. Because both sets from the CALC records to the junction
record are sorted, the effect is to set up a CALC-to-CALC sorted set,
one of the most dangerous structures in IDMS. With the implementation of integrated indexing/pointer arrays, however, the performance hazards of this structure are dramatically reduced.

```
ADD RECORD NAME IS JOB-ASSIGN-HDR.
02 JOB-ASGN-IDENT                PIC X(12).
02 JOB-ASGN-CODE                 PIC X(6).
02 JOB-ASGN-TITLE                PIC X(40).
02 JOB-ASGN-SAL-GRADE            PIC 99.
```

Figure 27-8 Header Record Structure.

Figure 27-8 illustrates the basic structure of the JOB-ASSIGN-HDR record, as well as the structure of the JOB-ASSIGN-DETL record.

As you can see from Figures 27-8 and 27-9, the header record is only a stub that contains control and status information. The meaningful data about the job assignment is located in the detail record.

Accessing The Job Data

Under normal circumstances, each occurrence of the PERSON record will have a single occurrence of the JOB-ASSIGN-HDR record. The header record can be readily obtained by using an OBTAIN NEXT JOB-ASSIGN-HDR statement. (While you can use OBTAIN FIRST and get the same results, OBTAIN NEXT operates more efficiently within IDMS.)

If you wish to save pointer space in the PERSON record, the JOB-ASSIGN-HDR record can be included in another unsorted set of

```
ADD RECORD NAME IS JOB-ASSIGN-DETL.
02   JOB-HIST-EFF-DATE.
     03   JOB-HIST-CENT-YR.
          04   JOB-HIST-CENTURY   PIC 99.
          04   JOB-HIST-YEAR      PIC 99.
     03   JOB-HIST-MONTH          PIC 99.
     03   JOB-HIST-DAY            PIC 99.
02   JOB-HIST-PD                  PIC X(8).
02   JOB-HIST-PD-TITLE            PIC X(40).
02   JOB-HIST-RATE                PIC 9(7).
```

Figure 27-9 Detail Record Structure.

which PERSON is the owner. You *must* use the OBTAIN FIRST option in this case to insure that the JOB-ASSIGN-HDR record will be obtained. See the section on forked sets for an explanation of the currencies involved.

Once the JOB-ASSIGN-HDR record has been obtained, the desired detail record is read. This is where the flexibility of this structure becomes evident. You can:

1. *Retrieve the current job assignment* by obtaining the first detail record within the set.
2. *Retrieve the first job assignment* by obtaining the last detail record within the set.
3. *Retrieve the job assignment as of any date* by obtaining a detail record using the desired date. It is likely that a record for that exact date will not be found. However, IDMS will stop the search when a comparison with the records in the set indicates that there is no equal date record. The NEXT record currency of the set points to the assignment detail record that has the closest date preceding the desired date. A simple OBTAIN NEXT of the detail record will retrieve the job assignment as of the desired date.
4. *An ascending chronological sequence* of job assignments, those assignments from the beginning of the person's employment, may be obtained by reading the set backward (OBTAIN PRIOR) from the header record.
5. *A list of job assignments* beginning with the most recent, may be obtained by reading the set from the front (OBTAIN NEXT).

It may be possible to bypass reading the detail record altogether if the header information indicates that the person had no detail data during the time period being scanned. If the date being queried precedes that of the earliest date on the header record, no search of detail data is necessary.

Archiving Detail Data

Over a long period of time, it is possible that the number of detail record occurrences will exceed that required for on-line inquiry. The unneeded data may be archived onto tape. How do we know when older data than what is on-line may be available?

The header record may contain two additional fields to cover this condition. The oldest data date field now takes on the meaning of the oldest data date *on-line*. A new field representing the initial date of job assignment and a count field indicating how many assignment records have been archived are added. When the person is first added to the database, the initial date and oldest date fields are identical with the archive count at zero.

When the archive limit is reached, a batch program transfers the bottom of the stack of assignments to the tape file. It is even possible to include a field that defines the archive limit, making a different limit for each person available. Some installations may also wish to include the date when the archiving function was performed in the header record.

OOAK Records

The one-of-a-kind record, otherwise known as the OOAK, is somewhat like a dinosaur that won't go away. It dates back to the early days of IDMS when secondary indexes were not available and a means was needed to be able to quickly reach all occurrences of a CALC record within an area.

Since a CALC record is itself usually an entry point, frequently without owners, reading all of the CALC records of a certain type required that the program sweep the entire area. If the area was large, this was very time-consuming.

The alternative was to create a record type that had all CALC records of one or more types as members. The database actually contained a single occurrence of this record, hence the one-of-a-kind label. All occurrences of the CALC members were included in the chain and the records could be more quickly located by walking the set.

Some schemas — the data dictionary is a good example — have a single OOAK record with all key CALC records linked to it. While this conserves on record types, it can be disastrous in a high-volume, on-line updating environment. (Most of us have experienced the frustration of having ADSO come to a halt while the DBA did a schema compile, even when we were not working with that schema.)

When an area containing an OOAK is opened in update mode, any record processed that connects to the OOAK causes the OOAK to be locked also. Where multiple CALC records are connected to the

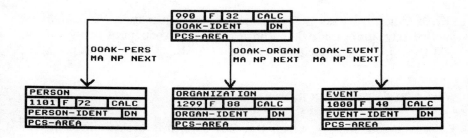

Figure 27-10   OOAK Record In A Database Structure.

OOAK, it is possible for one user to lock out another who is working in an entirely different application. Figure 27-10 illustrates the kind of OOAK structure that can cause problems in multi-user environments.

If an OOAK record is really desirable, a separate OOAK record should be defined for each CALC member record type. This will eliminate cross-application lockout. Figure 27-11 illustrates the same CALC records as in Figure 27-10, but with separate OOAK records.

When To Use OOAK Records

If secondary indexes do the same job as an OOAK (they actually do it better), why should we use any OOAK records? Many databases have key control counts or sequences that must be maintained. The

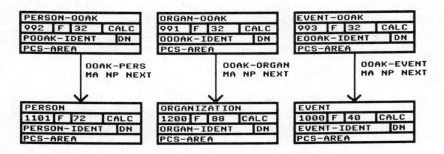

Figure 27-11   Multiple OOAK Records In An Application.

OOAK is a good place to put this kind of information. An OOAK is particularly applicable when those counts or sequences apply to the CALC record type associated with the OOAK.

When NOT To Use OOAK Records

When the sequence in which the CALC records are obtained is important, an OOAK should not be used. Sorting the set between the OOAK and its CALC member has the effect of creating a CALC-to-CALC sorted set. (See sorted sets for a further explanation of this phenomenon.

OOAK records should not be used when the volume of CALC records is such that an area sweep would be at least as efficient as walking the chain. For example, an area of 500 pages contains 600 CALC records associated with an OOAK. An area sweep requires a maximum of 500 physical I/Os while walking the OOAK-CALC set will probably result in nearly 600 I/Os. As a rule of thumb, the CALC volume in the OOAK-CALC set should not be greater than 50 percent of the number of pages. Remember that it is probable that several pages will contain more than one CALC record, resulting in a single physical I/O for retrieving multiple records during a sweep.

OOAK records used for sequential processing make contention more likely if the sets are long and volatile. The frequency with which the set is updated is critical to the use of the OOAK.

Alternatives To OOAK Records

The principal alternative to an OOAK record is a secondary index. The index has several advantages over the OOAK:

1. *It can be sorted*, permitting retrieval of the CALC records in a desired sequence.
2. *The sequence of CALC records can be scanned* without actually reading each record, saving many I/Os.
3. *In an on-line environment, updates to a CALC record do not lock out other transactions.*

Figure 27-12 illustrates the use of a standalone OOAK and a secondary index to replace the OOAK-CALC sets of Figure 27-11.

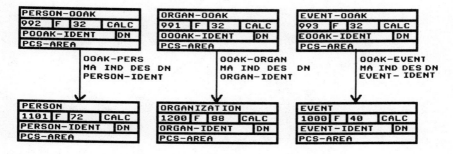

Figure 27-12   OOAK Structure Using Secondary Indexes.

Where key and control information must be maintained, simply create the OOAK without any sets. This will provide the repository for that special one-time information without creating other overhead. Consider creating such a record for each separate application, maybe even more than one for different functions of the same application. Remember that ANY OOAK record becomes an on-line bottleneck when it must be updated by multiple transactions.

28

Multiple Dictionary Elements

"In the beginning" there was only one dictionary per IDMS region. User requests first made more dictionaries available. Then we found that multiple dictionaries were only of limited use without corresponding load areas. Now we have both.

The multiple dictionary capability gives IDMS, particularly in the large, multisystem environment, a great deal of added flexibility. This chapter will address when we should begin to plan for multiple dictionaries, how to set them up, and how to manage them. Of necessity, we will also discuss the IDMS processing regions that are part of the whole dictionary picture.

When To Use Multiple Dictionaries

For years, I was a strong proponent of limiting the number of dictionaries to only a few on the development system and one on the production system. Improvements in the IDMS processing facilities have made it much easier to manage more dictionaries.

That doesn't mean that we should create dictionaries for everything, though. Easier management is relative. Dictionary management can be very time-consuming; if your DBA staff is small, fewer dictionaries should be the rule.

The Basic Configuration

Most IDMS installations have at least two CV regions, production and development. Many have added one or two more, a DBA test region for new releases, and a staging region for transitioning development to production. The latter two are run only when required.

Each of these regions normally has at least one dictionary. The production region, in most cases, has only one. The reasons for this relate primarily to performance. IDMS works better when it is using a single dictionary and load area. Placing all production into the same dictionary also makes system management easier and more consistent.

Dictionary Sharing Between Regions

It is quite normal for certain dictionaries to be shared between IDMS regions. Looking at Figure 28-1, we see that the production region primary dictionary is shared with the staging region. The development region's primary dictionary is also shared with the staging region. The staging region, on the other hand, does not share its dictionary. This permits the transfer of dictionary material from development through staging to the production environment faster and more accurately.

Dictionary sharing between regions should be established during the early days of the installation. While it can be added at any time, setting the arrangement up at the outset will allow for better overall planning of the installation.

The Primary Dictionary

Every IDMS CV must have a primary dictionary. Actually what is termed a "primary dictionary" is really several dictionary files/areas. Figure 28-2 illustrates this environment.

As we see, the data dictionary as we know it is only one part of the overall primary dictionary.

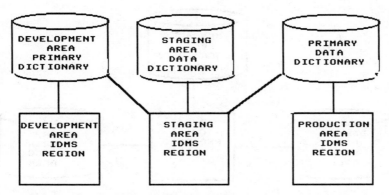

Figure 28-1   Shared Dictionaries Between Regions.

Contents Of The Primary Dictionary

The physical content of the DDLDML area of the primary dictionary will vary somewhat based on its purpose. For example, a primary dictionary supporting the production region may contain all elements, records, dialogs, and other entities that are used to operate the production environment.

The primary dictionary in the development region, on the other hand, may contain only an abbreviated set of items that are commonly used (assuming that multiple development secondary dictionaries are used for development projects). Let's look at what this abbreviated dictionary should contain:

1. *System sysgen information.* The system parameters and control data must be kept in the primary dictionary.
2. *User information.* The development users (the programming staff and supporters) are recorded in the primary dictionary. This provides the basis for access authorization to secondary dictionaries.
3. *Global DMCL.* This must be in all primary dictionaries.
4. *Schemas for applications* being developed in the secondary dictionaries. These may be the full schema or a skeleton used only to build the DMCL.

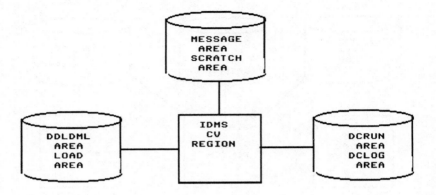

Figure 28-2   Primary Dictionary Organization.

5. *Standard dictionary report parameters.* Those dictionary reports useful to the development effort should be placed in the development primary dictionary.

Primary Dictionary Access

The primary dictionary is the most critical element in the operation of an IDMS region. Properly set up, every control and parameter associated with the system resides in the dictionary. Restricting use of the primary dictionary, therefore, is a critical security issue. Only data administration staff members, and not all of those, should be allowed to update the dictionary.

Restricted retrieval authority may be provided to persons outside of Data Administration. The type of retrieval needs to be carefully evaluated since the nature of IDD operation will permit anyone who can retrieve data to copy it to another dictionary.

The Secondary Dictionary

The secondary dictionary is normally used for application development. In this dictionary, we should normally find:

1. *Development user information.* The access authorization can be different for each dictionary; each one should identify those users authorized for that specific dictionary.
2. *Record and element definitions.* All elements and records required to support the application are stored in the dictionary.
3. *Schemas, local DMCL, and subschemas.* The schemas are used primarily for local mode processing and application development reference.
4. *Process, dialog, and map source.*

Each development dictionary should also have a corresponding load area to support dialog generation.

Multiple Development Dictionaries

As long as there is only one development project going on under IDMS, it is easy to justify having a single development dictionary. The DBAs should, however, have a small dictionary where the standard elements, records, modules, and other entities are kept. Then there is the dictionary to hold tested application code. When you stop to think of the ways extra dictionaries can be used, the number climbs rapidly.

When multiple projects are in progress, each should have its own dictionary. Before handing a project manager a dictionary, however, some preparation needs to be done.

Most IDMS installations have established some standards regarding elements, records, screen design, and program design. If the development team is provided with copies of standard items, they are more likely to use them than to invent their own. The development dictionary, therefore, should be provided with prestored standard items that the development team is *expected* to use.

Figure 28-3 illustrates an example of a complete development, staging, and production environment. This includes multiple development dictionaries. As you can see, the development dictionaries are also linked to the staging region. This makes migration of an application easier to perform and control. (When a development dictionary is placed on-line with the staging system, it is set off-line to development, preventing changes during the migration.)

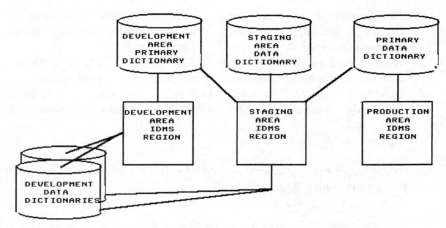

Figure 28-3   Full Three System IDMS Dictionary Configuration.

Installing The Secondary Dictionary

New secondary dictionaries are not difficult to install. They are a bit time-consuming, however. When creating one, you might give consideration to doing two or three at one time. The steps required to install the secondary dictionary are:

1. *Define the page ranges* that you will assign to a series of secondary dictionaries.
2. *Create a skeleton schema* in the primary dictionary for the new areas and files. If you plan for the secondary areas to be called DDLDML and DDLDCLOD, alias will be required in the global DMCL.
3. *Add the new areas into the global DMCL.* Compile and link the DMCL.
4. *Run IDMSRNWK for each network subschema.* The subschema name should be the new area name and the DMCL should be the global DMCL. The ranges for the dictionary and load areas should be those specified in the new schema. The source subschema module is also required. Concatenate the source to the input parameters. IDMSRNWK produces an object module that is directed to SYSPCH. SYSPCH needs to identify a new file name.

5. *Execute LNKRNRWK.* Change the linkage editor control statements to reflect new subschemas.
6. *Allocate space for the new areas.*
7. *Populate secondary dictionary.* The quickest way to set up a development dictionary is to build a standard dictionary, load it with your standard items, and do an IDMS unload. Run a complete IDD report list of all of the contents, too. When a new development dictionary is required, allocate the space and then reload the unloaded file, changing the page range to that of the new dictionary.
8. *Update the startup JCL.*
9. *Update the dbname tables in the sysgen.* The subschema statement maps the name of the subschema for the secondary dictionary to the same subschema for the primary dictionary. For example:

```
MODIFY SYSTEM 60
DBNAME TYPADICT
SUB IDMSNWK?
MAPS TO TYPANWK?.
```

10. *Bring CV down and back up.* The new areas will be on-line when CV comes back up.
11. *IDMSDIRL.* Under OS, the execute card will look like:

```
//DIRLRUN=IDMSDIRL,REGION=400K,PARM='DBNAME=TYPADICT'
```

Managing The Dictionary Interfaces

It is important that consistency be maintained between dictionaries. The standard item load described earlier begins the process by supplying commonly used items to be used across all systems. But this only covers part of the definition process that goes on in every application development.

Management of standards is enforced during migration from one dictionary to another, usually from the development to the staging area. If only those items that meet standards are permitted to migrate, the developers learn quickly to approach their design and development with standards in mind. The thought of having to do over parts of their application that are non-standard is usually adequate incentive to follow the rules.

Migrating Between Dictionaries

Migration is the Achilles Heel of multiple dictionary environments. While now supported by a variety of tools, migration still is time-consuming and must be done with great care to avoid failures in the migrated software.

Aids To Migration

The first decision that has to be made is what to migrate. Not everything in a development dictionary should be migrated to production. It is unnecessary, for example, to migrate those standard items that were generated with the dictionary. They are already present in the production dictionary.

Using an IDD class/attribute combination, APPLICATION IS XXX, where XXX as the application under development is an easy way to identify each entity occurrence within the dictionary that belongs to an application. As each entity occurrence is stored, APPLICATION IS XXX is added to the syntax. A listing of the attribute XXX will, at any time, provide a complete list of all entity occurrences in the dictionary associated with the application.

Sequence Of Migration

The dictionary entities should be migrated in a specified sequence. Since IDD entity occurrences link to each other in a building block fashion, it is important to dump the data in the right order to avoid loading errors. Data dumping order is:

1. *Class/attributes.* Punch all class/attribute combinations that were created specifically for this application.
2. *UDC/UDN.* Punch all user-defined comments and user-defined nests that were created specifically for this application.
3. *Elementary elements.* Punch those elements that are not further subdivided.

4. *Group elements*. Punch elements that are made up of other elements. Here it is desirable to place group elements that are part of other group elements ahead of those they build. This is difficult to achieve without manual intervention or rerunning the element load several times until the elements are all properly linked.

5. *Records*. Punch all records, both schema and work records. Run record detail reports to be sure that all record elements are correctly structured. It is not unusual for an incomplete record to be generated if the record elements have not been correctly migrated.

6. *Tables*. Punch all tables. Sometimes it is useful to punch all of the edit tables and then the decode tables.

7. *Schema, DMCL, and subschemas*. Load and generate each in the receiving dictionary. Look carefully at the reports to be sure everything required was present.

8. *Maps*. Decompile maps from the old dictionary using RHDCMPUT and recompile them in the new dictionary using RHDCMAP1.

9. *Processes*. Punch all processes and load them in the new dictionary.

10. *Dialogs and programs*. Move all source and descriptions; generate dialogs using ADSOBGEN.

11. *ADSA applications*. Unload ADSA applications from the old dictionary using ADSAUNL and load them to the new using ADSOALOD.

DATABASE ACCESS AND MAINTENANCE

This part focuses on the physical functionality of IDMS/R. It is intended as a reference to the generic functions that are basic to IDMS/R; these functions, while modified slightly to serve new systems software, have remained largely unchanged and intact through the many releases of the product.

29

Currency

Currency is the key to understanding IDMS and using it effectively. It is at once very simple and very complex. Currency is expressed in terms of a database record occurrence being the current data that IDMS is processing.

The Four Levels Of Currency

IDMS looks at data at four levels. Each of these levels has a currency or currencies. The more detailed the level, the fewer the number of currencies that typically exist. Figure 29-1 illustrates the inverted pyramid of currency occurrences. We will deal with each of the currencies in detail later in this chapter. Briefly, however, the four currency levels are:

1. *Record currency.* Each time IDMS accesses a specific record type, the occurrence of that record type becomes the CURRENT OF RECORD TYPE. IDMS, therefore, maintains a currency of the last accessed occurrence of every record type in the database subschema.
2. *BISet currency.* IDMS maintains a currency for every set in the subschema, identifying the last processed record occurrence **of**

Figure 29-1   Inverted Currency Pyramid.

    any type defined to that set. This currency is known as the
CURRENT OF SET.

3. *BI Area currency.* Within a schema, each area is composed of a
    number of record types. The most recently record occurrence *of
    any type within the area* is maintained by IDMS and is known as
    the CURRENT OF AREA.

4. *BI Run-unit currency.* IDMS identifies the most recent database
    record accessed as the CURRENT OF RUN-UNIT, regardless of
    type or where it is residing in the database. Run-unit currency
    is particularly important when MODIFY and ERASE DML
    verbs are employed, as IDMS insists on operating against the
    CURRENT OF RUN-UNIT for these functions. The CURRENT
    OF RUN-UNIT therefore must also be the CURRENT OF
    RECORD TYPE before modify or erase will operate.

How Currency Is Established

Every time IDMS issues a request for a record occurrence, the
retrieved record becomes current of: (1) the IDMS run-unit processing
the request, (2) the record type of the retrieved occurrence, (3) all of
the sets in which the record participates, and (4) the area in which
the record resides. As IDMS continues to access the database, other
record occurrences replace their predecessors in one or more
categories. It is important to understand that reading a record in area
B after reading a different type of record in area A does not change
the area or record currency of the record in area A.

How To Use Currency

Currency information is physically stored in the variable portion of the subschema. Within the subschema table, a place is provided for every possible currency that can occur under that subschema definition. As IDMS processes database requests, it remembers the most recent request of each of the four currency types.

This can be particularly useful to the programmer who must bounce around the database. The program may wish to process several records at once. As each record type is accessed, the occurrence of that type becomes the current of the area, set, record type, and run-unit in turn. If the subsequent record type accessed is within the same area and set, the newest occurrence replaces the previous one as the current of area and set.

When we walk a set, the occurrence of the member record most recently retrieved becomes the current of area, set, record type, and run-unit. The next occurrence accessed replaces all of these currencies.

Record Currency

Record currency is the simplest of all of the currencies. Simply put, *the last occurrence of a record type to be accessed is the current of that record type.* IDMS maintains a dbkey for every record type in the subschema.

Record currency data occupies most of every subschema. It is somewhat ironic that this currency is the least used of any of the currency types. The only time IDMS, through the programmer, uses record currency is when an OBTAIN CURRENT or ACCEPT CURRENCY OF type commands are issued. The principal DML verbs use current of run-unit, set, or area for their currency reference.

For example, the most used OBTAIN verbs (NEXT, PRIOR, FIRST, LAST, SORTED) use the current of set or area. OBTAIN CALC uses the current of the CALC set. The MODIFY and ERASE verbs use the current of run-unit. STORE simply establishes the current of record type.

Set Currency

Set currency gets very complicated if you let it. There are a wide variety of currencies that occur under the set banner, each of which has its own peculiarities. Within each currency are the functional considerations associated with the DML verbs STORE and OBTAIN.

Current Of Set

Within the subschema is a set of currency tables. All possible currencies are maintained in the currency table. The portion of the table devoted to sets contains one entry for each set identified to the subschema. *Once the first record occurrence in a set has been found, the subschema maintains a current record for that set.* The current of set, therefore, is the occurrence of *one record type* associated with the set that has become *at some time during the processing the current of run-unit.*

Every set, sooner or later, establishes currency to one of the record types associated with the set. This may be the owner record type or one of the member record types. We must keep in mind that the current of set can be, and frequently is, the *owner record type occurrence.*

Area Currency

Area currency is one of the trickiest of the currencies to work with. The thing we must keep in mind is that *any* record type may be current of its area at any time. Just because you are accessing a particular record type in an area sweep does not mean that the record type remains current of area during the sweep process.

Let's look at an example. The program is sweeping the area reading the next ABC record. In between obtains of the ABC record, the program processes other records, too. The logic of this program is shown in Figure 29-2.

In this logic, the program starts with an OBTAIN FIRST ABC WITHIN X AREA to establish the area currency at the first ABC record. Then subroutine GET CDE is called as part of the beginning of a WHILE loop. Once GET CDE is completed, the next ABC record is obtained. At least that is what the programmer had in mind.

```
OBTAIN FIRST ABC WITHIN X AREA.
WHILE NOT DB-END-OF-AREA
  REPEAT.
     CALL GETCDE.
     OBTAIN NEXT ABC WITHIN X AREA.
  END.

SUBROUTINE GETCDE.
WHILE NOT DB-END-OF-SET
  REPEAT.
     OBTAIN NEXT CDE WITHIN ABC-CDE.
  END.
```

Figure 29-2   Area Sweep Processing Example.

What actually happens, however, is that the program goes into a loop. It is reading the *same* ABC record each time. Why? Looking at Figure 29-3, a cross-section of the area, we see that there are several ABC record occurrences (the [A] records) and one CDE record (the [C] record).

When the program in Figure 29-2 executes, area currency is initially established at the ABC record (A1) in the first page of the area (101). The execution of the GET CDE routine obtains the CDE record and *moves the area currency to the CDE record (102).* The OBTAIN NEXT of the ABC record within the area therefore *starts at that point of the area,* retrieving the ABC record at (A3) instead of the desired ABC record at (A2). This is the first of the problems created by Figure 29-2s program logic. Here we have simply bypassed one of the ABC records in the database.

The next problem is more serious from an operational view. As we continue to read forward through the area, we encounter ABC record A5 on page 107. Executing the GETCDE subroutine retrieves the CDE record on page 105, two pages back. Since the CDE record is obtained each time the WHILE loop executes, the ABC record A4 is always the next one in the area and an endless loop is created.

In many ways, the second problem of an endless loop is preferable to the first problem of missing a record. The loop is very visible and triggers analysis to correct the bug. Missing the record, the most common problem of area sweeps, can be a subtlety that remains hidden for a long time.

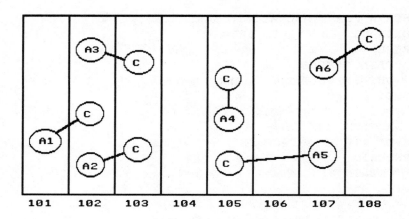

Figure 29-3   Database Area Cross Section.

Figure 29-4 illustrates the correct logic to handle this type of processing. The dbkey identifying the area position of the next ABC record read is held after each ABC record is read. The currency is reestablished each time by FINDing the ABC record identified by the dbkey. The program then accesses the next ABC record by using the OBTAIN NEXT ... AREA command.

Run-Unit Currency

IDMS identifies the most recent database record accessed successfully as the CURRENT OF RUN-UNIT, regardless of type or where it is residing in the database. Run-unit currency is particularly important when the MODIFY and ERASE DML verbs are employed, as IDMS insists on operating against the CURRENT OF RUN-UNIT for these functions. The CURRENT OF RUN-UNIT must also be the CURRENT OF RECORD TYPE before the modify or erase will operate.

```
OBTAIN FIRST ABC WITHIN X AREA.
MOVE DBKEY TO W-DBKEY.
WHILE NOT DB-END-OF-AREA
 REPEAT.
   CALL GETCDE.
   FIND ABC DB-KEY W-DBKEY.
   OBTAIN NEXT ABC WITHIN X AREA.
   MOVE DBKEY TO W-DBKEY.
 END.
```

Figure 29-4   Correct Database Area Sweep Logic.

30

DML

Data Manipulation Language (DML) is the access language for IDMS. It comes in various forms to fit the programming language that it supports. Currently there is a DML form for COBOL, PL/I, FORTRAN, assembler, and ADS/O. This chapter will use the ADS/O form of DML since it closely resembles both COBOL and PL/I.

With the exception of ADS/O and assembler, the program source containing DML is passed through a Cullinet-supplied preprocessor that converts the DML syntax to the call structure of the host language. The preprocessor handles all IDMS-related statements, including the control and IDMS COPY statements that perform other functions than program logic.

The purpose of the preprocessor was to permit the programmer to code DML statements as readable syntax versus difficult CALL sequences. This has been shown to improve the performance and productivity of programmers wherever implemented.

Types Of DML Statements

DML statements can be broken into six general types, each of which will be discussed in detail in subsequent sections of the chapter:

1. *Database maintenance verbs*. This set of statements manipulates the contents of the database by adding, changing, and deleting the database records. Also included in this group are two verbs for manual association of records and the means to break that association.
2. *Database access verbs*. This group provides the means to access the database records.
3. *Database key verbs*. These verbs provide the ability to retrieve location keys of records stored in the database.
4. *Utility verbs*. This is a set of special-purpose verbs that perform unusual functions.
5. *Recovery verbs*. Last but certainly not least are the verbs that identify the boundaries of a run-unit and tell IDMS when to accept or reject the updates to the database.
6. *Miscellaneous verbs*. These verbs hold control over records to prevent them from becoming current of other run-units and test set status.

This book will not attempt to discuss every DML verb that IDMS supports. Some are available only with specific language interfaces and others get almost no use. The chapter will concentrate on bringing together useful information on the most often used (in some cases those that *should* be used often).

Error-Status Codes

Before we get into the DML statements themselves, it is useful to have an understanding of the error status codes that may be returned by IDMS to the program. The ERROR-STATUS field itself is a four-digit display mode field. It is broken into two sections: the major code and the minor code.

The Major Codes

The major code identifies the DML group being executed when the error was detected. There are many of these and for the complete list you should refer to Cullinet's manuals (the list changes as new system features are added). The principal codes, ones that you will see frequently, are:

01. FINISH
02. ERASE
03. FIND/OBTAIN
07. CONNECT
08. MODIFY
09. READY
11. DISCONNECT
12. STORE
15. ACCEPT
16. IF

The Minor Codes

In most cases, the minor codes identify specifically the cause of the error. These codes can themselves be separated into two groups: those that occur as a result of database conditions, and those that are caused by design or program logic errors.

Let's first look at those caused by database conditions:

00. No error has occurred; the statement executed properly.
05. A duplicate record was encountered where duplicates are not allowed. This error is common when storing CALC records or sorted VIA set members with the DUPLICATES NOT AL-LOWED option active.
06. There is no occurrence of the requested record or set.
07. The end of the set or area has been reached.
10. Attempted security violation. This code, under the currently established DBMS, can occur only when a database procedure has been implemented to enforce security.
11. The database is full. This can occur on store or modify.
26. The requested record was not found. This error is normally associated with an OBTAIN where the CALC key value is specified, sorted set key value is specified, or dbkey is specified.

The remainder of the minor codes can be considered to occur as a result of *our* error. If the minor code that is returned does not exist in the preceding list, look to the program as the source of the problem. Only the most common of these internal goof errors will be listed:

04. Set name for VIA record not in subschema.

06. There is no current record for a named record or set.

08. The record or set name is invalid.

09. Areas readied with an incorrect usage mode. Look at the ready statement location. This error usually occurs when trying to update the database while in retrieval mode.

13. No current of run-unit has been established. The program is trying to retrieve dbkeys before any records have been read or written.

14. The record is defined as MA and a DISCONNECT cannot be performed.

15. The record is defined as MANDATORY and a DISCONNECT cannot be performed.

16. The record is already a member of the target set and cannot be CONNECTed to the set again.

20. The target record type is not the current of run-unit. This occurs when an attempt is made to MODIFY or ERASE a record without making it current first.

22. The target record is not connected to the target set. Either it was a MANUAL set and not connected or has been DISCONNECTed by a prior database action.

31. The DML statement and the record type conflict. This usually occurs when an attempt is made to use the Format 6 (sorted set) OBTAIN against an unsorted set.

69. The DBMS is not active. This occurs with on-line transactions when IDMS goes down unexpectedly. It occurs with batch jobs when the DBMS setup is incorrect.

Database Maintenance Verbs

This section reviews the principal database maintenance verbs in the IDMS DML stable. When using this group of verbs, *testing of the error status is mandatory*. Omission of this step *will* result in a damaged database sooner or later, probably sooner.

STORE   record-name

[error-expression] .

Figure 30-1   STORE Command Syntax.

STORE (Figure 30-1)

The store command writes *new* data records to the database. The efficiency of the verb depends on the database structure. Storing a VIA record into a NEXT set is the most efficient while storing a CALC record into a sorted set is the least efficient.

Let's look at a few general considerations when storing data:

1. CALC records that are members of a set can have considerable overhead when stored. Not only must the record be placed in its CALC set but it must be inserted into those sets in which it is a member. If the CALC record is a member of a sorted set that is using standard chain linking (a very poor idea in the first place), performance will degrade as the set population increases. Unfortunately, establishing currency within the set ahead of the store does not help as IDMS will still walk the sorted set to locate the insertion point for the new record.

2. VIA records stored NEXT and PRIOR are the most efficient because IDMS accepts the currency of the set as is. If the owner is the current of set, the record is stored at the front of the set (NEXT) or end of the set (PRIOR), equivalent to FIRST and LAST, respectively.

   Since it is always necessary to establish currency to the owner of the set in order to store a record as FIRST or LAST (IDMS does it automatically beneath the covers), why not do it yourself and use NEXT or PRIOR instead? NEXT or PRIOR ordering gives the programmer additional flexibility to insert a record in the middle of the chain.

3. Junction records require that currency be established to both owners in most cases. One of the sets (normally the VIA set unless pointer arrays are used) may be sorted. This improves the speed of walking the set when retrieving.

The error status conditions that may occur with the storing of data are numerous. They can be broken into errors that are the result of design or programming logic and those that occur because of database conditions.

Database activity oriented codes are:

1205. Storing the record will violate duplicates not allowed restrictions for either a CALC record or a sorted set.

1210. A security violation has occurred that prevents storing the data.

1211. The database is full.

Design and programming logic problem errors are **1202, 1208, 1209, 1212, 1221, 1233,** and **1255.**

MODIFY record-name

[error-expression] .

Figure 30-2 MODIFY Command Syntax.

MODIFY (Figure 30-2)

The key to successful use of the MODIFY verb is to remember that modify *operates only against the current of run-unit.*

Here are a few pointers:

1. *Always* issue a FIND CURRENT of the record to be modified immediately before executing the modification. This will ensure that no other record type has been made current between the retrieval of the record and the modify.

2. *Do not* reestablish currency with an OBTAIN. This overwrites all of the changes made to the current record with the original data and the modify will simply put the record back the way it was read.

Error status codes caused by database activity are:

0805. The modification changes a key field in the record in such a way that it now duplicates the key value of an existing record.
0810. Security violation.

Other error status codes, caused by design or program logic, are: **0806, 0809, 0813, 0820, 0821, 0825, 0833,** and **0855.**

ERASE   record-name

[error-expression].

Figure 30-3   ERASE Command Syntax.

ERASE RECORD (Figure 30-3)

The various options of the erase verb can be confusing. The plain ERASE RECORD verb, however, is fairly straightforward.

The processing of this verb is very similar to that of MODIFY:

1. The ERASE verb, all forms, operates against the current of run-unit. Currency must be established to the proper record type occurrence before issuing the erase verb.
2. Unlike the MODIFY, it is normal to OBTAIN the target record before erasing it. It is a good idea to display the target record and get the operator to verify that this is the proper occurrence to delete.

The error status codes for this form of ERASE apply to all of the following forms, too. Database activity codes are:

0210. A security violation has occurred that prevents the record from being erased from the database.

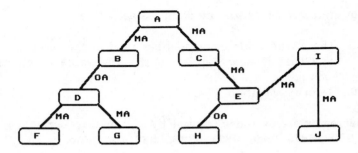

Figure 30-3a   General Occurrence Chart.

0230. The erase attempted to remove the owner of a set while there are still members present (effective only for the singular ERASE RECORD command).

The error status codes that can be traced to design and program errors are: **0209, 0213, 0220, 0221, 0225,** and **0233.**

To make the effect of the different options of the ERASE verb easier to understand, we will use a chart of record occurrences to illustrate which of those occurrences are deleted by each ERASE option. Figure 30-3a illustrates this chart.

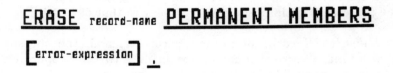

Figure 30-4   ERASE PERMANENT Command Syntax.

ERASE PERMANENT (Figure 30-4)

The PERMANENT option of the ERASE verb deletes all mandatory members of the target record even if they are members of another set. Optional members are disconnected.

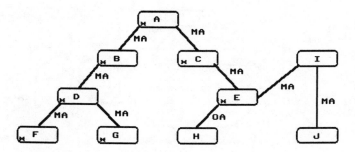

Figure 30-5 Effect Of ERASE PERMANENT.

Figure 30-5 shows a data structure that we will use to demonstrate the effect of the PERMANENT option of the ERASE verb. In this illustration, all records with asterisks are erased.

CAUTION: This option of ERASE can leave orphan member records in the database. See record *H* in Figure 30-5.

ERASE record-name SELECTIVE MEMBERS

[error-expression]
.

Figure 30-6 ERASE SELECTIVE Command Syntax.

ERASE SELECTIVE (Figure 30-6)

This option, as its name implies, is a bit more selective in what records are erased. The SELECTIVE option erases those member records that are mandatory members of the target record and those optional members who are not currently members of another owner who is not subordinate to the target record.

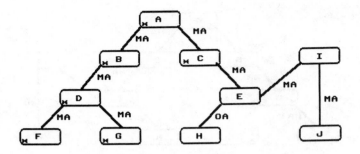

Figure 30-7   Effect Of ERASE SELECTIVE.

Figure 30-7 illustrates this condition; those records with asterisks are erased.

$$\underline{\text{ERASE}}\ \text{record-name}\ \underline{\text{ALL MEMBERS}}$$

$$\Big[\text{error-expression}\Big]\ \underline{.}$$

Figure 30-8   ERASE ALL Command Syntax.

ERASE ALL (Figure 30-8)

The ALL option of the ERASE verb is also simple in its execution but dangerous too. As the option implies, *all* subordinate records of the target record are erased.

Figure 30-9 illustrates the effect of this verb. Notice that records *E* and *H* are also erased. It is important to understand the database structure and the intent of the relationships between owner records (in this case between *A* and *I*) before using the ALL option. It is very easy to destroy a database with the ERASE ALL verb option.

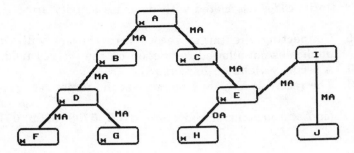

Figure 30-9   Effect Of ERASE ALL.

CONNECT record-name **TO** set-name

[error-expression **]** .

Figure 30-10   CONNECT Command Syntax.

CONNECT (Figure 30-10)

The CONNECT verb is usable only when the set is defined as OP-
TIONAL or MANUAL. If a set is identified as AUTOMATIC, the
connection is performed as part of the storing of a record. If the set
is also defined as MANDATORY, it is not possible to disconnect a
member from the set without erasing it. The CONNECT verb, therefore, can be used to connect a record stored as part of a MANUAL
set or one that was previously disconnected from an owner of a set
defined as OPTIONAL.

It is important *that currency be established to both owner and
member* before issuing the CONNECT as IDMS will connect the
member to whatever owner is current of that record type.

Error status codes associated with database activity are:

0705. Connecting the target record into the set will violate a duplicates-not-allowed restriction on the set key field.
0710. A security violation has occurred.
0716. The record is already a member of the target set.

The design and logic error codes are: **0706, 0708, 0709, 0714,** and **0721** .

DISCONNECT record-name FROM set-name

[error-expression] .

Figure 30-11 DISCONNECT Command Syntax.

DISCONNECT (Figure 30-11)

The DISCONNECT verb may be used only with member records defined as having OPTIONAL membership in a set. The record is removed from the named set and becomes an orphan until reconnected to another set. Programmers should be very careful to immediately provide for reconnecting the member to another set; leaving the record unconnected for any amount of time is asking for trouble. Be sure also not to issue a COMMIT between the disconnect and the subsequent connect. An abend would leave the disconnected record an orphan with little chance of recovery (without manual intervention).

Database activity error status codes are:

1110. A security violation has occurred.
1122. The object record is not a member of the set. It either was never connected to the set or has been previously disconnected.

Design and logic-oriented error codes are: **1106, 1108, 1109, 1115,** and **1121**.

Database Access Verbs

The database novice frequently looks at database maintenance and retrieval as two different environments. In fact, however, very few of the database maintenance verbs (storing a CALC or DIRECT record are the exceptions) can be correctly executed without a preceding access of the database. MODIFY and ERASE are good examples. They act *only on the current record of the run-unit.* Review the model software modules in Appendix B for examples.

At the beginning of this section we will discuss two less frequently used verbs, FIND and GET. They are placed at the beginning because the two of them constitute an OBTAIN. There are times when it is desirable to break up the OBTAIN into its components.

FIND

FIND uses all of the DML statement extensions that are available for OBTAIN. So as you progress to the OBTAIN extensions later, remember that those same statements can be used for FIND.

FIND is used when we desire to *establish currency without retrieving the data* of a record in the database. There are several reasons for choosing FIND over OBTAIN. Here are the two most important:

1. *Establishing currency to a record* just before MODIFY or ERASE verb execution. FIND is particularly important to use before MODIFY because the program has usually changed the record contents (or why would we modify it) and using OBTAIN to reestablish currency would wipe out the changes.
2. *To check on the presence of a record* without incurring the overhead of actually moving the record from the page buffer to your working storage.

The database activity error status codes are:

0310. A security violation has occurred.
0326. The requested record cannot be found.
0332. An attempt to retrieve a duplicate CALC record failed.

Design and logic error codes are: **0306, 0308,** and **0331.**

GET [record-name]

[error-expression] .

Figure 30-12   GET Command Syntax.

GET (Figure 30-12)

GET is the other half of OBTAIN. It simply moves the *current of run-unit* from the page buffer to the working storage of your program. GET is very seldom used by itself. The one place that I have found GET useful has been in the final stages of an analytical query that has been walking the database using FINDs to reduce overhead. The records finally selected can be brought into the working storage by issuing a GET *after being made current of run-unit*. If the GET includes a record name, that record type *must be current of run-unit or a 0520 error will occur.*

Only one error status code is associated with database activity:

0510.   A security violation has occurred.

Design and logic error status codes are: **0508, 0513, 0518,** and **0520.**

OBTAIN RECORD DBKEY (Figure 30-13)

IDMS provides the field DBKEY as an external access point in which the database key of the current of run-unit is stored. Having this data available, we are able to store the dbkey in a hold field or table for future use.

Obtaining a database record by its dbkey is the most efficient of the OBTAINs. IDMS does not have to resolve anything or compute anything. It just goes and gets the record.

Where do we use this type of statement? Well, one of the most common is to hold the position of a nest record when walking a multilevel bill of materials.

Error status codes associated with database activity are:

$$\left\{ {FIND \atop OBTAIN} \right\} \left[KEEP \ \left[EXCLUSIVE \right] \right]$$

$$\left[record\text{-}name \right] \ DB\text{-}KEY \ IS \ dbkey\text{-}field\text{-}name$$

$$\left[error\text{-}expression \right] \ \underline{.}$$

Figure 30-13 OBTAIN Record By Dbkey Command Syntax.

0310. A security violation has occurred.
0326. The requested record is not in the database.

Design and logic error codes are: **0302, 0308,** and **0371.**

$$\left\{ {FIND \atop OBTAIN} \right\} \left[KEEP \ \left[EXCLUSIVE \right] \right]$$

$$CURRENT \ \left[record\text{-}name \right]$$

$$\left[error\text{-}expression \right] \ \underline{.}$$

Figure 30-14 OBTAIN Current Command Syntax.

OBTAIN CURRENT (Figure 30-14)

This verb is really nothing more than a move of record data from the page buffer to the working storage. It does the same function as GET but for a named record type. *A test of error status is NOT necessary after this verb.* Any normal error would have occurred when the record occurrence was originally retrieved.

The security violation error status code, **0310,** is the only database-oriented error code for this command. Design and logic codes are: **0306, 0308, 0313,** and **0325.**

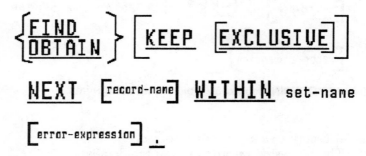

Figure 30-15   OBTAIN NEXT Record Command Syntax.

OBTAIN NEXT (Figure 30-15)

This is probably the most-used retrieval verb in the entire set of DML statements. The next available record within either a set or an area for the named record type is brought into working storage. This verb is used for walking forward in a set. If the end of the set is encountered, a 0327 error status (end of set) is returned by IDMS.

IDMS assumes that the program has established currency in the named set or area. One of the more common errors in programming using this verb is failing to establish currency to the desired owner record before beginning to walk the set.

The error status codes for the PRIOR, FIRST, LAST, and sequence OBTAIN commands are the same as those for NEXT. The database activity-oriented error codes are:

0307. The end of the set or area has been reached or the set is empty.
0310. The usual security violation.
0326. The record cannot be found (occurs for FIRST, LAST, and sequence options only).

The design and logic error codes are: **0306, 0308, 0318,** and **0323.**

$$\left\{\begin{matrix} \text{FIND} \\ \text{OBTAIN} \end{matrix}\right\} \left[\underline{\text{KEEP}} \quad \left[\underline{\text{EXCLUSIVE}}\right]\right]$$

$$\underline{\text{PRIOR}} \quad \left[\text{record-name}\right] \quad \underline{\text{WITHIN}} \quad \text{set-name}$$

$$\left[\text{error-expression}\right] \underline{\quad}$$

Figure 30-16   OBTAIN PRIOR Command Syntax.

OBTAIN PRIOR (Figure 30-16)

This verb is used to walk sets backward. It otherwise operates exactly like OBTAIN NEXT. *The set must have prior pointers for this verb to execute.*

$$\left\{\begin{matrix} \text{FIND} \\ \text{OBTAIN} \end{matrix}\right\} \left[\underline{\text{KEEP}} \quad \left[\underline{\text{EXCLUSIVE}}\right]\right]$$

$$\underline{\text{FIRST}} \quad \left[\text{record-name}\right] \quad \underline{\text{WITHIN}} \quad \text{set-name}$$

$$\left[\text{error-expression}\right] \underline{\quad}$$

Figure 30-17   OBTAIN FIRST Command Syntax.

OBTAIN FIRST (Figure 30-17)

This verb *always* establishes currency to the first record of the set or area before retrieving its record. The overhead of this activity can have an effect on performance if it is done indiscriminately.

Let's look at an example. We want to retrieve the first record of a set as preparation for walking the set. In Figure 30-18, the program-

```
OBTAIN CALC EVENT.
IF DB-ANY-ERROR
   DO.
      MOVE 1 TO DB-EVENT-FLG.
    GOBACK.
   END.
OBTAIN FIRST ASSIGNMENT WITHIN EVENT-ASSIGN.
IF DB-ANY-ERROR
   DO.
      MOVE 1 TO DB-ASSIGN-FLG.
      GOBACK.
   END.
CALL ASSIGN-PROCESS.
WHILE NOT DB-ANY-ERROR
   REPEAT.
      OBTAIN NEXT ASSIGNMENT WITHIN EVENT-ASSIGN.
      IF DB-ANY-ERROR
         DO.
            MOVE 1 TO DB-ASSIGN-FLG.
            GOBACK.
         END.
      CALL ASSIGN-PROCESS.
   END.
GOBACK.
```

Figure 30-18   OBTAIN First Record Of A Set (A).

mer retrieves the owner record, issues an OBTAIN FIRST, and then enters a logic loop to retrieve each member of the set.

The same effect can be accomplished by using the logic in Figure 30-19. In this instance we accomplish two things:

1. *The extra OBTAIN is eliminated.* There is no need for an OBTAIN FIRST since the next record from the owner is the first record of the set.
2. *A double currency establishment is eliminated.* OBTAIN FIRST reestablishes the currency just set up by the OBTAIN of the owner, needless system overhead.

```
OBTAIN CALC EVENT.
IF DB-ANY-ERROR
   DO.
      MOVE 1 TO DB-EVENT-FLG.
      GOBACK.
   END.
WHILE NOT DB-ANY-ERROR
   REPEAT.
      OBTAIN NEXT ASSIGNMENT WITHIN EVENT-ASSIGN.
      IF DB-ANY-ERROR
         DO.
            MOVE 1 TO DB-ASSIGN-FLG.
            GOBACK.
         END.
      CALL ASSIGN-PROCESS.
   END.
GOBACK.
```

Figure 30-19   OBTAIN First Record Of A Set (B).

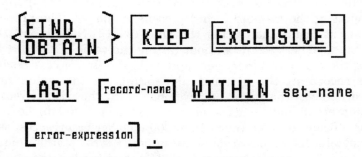

Figure 30-20   OBTAIN LAST Command Syntax.

OBTAIN LAST (Figure 30-20)

This verb is used to retrieve the last record in a set. It otherwise operates exactly like OBTAIN FIRST. Again, *prior pointers must be defined for the set.*

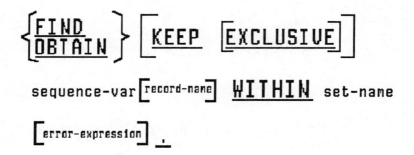

Figure 30-21   OBTAIN n Command Syntax.

OBTAIN _n_ (Figure 30-21)

This version of the OBTAIN statement retrieves the _n_th occurrence of the set. The value associated with _n_ may be either positive or negative. If negative, the set must have prior pointers.

This statement has been used to perform binary searches on a long set. The set must be sorted in order to make a binary search possible. The owner record must also contain a count of the number of occurrences of the member record present in the set. The processing is somewhat faster than using the OBTAIN USING format. IDMS passes the member records without testing the value of the sort key.

Using the standard binary sort approach, the first access reads the middle record in the set and, depending on the value found, repeatedly halves the upper or lower half until the desired record is found (or not found). This approach has been found to be nearly twice as efficient on long (more than 200 member occurrences) sets.

This obtain option has a database oriented error status unique to its function. The error status code **0304** indicates that the sequence number requested was zero.

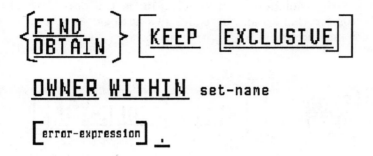

Figure 30-22   OBTAIN OWNER Command Syntax.

OBTAIN OWNER (Figure 30-22)

This OBTAIN option is frequently used when walking a many-to-many set. One owner is obtained, a junction member is retrieved, and the other owner of the junction member is retrieved through use of OBTAIN OWNER.

For this verb to be efficient, the set should be defined with owner pointers. *IDMS will e   ecute OBTAIN OWNER without owner pointers,* but it must walk the set to its end instead of jumping directly to the owner. Obviously, on long sets, the owner pointer directly contributes to higher performance.

OBTAIN OWNER is another DML statement that does not normally need error status testing if the set being tested is MANDATORY AUTOMATIC. Because IDMS insists on the presence of an owner record occurrence in order to insert a member in the set, only a serious system malfunction would result in am error condition being returned after executing this verb. Error status testing *should* be performed for all other set membership options.

The security violation error code, **0310,** is the only database activity error for this option. Two design and logic error codes, **0306** and **0308** may occur.

```
{FIND   }  [KEEP  [EXCLUSIVE]]
{OBTAIN }

{CALC (ANY)}  [record-name]
{DUPLICATE }

[error-expression].
```

Figure 30-23   OBTAIN CALC Command Syntax.

OBTAIN CALC (Figure 30-23)

The CALC record is a random-access record that is normally accessed based on the value of key fields within the record. CALC records are the entry points of the database.

IDMS obtains the record based *on the current contents of the key fields within the record.* The programmer is responsible for ensuring that the key fields are loaded before issuing the OBTAIN.

Associated with the OBTAIN CALC command is the OBTAIN DUPLICATE command. If the schema definition indicates that a CALC record may have duplicate keys (something we should avoid if at all possible), the only way to test for the presence of a duplicate record is to issue an OBTAIN DUPLICATE. As we discussed in Chapter 15, permitting duplicate CALC records will have a significant impact on the amount of logic written to process that record type. Program performance will suffer too as more tests have to be run (checking for one or more duplicates) each time the record type is accessed.

When the OBTAIN CALC (or OBTAIN DUPLICATE) command fails to find a matching database record, a 0326 error status is returned to the program.

The database activity error codes are:

0310. A security violation has occurred.
0326. The requested record is not in the database.
0332. A request for a duplicate record is unsuccessful.

The design and logic error codes are: **0306, 0308,** and **0331**.

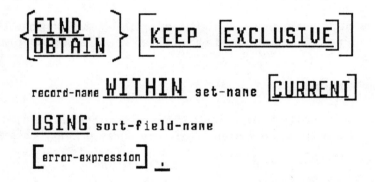

Figure 30-24   OBTAIN Record USING Command Syntax.

OBTAIN USING (Figure 30-24)

This statement type is used to retrieve specific member record occurrences within a sorted set. The same warnings about allowing duplicate CALC records applies to the sorted set. Allowing set keys to be duplicated means that an OBTAIN NEXT (or PRIOR if set is sorted in descending order) must be executed to cover the possibility of duplicates.

The security violation error code, **0310,** and the record not found error, **0326,** are the only database activity errors for the this command. The design and logic error codes are **0306, 0308,** and **0331.**

DBKEY Verbs

The dbkey verbs are a special breed. Their job is actually a glorified move statement. The move, in this case, is the value of one or more specific dbkeys from the subschema table to the program. There are often times during database set navigation, particularly when dealing with nest structures, that holding a dbkey for further reference is useful.

One point to remember when attempting to boost performance is that obtaining a database record by its dbkey is the fastest approach.

Why Play With Dbkeys?

Dbkeys are one of the advanced features of IDMS that can be used to make programs perform better. There are three primary uses for dbkeys:

1. Save a reference to a database record that the program may wish to recall later in the processing.
2. Mark a reference point in an area or set. This is particularly useful when sweeping an area and the program will access records related to the record that is the object of the sweep. (If the related record is located on a page previous to the object record, it becomes current of area and a processing loop occurs.)
3. Comparing record occurrences. The dbkey of a target record can be used to check a set to see if it is already a member of the set. This technique is quite useful in checking a nest structure to determine if a record being added to the nest is already

present in the nest at a higher level. Such conditions also cause program looping.

Holding Dbkeys

Before we go on to describe the dbkey verbs, it is important to understand the characteristics of dbkeys. A dbkey:

1. Is 4 bytes long and formatted binary (S9(8) COMP SYNC).
2. Is signed. This is important because negative numbers are legal.
3. Contains a value of -1 when empty, if in a member record.
4. Contains a value of 0 when empty, if in an owner record.

One note of caution: Do not keep dbkeys in a file that is retained after the program has terminated. If an unload and reload of the database were to occur between program executions, the dbkey value for a record could change.

ACCEPT DB-KEY INTO dbkey-field-name
FROM CURRENCY
[error-expression].

Figure 30-25 ACCEPT RUN-UNIT CURRENCY Command Syntax.

ACCEPT RUN-UNIT CURRENCY (Figure 30-25)

This is the first of four options of the accept dbkey from currency command. Each will be shown separately.

This command, as shown, moves the dbkey of the *current of run-unit regardless of its record type* to a program field. No error status test is required because the only way an error could occur would be if *no database records had been processed* by the program.

Performance may be improved slightly by replacing this command with a simple **MOVE DBKEY TO xx**. Both approaches accomplish the same thing; the simple move statement avoids the DML call to IDMS.

ACCEPT DB-KEY INTO dbkey-field-name
FROM set-name CURRENCY
[error-expression].

Figure 30-26 ACCEPT CURRENCY SET Command Syntax.

ACCEPT SET CURRENCY (Figure 30-26)

This is the second of the dbkey currency command options. This command allows us the retrieve the dbkey of the current of any set in the subschema, regardless of the record type.

A note of caution: It is poor practice to use this command when dealing with forked sets unless you know specifically which record type you are dealing with. If you obtain the record by dbkey without specifying its name (yes, it is permitted), any database procedures associated with that record type are bypassed. This can prove a problem if the record is compressed or otherwise specially handled by a procedure.

Two error status codes can occur. Both are caused by errors in design or programming logic:

1506. Currency was not established for the set. The program has not had activity against any record occurrence in the set.

1508. The set is not in the subschema. This is one of those errors that should never occur.

```
ACCEPT DB-KEY INTO dbkey-field-name
FROM record-name CURRENCY
[error-expression].
```

Figure 30-27   ACCEPT RECORD CURRENCY Command Syntax.

ACCEPT RECORD CURRENCY (Figure 30-27)

The third of the accept dbkey command group, this command retrieves the dbkey of the identified record from the subschema tables. This dbkey represents the current of the record type.

```
ACCEPT DB-KEY INTO dbkey-field-name
FROM area-name CURRENCY
[error-expression].
```

Figure 30-28   ACCEPT AREA CURRENCY Command Syntax.

ACCEPT AREA CURRENCY (Figure 30-28)

The fourth and last of the accept dbkey command group, this command identifies the dbkey of the current record of the named area, *regardless of the record type.* This command is useful for establishing a checkpoint during an area sweep; otherwise it is dangerous because the record type may be unknown, setting the ground for other processing problems.

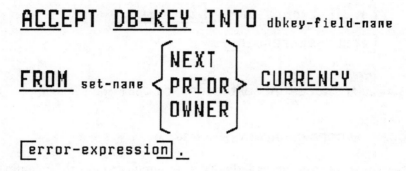

Figure 30-29   ACCEPT DB-KEY FROM CURRENCY Command Syntax.

ACCEPT DB-KEY FROM CURRENCY (Figure 30-29)

This command permits the programmer to get the dbkey of a record within a specified set without having to read the actual record. This is particularly useful when walking a set and you wish to take a checkpoint before walking down another path.

Two possible error status codes are returned by this command, both design and logic associated: **1506** and **1508**.

RETURN DB-KEY FROM CURRENCY (Figure 30-30)

The RETURN DB-KEY command originates with SPF and has been carried forward to integrated indexing. There are six options, which we will review in this section.

The intent of the RETURN command is to permit us to search an index without actually reading the records linked to the index. The dbkeys desired as part of the index search can be retrieved and then the specific database records accessed.

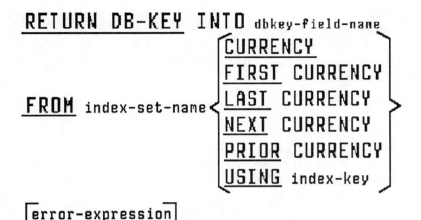

RETURN DB-KEY INTO dbkey-field-name

FROM index-set-name
- CURRENCY
- FIRST CURRENCY
- LAST CURRENCY
- NEXT CURRENCY
- PRIOR CURRENCY
- USING index-key

[error-expression]

Figure 30-30   RETURN DB-KEY FROM CURRENCY Command Syntax.

The six options are:

CURRENCY. The current record dbkey of the index set is returned.

FIRST. The first dbkey in the index set is returned.

LAST. The last dbkey in the index set is returned.

NEXT. The next dbkey in the index set currency is returned.

PRIOR. The previous dbkey in the index set currency is returned.

USING. A specific index key value is the object of a search through the index.

The key to using the index set is that currency must be established by use of the OBTAIN verb. Reading a record that participates in the index makes that record current of the index. *Using FIND does not establish currency to the index.*

Two error codes, **1707** (end of index), and **1726** (index entry not found), are database activity oriented. Error code **1725** is design and logic oriented.

Utility Verbs

There are a series of verbs within IDMS that do not fit easily into one of the other categories. They provide a variety of services; I call them utility verbs.

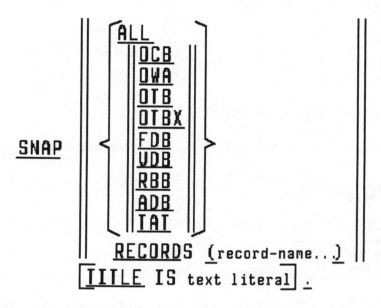

Figure 30-31   SNAP Command Syntax.

SNAP (Figure 30-31)

The SNAP command requests a dump of a variety of data to the system log. The command can be used to evaluate tricky logic in a transaction. Its use is not encouraged because it affects system performance and fills up the log.

The options of the command are:

ALL. All areas of memory associated with the issuing program are dumped to the log. This option is very dangerous; a program with large resource requirements can fill the system log. If several SNAPs occur in rapid succession, the entire system may hang.

OCB. The ADS Online Control Block contains the ADS system parameters defined at sysgen time.

OWA. The ADS Online Work Area. This is a temporary buffer for the ADS application during runtime.

OTB. The ADS Online Terminal Block. The area holds information about the current ADSO session.

OTBX. Online Terminal Block Extension. It contains pointers to the Task Application Table (TAT), the ADSO application global record, Application Definition Block (ADB), and the Record Buffer Block (RBB).

FDB. This is the ADS Fixed Dialog Block, the actual load module of a ADS dialog. Dumping the FDB is normally a waste of time as it does not contain any variable data.

VDB. The Variable Dialog Block is the meat of the dialog. Here is all of the variable data associated with the transaction execution.

RBB. The Record Buffer Block is the repository for all records associated with a dialog.

ADB. The Application Definition Block is a load module created by the ADS application generator. It is compiled data and serves little use to dump.

TAT. The Task Application Table identifies the names of task codes created using the application generator.

RECORDS. This option permits you to dump the contents of specific records.

TITLE. A title is linked to the dump to more easily identify the dump data.

No error status codes are associated with the SNAP command.

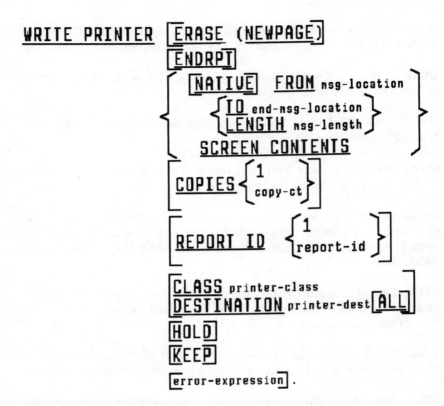

Figure 30-32   WRITE PRINTER Command Syntax.

WRITE PRINTER (Figure 30-32)

The write printer command permits the program to actually create a report from an on-line transaction. With few exceptions, this is not a good idea. It ties up database resources and I/O resources. Should a number of these reports execute concurrently, the entire system can be affected. Performance as a whole will suffer because of the overhead required to support on-line report printing.

The write printer option, therefore, should be used for exception situations that need to be recorded in hard-copy form.

As you can see from Figure 30-33, the syntax of the command contains several options. The remainder of this section will look at the most practical of the options:

NEWPAGE. This option causes the report to eject to a new page before printing begins, a good idea for most situations.

ENDRPT. The principal feature of this option is to force the *complete* printing of the report *before the task completes*. This means that the terminal operator is unable to proceed with other transactions until printing is done. What happens if the printing is queued and does not print for a few hours? The same thing! This option should be avoided.

NATIVE. If used, this option requires the program to insert line control.

FROM. This parameter identifies the location in the record buffer, usually a field, that starts the printed output.

TO. This parameter specifies the end of the printed output. *The output does not include the data in this field.*

LENGTH. As an alternate to the TO parameter, the actual byte length of the data to be printed is provided.

NOTE: If neither TO or LENGTH parameters are used, the length of the FROM parameter is used.

SCREEN CONTENTS. This option causes the screen image (327x devices only) to be printed.

COPIES. You can specify the number of copies to print. One is the default.

REPORT ID. This option allows you to specify a number from 1 to 255 to identify the report. The default is one; to date I have not found a good reason for using this parameter.

CLASS. This option permits identifying a specific print class, ranging from 1 to 64, that the report will be assigned to. The default is that of the physical terminal.

DESTINATION. This option allows the report to be routed to a defined destination code in IDMS. A 1-8 character variable or a field containing the variable sets up the routing. The default is the physical terminal. The ALL option prints the report on all terminals of the destination, otherwise the report is printed on only one terminal.

HOLD. The report is not printed until the system operator releases it. This feature is useful for overnight report printing.

KEEP. The report is held after printing instead of immediately purging it from the system. This option should not be used unless some means of managing the retention of reports has been implemented.

The processing oriented error code is **4807** indicating that an I/O error occurred when loading the record to the print queue. The remaining error codes, **4818**, **4821**, **4838**, **4845**, and **4846**, are related to design and logic errors.

Accept Statistics

This is an interesting if useless command. It provides a number of statistics that are interesting in themselves, but seldom serve much useful purpose to the executing program. Anything that can be retrieved is also available to the system managers by turning on statistics for the system.

Those fields that have some use to the program, DATE-TODAY, TIME-TODAY, RUN-UNIT-ID, TASK-ID, LOCAL-ID, are all available from the ADSO extended MOVE statement. The only use for the command, therefore, is in VERY complex debugging. Once debugging is done, the command should be removed.

Figure 30-33   INTIALIZE Command Syntax.

INITIALIZE (Figure 30-33)

The initialize command receives far too little attention, particularly in on-line dialogs. This command, in one motion, clears and sets an initial value in every element within a record (or all records, if desired).

MOVE commands take up space in the program. Too often, I have observed line after line of moves setting up a program's environment. This is a gross waste of space and computer time when, with a little planning, INITIALIZE could do the job.

Recovery Verbs

This group of verbs, with the exception of BIND, controls the hand-shaking between IDMS and the journal file. They are a foundation part of the IDMS backup and recovery facility, the best in the DBMS industry.

BIND

The BIND command is invisible to the ADS programmer; it is performed automatically by the software. In other languages, such as COBOL, the BIND command is issued at the beginning of the program. Its function is to tell IDMS where the control areas and record buffers are located in the program. These addresses are stored in the subschema and permit IDMS to provide records and status information to the program and to accept data from the program for database activity.

The BIND commands may be copied as a group into the program, the usual approach, or tailored with each specific bind of a record coded separately. Separate coding is often done to reduce the memory requirements of a program by eliminating those binds that are not required for the program to operate.

Figure 30-34   READY Command Syntax.

READY (Figure 30-34)

The READY command initiates an IDMS run-unit. It tells the DBMS that the program is ready to communicate with the DBMS and whether the program will update the database or just retrieve data. It is important to wait and ready the database only when access is required. Readying the database at the start of the program may tie up IDMS resources for some time before actual database access begins

Often it is possible to ready the database in retrieval mode during most of the transaction's running and then switch to update mode when changes are required. Some caution is required in these cases, however. It is possible to create a deadlock condition by having shared locks on a record and then requesting an exclusive lock later. If another run-unit, using the same transaction program, requests the same physical record, a deadlock is probable. In these cases, the program should issue a KEEP LONGTERM EXCLUSIVE to reserve the database record for its later use.

FINISH.

Figure 30-35   FINISH Command Syntax.

FINISH (Figure 30-35)

The FINISH command terminates the IDMS run-unit. A checkpoint is written to the journal and all database updates to that point are considered to be accurate.

COMMIT [TASK] [ALL].

Figure 30-36   COMMIT Command Syntax.

COMMIT (Figure 30-36)

The COMMIT verb is most often found in batch update programs. It is one of the most misused verbs in the command set. The COMMIT functionally performs a FINISH followed by a READY without the overhead of closing the program's run-unit.

A COMMIT, therefore, is a checkpoint of the database. Like the FINISH, IDMS expects that all updates to the database performed prior to the COMMIT are accurate; later rollbacks will have not effect on them.

To use COMMITs effectively, these points must be considered by the programmer:

1. *The database updating activity must be at a logical quiesce point.* That is, all updates for the completion of a logical activity must be done. It can be disastrous to issue a COMMIT in the middle of an update that requires changes to five records in order to be complete.

2. *Restart logic must be included in the program.* The program must know where the last COMMIT took place and be prepared to roll past the input data to reach that point before resuming updating.

ROLLBACK [TASK] .

Figure 30-37   ROLLBACK Command Syntax.

ROLLBACK (Figure 30-37)

The ROLLBACK verb is invoked to restore the database to its condition as of the last FINISH or COMMIT. ROLLBACK is executed when the program identifies an error condition that indicates the database has been corrupted or would be corrupted if updating were permitted to complete normally.

Miscellaneous Verbs

This group of verbs includes two to lock records and two others to test sets.

KEEP LONGTERM

We could almost write a chapter on this verb alone. It has so many options and such serious consequences are possible with its use that it deserves serious review. The command is used primarily to set record locks across run-units. The program can also test the status of a selected record over time.

Each keep longterm command can apply to one longterm identifier (except for RELEASE, that can use ALL to release all keeps at the same time). A separate command identifier must be assigned to each keep longterm function separate.

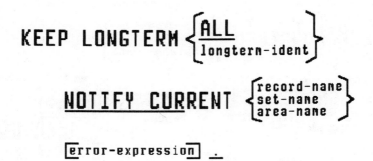

Figure 30-38   KEEP LONGTERM NOTIFY CURRENT Command Syntax.

The error status codes are largely database activity oriented (a change from most we have seen so far where most errors are logic error oriented):

5101. The keep specified NODEADLOCK and a deadlock condition was detected.
5105. The requested record is not in the database.
5149. The keep specified NOWAIT and a wait is necessary.

Those errors attributable to design or logic errors are: **5105** (currency not established), and **5121**.

There are actually three principal functions associated with this command. A fourth, RELEASE, terminates the other three. It is easier to discuss each function separately and break the syntax down into that necessary for the function.

NOTIFY CURRENT. This keep option is illustrated in Figure 30-38. The DBMS tracks a specific record occurrence that is the current of a record, set, or area. Normally, the command is issued immediately after establishing currency to a specific record occurrence.

SHARE/EXCLUSIVE. This option, illustrated in Figure 30-39, *attempts* to place a longterm lock on the record that is the current of record, set, or area. The emphasis on attempt highlights the extra options available:

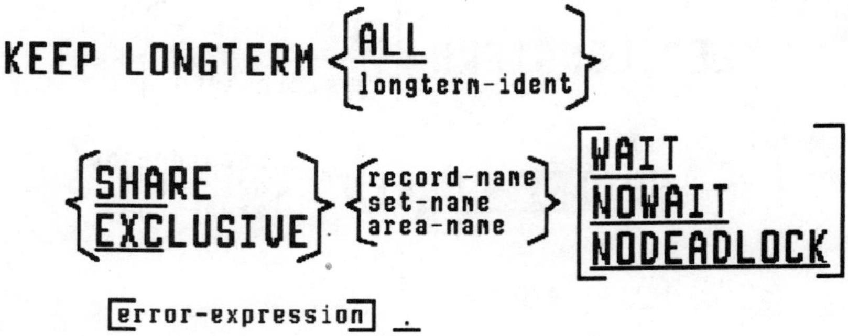

KEEP LONGTERM { ALL / longtern-ident }

{ SHARE / EXCLUSIVE } { record-nane / set-nane / area-nane } [WAIT / NOWAIT / NODEADLOCK]

[error-expression] .

Figure 30-39 KEEP LONGTERM SHARE/EXCLUSIVE Command Syntax.

1. *WAIT. The run-unit waits until the lock can be placed* on the record selected. If a deadlock will occur as the result of waiting, the run-unit is abended.
2. *NOWAIT. The run-unit continues processing* and the keep longterm is ignored.
3. *NODEADLOCK. The run-unit waits unless a deadlock may occur.* If a possible deadlock is detected, the keep longterm is ignored and processing continues.

UPGRADE SHARE/EXCLUSIVE. This option, shown in Figure 30-40, updates an already existing keep longterm command. The lock is made either shared or exclusive. The WAIT, NOWAIT, and NODEADLOCK options are as described earlier. An additional option, RETURN NOTIFICATION, permits the program to check on activity of the kept record that has previously included the NOTIFY CURRENT option.

TEST RETURN. This option tests the activity against a keep longterm NOTIFY CURRENT previously issued. The program can

KEEP LONGTERM $\left\{\begin{array}{l}\text{ALL}\\\text{longterm-ident}\end{array}\right\}$

UPGRADE $\left\{\begin{array}{l}\text{SHARE}\\\text{EXCLUSIVE}\end{array}\right\}$

$\left[\text{RETURN NOTIFICATION INTO return-locat}\right]$

$\left[\begin{array}{l}\text{WAIT}\\\text{NOWAIT}\\\text{NODEADLOCK}\end{array}\right]$

Figure 30-40   KEEP LONGTERM UPGRADE Command Syntax.

check the fullword binary field for one or a combination of the following statuses:

1. *The record was obtained* by another run-unit.
2. *The data portion of the record was modified* by another run-unit.
4. *The pointer portion of the record was modified* by another run-unit. This modification is usually caused by a CONNECT or DISCONNECT of the record within a set.
8. *The record was logically deleted* by another run-unit.
16. *The record was physically deleted* by another run-unit. A combination of the preceding conditions can be checked by testing the numerically added separate conditions. For example, a value of 2 to 7 indicates that the record was modified.

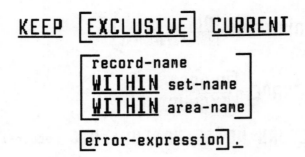

Figure 30-41   KEEP CURRENT Command Syntax.

KEEP CURRENT (Figure 30-41)

This command issues a record lock explicitly on a single record occurrence that is current of run-unit, record type, set, or area. Optionally, the lock may be a shared lock or exclusive lock.

Only two error status codes apply to this verb. The first, **0610**, relates to a security violation; the second, **0606**, is a design and logic error type.

$$\text{IF } \underline{\text{SET}} \text{ set-name IS } [\underline{\text{NOT}}] \text{ EMPTY}$$

connand-statenents .

Figure 30-42   IF EMPTY Command Syntax.

IF EMPTY (Figure 30-42)

This verb lets you quickly determine if a set has any member occurrences. It is equivalent to issuing a FIND FIRST of set command and checking the error status. In this case, the error status is zero if the set has no members for the selected owner. The *true* path of the IF command is executed if the set is empty.

IF SET set-name MEMBER

command-statements .

Figure 30-43   IF MEMBER Command Syntax.

IF MEMBER (Figure 30-43)

This verb tests to see if a record occurrence is a member of a set. It is useful only for optional or manual sets where the member occurrence may not have been connected to a set. The *true* path of the IF command is executed if the record *is* a member of the named set.

31

Locks

IDMS uses a sophisticated locking facility to aid in ensuring that the integrity of data is kept intact when operating in a multiuser environment. Since on-line operation is always assumed to be multiuser, the locking facility has a direct impact on each and every on-line user.

The concept behind the locking facility is to flag each record occurrence active in update mode and prevent some other user from updating such active records until the current user releases them. This is implemented by holding the dbkeys of each record occurrence that is processed by a run-unit until the run-unit is terminated or issues a COMMIT.

IDMS uses two basic types of locks: area and record. Each serves a particular purpose. They are described in detail in the following sections.

Problems Associated with Locks

Application programs updating the database find three basic problems associated with locks. We will discuss them in more detail later in the chapter:

1. *Deadlock/deadly embrace.* This is one of the most serious problems that can and does occur in multiuser environments when two or more users want the same data item at the same moment in time.
2. *Timeout waiting for data.* This is the most serious problem associated with the concurrent updating of the database by a batch program during times of on-line usage. Unless the batch program issues frequent COMMITs (checkpoints), an on-line request may exceed the allowed waiting time before database access is available.
3. *Too many locks.* This problem is also associated almost exclusively with batch update programs. In shared update, all programs issued implicit locks against the data updated *until end of task or a COMMIT is issued.* IDMS will continue to assign space for lock flags as long as storage pool space is available. When the storage pool fills, the run-unit abends and a *very* time-consuming rollback occurs.

Area Locks

Area lock flags, located in the first space management page of the area, are set whenever an area is opened in update mode. The locks are used principally to:

1. *Prevent concurrent update by multiple local run-units.* Local-mode run-units have no way of knowing if some other program is attempting to update the database. The area lock is set whenever one run-unit accesses the area in update mode; until that local program has completed processing no other local program can update the area.
2. *Prevent concurrent update by multiple central versions.* IDMS permits multiple central versions to access the same database. As with local-mode processing, there is no one point of control for the central versions so they could erroneously update the same data at the same time. The area lock keeps one CV waiting while the other processes shared data.
3. *Control rollback access.* While a database rollback is in progress, no other run-unit may access the areas involved in the rollback. This is one reason why rollbacks, if they occur frequently, can have a very detrimental affect on performance.

CV attempts to lock all database areas defined in its DMCL when it comes up. If an area is shown as already in use, CV will warn the operator and finish its startup *with that area offline.* Attempts to use that area through CV will result in a run-unit abort.

Local run-units check the area locks and when:

1. *The lock is set,* the run-unit is sent an error status of 0966 and area access is prevented.
2. *The lock is not set,* the run-unit sets the lock and forces the space management page to be immediately written so that the lock is visible to any subsequent run-unit.
3. *The run-unit abends,* the area lock remains set to signal subsequent users that the area may be contaminated. Updating is prevented until the area is recovered.

When operating under central version, CV checks area locks and when:

1. *The lock is set,* the *console operator* is warned by message and the area is isolated from *any* further access. CV will continue operation but any other run-unit requesting the area will receive a 0966 error status.
2. *The lock is reset after startup,* the operator must manually place the affected area back on-line. CV does not itself allow run-units to set the area locks; run-unit conflicts are avoided by other CV logic.

Record Locks

Record locks are a CV facility to prevent concurrent update of a specific database record *or the pointers in a related record.* It is important to understand this point! CV will lock records that are related by set to a record being modified on the premise that a change to a record may require pointer changes within other records. (This happens often when the sort key of a set is changed in one record occurrence in the set.)

Record locks perform three services:

1. *Selectively protect a run-unit from the possible retrieval or update* by another run-unit.

2. *Protect a record occurrence from concurrent update* by two or more programs.
3. *Prevent records that are current of run-unit in one* program from being updated by another program.

Record locks come in two forms: shared and exclusive.

1. *Shared locks* permit access to a record occurrence, but prevent any run-unit other than the locking one from updating the record. IDMS permits many run-units to place a shared lock on a record occurrence as long as no exclusive lock is placed on the record occurrence. Shared locks defer to exclusive locks.
2. *Exclusive locks* prevent access by *any* other run-unit until the lock is released. IDMS does not allow an exclusive lock to be set on a record occurrence while there are any shared locks present. A run-unit trying to place an exclusive lock on a record already under shared locking must wait until all shared locks are released. *This is a strong argument for banning exclusive locks in an on-line environment* except for special situations.

Management of locks can have dramatic effects on the performance of an application. Since on-line systems often wish to use the same record occurrences concurrently, improper use of locks can stack transactions into a queue waiting for access. When this occurs, even momentarily, performance suffers. Taken to an extreme, the entire DBMS run-unit complement can be filled, preventing further use of the DBMS until one run-unit lets go. Unfortunately, this frequently leads to run-unit timeout and user upset.

Programmer Set Record Locks

The programmer can overtly set record locks by using the DML command *KEEP*. This verb, on the FIND or OBTAIN verb, places a shared lock on a record. Adding *EXCLUSIVE* to the statement makes the record lock exclusive. Placing a lock on data while the program is running is asking for trouble. It is an invitation to "deadly embrace."

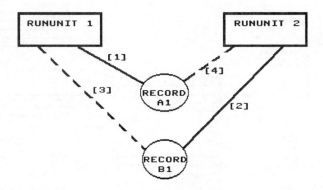

Figure 31-1   Deadly Embrace Locking.

Deadly Embrace/Deadlock

Deadly embrace or deadlock occurs when two run-units each ask for data that the other controls. IDMS tries to avoid the problem by monitoring the requirements of a run-unit at its startup time. This is similar to that performed by MVS; if one run-unit asks for an area exclusively, no one else can get in. Figure 31-1 illustrates this condition. Run-unit 1 requests and locks record A1 and run-unit 2 requests and locks record B1. Run-unit 1 then asks for record B1 while run-unit 2 is asking for record A1. Neither run-unit can continue without the other releasing the record it holds.

In an on-line environment, however, we seldom see an area locked. Instead, individual run-units access and lock specific records within the database. Deadlock, in the on-line world, becomes an issue of sharing records (and their dbkeys), rather than sharing areas.

Once a run-unit is in operation, however, the sequence in which it requests data records can directly affect the potential for deadlock. Backward movement in the database by one run-unit at the same time some other run-unit is working forward through the same data can increase the chances of deadlock.

Deadlock can be avoided by being consistent in the way data is handled in all areas. If all programs walk through the database in the same basic way, the chances of deadlock are dramatically reduced. Figure 31-2 illustrates a many-to-many data structure that, under high-volume conditions, would be prone to deadlocking. In this

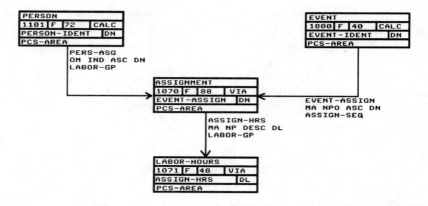

Figure 31-2   Deadlocking The Schema.

illustration, it is normal to walk the path from EVENT to ASSIGN-MENT and then to LABOR-HOURS. If the processing path also included retrieving the PERSON record as a normal event during update, we have set the scene for a deadly embrace. Another run-unit, using a processing path from PERSON to ASSIGNMENT and LABOR-HOURS, could deadlock on the ASSIGNMENT and PERSON records.

Using this schema, let us assume that run-unit #1 has retrieved the PERSON record for *John Jones* and is planning to update the LABOR-HOURS data for John's current weekly efforts. This will require that the program read John's PERSON record and then read those ASSIGNMENT records that correspond with John's timecard entries. John's PERSON record is locked, as are each of the ASSIGNMENT records in turn.

From the other side, another run-unit (#2) is updating corrections to labor entries (transferring some entries from one ASSIGNMENT to another). Project *W05221* reads its assignment records, one of which, *W05221-22,* is John's (but not one that run-unit #1 is currently processing). As part of the processing of a change, it is necessary to retrieve the PERSON record to get labor rate data. Run-unit #2 attempts to read John's PERSON record but can't because run-unit #1 currently has the record locked.

The plot thickens as run-unit #1 now asks for ASSIGNMENT record *W05221-22. Since run-unit #2 has locked this record,* run-unit #1 can't get it and begins to wait. Now run-unit #1 waits on *W05221-*

22 and run-unit #2 waits on *Jones, John.* Neither can continue and deadly embrace has occurred.

Reducing Deadlocks

IDMS "solves" the deadly embrace situation by sensing which program has made the second request for a specific piece of data. IDMS aborts the second program to break the embrace. Obviously, this is a brute force method that leaves the application users saying unkind words about the MIS organization. Other solutions are possible without reaching the point where IDMS has to step in.

Proper database and program design can eliminate most deadlocks. Returning to our previous example, we could have prevented the problem if the labor rate data was present in the ASSIGNMENT record. It would, therefore, have been possible for run-unit #2 to avoid reading John's PERSON record. Redundant data is deliberately introduced to improve performance.

A point to remember: Many-to-many and nest structures are the most prone to deadly embrace. Every such structure must be designed with deadly embrace possibility in mind; each use of the structure must be mapped and *the structure adjusted if a deadlock possibility exists.*

IDMS Handling Of Deadlocks

There are two general methods of handling deadlocks: detecting the deadlock when it occurs and doing something about it; or detecting the probability of deadlock and preventing the occurrence. Obviously, the second method, prevention, is the most desirable. IDMS approaches deadlock from the prevention method.

Shared vs. Exclusive Ownership Of A Record

IDMS allows multiple run-units to share a database record. As we see in Figure 31-3, three run-units can each retrieve a single record occurrence. The problems begin when one of the three wants to update the record. To do the update, exclusive ownership must be obtained.

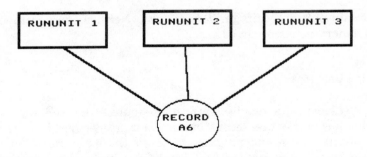

Figure 31-3   Multiple Run-Unit Sharing Data.

Exclusive ownership cannot be obtained by our update run-unit until *all* shared owners give up their claim to the record. If another of the run-units decides to update this record, a deadlock situation exists.

Deadlock And Wait Processing

IDMS tests for potential deadlocks at the time a run-unit issues a wait. The run-unit is tested to see if it is likely that the wait is caused by a possible deadlock. There are four pieces of information necessary, all kept within IDMS, used to determine if a deadlock is likely:

1. What systems are running
2. What processes are running within those tasks
3. What, if anything, are the active tasks waiting on
4. Who can satisfy other tasks' waits.

Conditional vs Unconditional Deadlock

When IDMS attempts to load a task and sufficient resources are not present for that task to load and execute, an *unconditional deadlock* is assumed. The system message DC001002 is displayed.

Once a task has actually begun executing, all waits are tested. If a potential deadlock is detected, this is known as a *conditional deadlock*. The system message DC204002 is displayed.

Summary

We could easily take this chapter and make it a book. In fact, Cullinet has issued a videotape on the subject. Let's summarize what we know about deadlocks and their prevention:

1. Deadlocks can be prevented through good database design. Deadlock prevention *begins with the first physical design efforts.* It must be considered at all times during the design phase.
2. Consistent use of the database can minimize the chances for deadlock. Programs that regularly use the same record types in the database should approach data, where possible, in a consistent pattern. Exceptions should be carefully reviewed for their potential for creating deadlocks.
3. *As a last resort,* IDMS will step in to prevent deadlocks. However, this is likely to result in an upset customer base.

32

Performance

Performance of the DBMS and the programs that operate with it will often make the difference between acceptance and rejection of an application system. Many otherwise excellent systems have been discarded because the user would not tolerate the slow response time. Performance, therefore, becomes an issue only when the system components (hardware, software, and communications) fail to provide sufficient resource at the speed required.

This chapter will look at the broad spectrum of IDMS and application performance. We will not, however, repeat many of the individual performance references found throughout the book. Refer to the index for these specifics.

Setting Performance Goals

On-line system performance requirements are quite different from batch. Applications that must serve both environments must be carefully tuned lest one kill the other. While we will concentrate on the on-line side, the side effects of tuning to enhance on-line performance will also be covered.

The bottom line of system performance is the ability of transactions to meet the business needs that are being supported. This is largely a perceptive judgment, based on the amount of work being performed and how fast it is performed. The amount of work is known as *throughput* while the speed of performance is identified as *response time*. Of major importance to the system developer is achieving a realistic definition of both of these parameters to the application and its individual components. Some transactions need five-second response time, others do not.

On-Line Performance Goals

On-line performance is typically measured in the response time to the entry of a transaction. To the end user (and they are the ones that count), response time is measured from the moment the ENTER or PF key is pressed until the results are displayed on the screen.

Performance goals should be based on rational need, not a blanket figure. Some applications, particularly those with a heavy data entry requirement, need very fast response time to keep up the productivity of the operators.

In other situations, casual users seldom need the speed as they use the terminal only occasionally. An extra couple of seconds has little impact on their productivity.

High-speed response time, therefore, should be focused on those transactions and applications where either the productivity of the terminal user or the activity being supported (like a production line where a label must be printed every 10 seconds to stay in sync with the line) demands a specific response level.

Service Levels

Most installations set service levels for computer performance. This is a good idea because it provides a basis for continuous monitoring of activity; performance trends signal operations personnel of potential problems before they occur. The mistake many installations make, however, is to set a single on-line service level.

There is no way that all transactions will respond in less than five seconds. Some simply do too much work to ever achieve that goal. But the longer transactions bias the overall picture and may obscure a developing problem. At least three levels of on-line service should be established:

1. *Response less than 3 seconds.* This is *internal* response time. It is very difficult to measure total terminal reponse time without a special recorder. Internal response time can be used *if we assume a basic fixed figure for line and controller delays.* This transaction uses little database access, normally fewer than 10 records accessed. Fifty percent of the transactions in any system should fall in this category.
2. *Response time of 3 to 8 seconds.* This transaction type typically does more database work, often accessing up to 25 to 30 records. Forty percent of the transactions in any application should fall in this category.
3. *Response time greater than 8 seconds.* There should not be very many of these transactions in any system. Most should be evaluated for conversion to batch jobs. If a system has more than 10 percent of the total on-line transactions in this category, the system design should be reviewed.

On-Line Performance Components

Several different components of the computer affect that response time figure. The efficiency of the program is only one of those components. Figure 32-1 illustrates these components. Each will be discussed in turn.

Looking at Figure 32-1, the path taken by a transaction is:

1. The terminal operator presses the ENTER key to send the transaction on its way. The transaction moves *serially* by coaxial cable to the terminal controller. This is the first place where performance can be affected. Large, cluttered screens transmit more data, taking more time to travel through the system.

RULE 1: Keep the volume of data to be transmitted low. This rule frequently conflicts with the desires of the user who wants to get as much done on one screen as possible. Remember this basic formula: Every 1000 characters transmitted slows response time by 1/10 second *for each leg of the transmission.*

2. Once the transaction data has completely reached the terminal controller, it is stored in the controller buffer. Here it waits

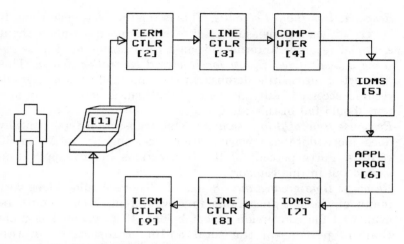

Figure 32-1   Components Of On-Line Response Time.

until the controller is polled by the computer's line controller. When the terminal controller is polled, it will transmit the first transaction in its queue.

Since the terminal controller can support up to 32 terminals (most only handle 16 or less), when the transaction is actually sent to the computer depends on the amount of activity by the other terminals attached to the controller.

3. When the transaction is transmitted, it travels from the terminal controller to the line controller at a standard rate of 9600 baud, normally in 512-byte bursts. Each burst is validated by the line controller and acknowledged before the next burst is sent. Sounds slow doesn't it? As long as the traffic volume is low and line quality is high, the process is very fast.

4. Once the entire transaction has reached the line controller, it issues an interrupt to the computer. The computer passes the transaction to IDMS.

5. IDMS recognizes an interrupt from the logical terminal and loads the application program (if it is not already loaded).

6. Our transaction program finally has the data and begins to execute. This is where we find out how fast *our* software is. The

program will interact with IDMS to access the database and perform the desired processing.

RULE 2: Keep database I/O to a minimum. To maintain consistent response time below five seconds, the transaction should access *no more than 10 to 15 database records.*

7. Processing completed, the transaction program instructs IDMS to send the results back to the terminal.
8. The line controller receives the transaction output, tests the transmission line and, when the line is available, sends the output back to the terminal controller. The time required is again dependent on the volume of data returned.

RULE 3: Return as little data as possible. The same technique is followed sending data back as when the line controller received data. At 9600 baud, each 1000 bytes takes a bit more than 1/10 second. Since data is sent back in 512-byte bursts, a response of fewer than 512 bytes saves time.

9. The terminal controller receives the data burst by burst. It immediately transmits the burst to the terminal screen. If the transaction response is displayed on the screen in sections instead of the full screen at once, this is a good indication that the load on the controllers is heavy.

What does this tell us about transaction response time? First, our program is only one part of the formula. Second, *if your terminal is remotely located from the computer, the best response time you can expect is about two seconds.* This figure will degrade as the number of active terminals increases. In a heavily loaded remote location, therefore, it is exceedingly difficult to achieve a five-second response rate even if your program does little or nothing.

What does this have to do with setting on-line performance goals? A great deal. There is little rationale in establishing a maximum five-second response time unless the transmission path and controller loading can be controlled to give the program a fair chance to meet the goal. Let's look at how we can shave time off the transmission.

Reducing Transmission Time

The first point in reducing transmission time is to reduce transmission volume. As a rule of thumb, every block of 512 bytes transmitted translates into about one second of total response time. Avoid transmitting blanks or underscores. Transmitting literals should be avoided wherever possible.

Since each data field is transmitted with its attribute byte, try to combine fields where possible. For example, send a date as six continuous digits (yymmdd) instead of three groups of two digits. If you have to use separators (yy/mm/dd), include the separators as part of the data. They take fewer bytes than the attribute and positional data for each separate field.

The next way to reduce transmission time is to utilize fiber optic transmission lines. Dramatic performance improvements are possible. The line controller can be located at your terminal site, making *local* mode processing possible. Line transmission speed can be up to 2 megabits per second, depending on the fiber installation. This is a BIG jump from the 9600 baud of remote operation. With fiber optics, response time can actually achieve subsecond speeds (if your program is fast, too).

Batch Performance Goals

A number of years ago an application was created to monitor sales performance. It was originally conceived as an on-line low-volume application that was to be used as a benchmark for the purchase of IDMS. Once completed, and IDMS purchased, the application became a standard product. Over time its data volume increased. On-line activity never materialized, but the system was run in batch mode each month.

After the second year, performance was noticed to degrade through the year as the data built up. In January, the monthly principal report took a few minutes. By December, it was taking several hours. Since computer time was available and there was no rush to getting the report, nothing was done about the problem.

Five years later, in November, the division president urgently needed the sales report for a special meeting called by the corporate president. Time was of the essence with the division president flying to New York in a few hours. The report, unfortunately, picked this month to run for nine hours. Needless to say, the division president had only the previous month's report to work from at his meeting.

Setting goals for batch processing performance is often overlooked because "batch is batch." While it is frequently easy to set up batch requirements to meet the turnaround goals of the project, the exceptions can be frustrating. This section looks at some of the tradeoffs that should be considered in the overall system design.

Identifying Turnaround Requirements

Every batch report user must be pressed to answer a few questions about their reports. These are among the most important:

1. Will the report be run at the same point (monthly closing, for example) every month?
2. Is the running of this report critical to any other decision making that makes its running at a certain time important?
3. Will the report be subject to ad hoc request? If so, what is the turnaround requirements of such a request?
4. What percentage of the database will be accessed to prepare the report?

These questions should cause other questions to be asked that are directly related to the application and report. The most critical consideration is the aspect of ad hoc requests. If ad hoc requests are expected frequently, turnaround requirements must be tightened. A multihour run may not be acceptable in that situation.

Each planned report should be put through the review. Those with special response requirements must be identified and the program tailored to meet requirements. Such tailoring may need only to permit the report to retrieve specific sets of data compared to printing all data.

CV vs Local Mode

Batch tasks act, to CV, like many transactions wrapped up into one. Since there is no break between transactions, as occurs in on-line mode, more CV resources are required to service a single batch task than an on-line task. Batch tasks use up one of the *maximum con-*

current task slots that the system can concurrently service. This means, in general, that a batch job requires more support from CV, per task, than almost any on-line task. If several batch jobs are running at the same time, on-line activity will suffer.

A batch job can process data as fast as it can get it from whatever input source it is using. It can tie up resources because it does not have to wait for an operator to press an ENTER key. Even set at low priority, the batch job is ready to run quicker than an on-line transaction, giving the batch transaction an "edge" that is difficult to overcome.

Batch programs tend to "hog" the database buffers because of the volume and frequency, they use the database. This will increase buffer paging and on-line transactions are paged out during their wait time, slowing on-line response because the database pages supporting the on-line transaction must be reread when the transaction continues. When should we run batch under CV? There are several good guidelines:

1. *Batch retrieval programs run in local mode.* There is no good reason to waste CV resources (and incur CV costs) by running a retrieval program under CV. No database updating is occurring and that is the main reason for running under CV (automatic backup and recovery).

2. *Long-running batch updates run in local mode.* These jobs should be run overnight. If an overnight local option is not available, the program MUST issue checkpoint COMMITs at regular short (approximately 50 to 100 logical transactions) intervals. Do not issue COMMITs too frequently as they themselves will have a degrading effect on performance.

   NOTE: Batch programs that issue COMMITs need to have some way to identify where the last checkpoint occurred and restart logic to pass the input to that point.

   NOTE: All batch jobs running in local mode must provide a three-step process: save the database; update the database; and restore the database if the update was not successful. *Do not separate these steps into different jobs!*

3. *Short-running or time-dependent batch updates run under CV.* CV backup and recovery is an important asset. If the batch job can operate effectively under CV without impacting on-line performance, let it. The job should be monitored over time,

however, as most batch jobs tend to grow in size and volume. There may be a time when the job should be moved to local mode.

Tuning For On-Line Performance

Up to this point the discussion has centered around physical considerations of on-line performance. Little impact on the batch environment will occur as a result of any tuning to this point. Once we begin tuning the database structure, the potential impacts on batch processing increase.

Let's look at database changes that can improve on-line performance (and the impacts on batch where applicable):

1. *Increase the number of CALC access points.* The fewer the records that must be read, the faster the program operates. The necessity of accessing a VIA record through a CALC entry point increases overhead.

   Increasing the number of CALC records generally extends the run time of a batch program, frequently forcing a sweep of the database instead of walking a chain.
2. *Assign secondary indexes.* This provides additional access paths through the database, making on-line access quicker. This technique has little impact on batch processing. In fact, some secondary indexes may improve batch performance.
3. *Eliminate sets.* Some sets are present primarily for ease of walking the database. Fewer sets reduce the number of currencies required. Batch processing can be impacted if desired set paths are removed, forcing batch processing to perform area sweeps.

IDMS provides such a variety of tuning possibilities that there is no one right or wrong way to tune a system. Each has its own idiosyncracies and its own needs. The best arrangement for a system today may be wrong in a year or two when the size, volume, and use of the database changes to reflect the change in business climate. The good DBA makes a point of reviewing each application every year to see if a performance trend has become visible.

Data Compression

We have mentioned data compression briefly elsewhere in the book, but it needs its own focus to provide a picture of the true pros and cons of compression.

First, over the years I have heard several DBAs say that they could come up with a better compression algorithm than that provided by Cullinet. A few have even demonstrated an improved technique. Fortunately, the idea of second guessing the vendor in this area has *not* caught on. Let me explain.

Assume your installation has implemented an installation stand-ard compression routine. All of your databases are compressed using the technique. For some reason your computer is out of service for several days and, to get the work out, you go to a local service bureau that supports IDMS. The service bureau, however, uses the vendor-provided compression routine as their standard.

Unless you can bring up your own CV region, you cannot operate within the service bureau's environment. You are nonstandard to the majority of IDMS users. The bottom line is this: Unless your com-pression routine is *critical* to your use of IDMS, stay with the ven-dor-supplied routines.

Guidelines To Using Compression

The following guidelines should help the decision-making process toward using compression. Remember, *compression does not have to be used on all records.*

1. Compression works best on records that have lots of empty space. This is particularly true where much of the record is text.
2. Avoid using compression on records that have many small fields. It is unlikely that significant compression can be achieved even though compression operates independently of field boundaries.
3. Short-lived records should not be compressed.
4. Largely static records, those not updated often, are good can-didates for compression. Since compression involves some sys-tem overhead, low-usage records can improve storage usage at minimum cost.

I/O Activity

The largest single piece of the transaction's time is typically spent in handling I/O. Since I/O is a physical activity, waiting for it is as time-consuming as the response time of the device. There are two basic ways to reduce I/O overhead:

1. *Reduce the number of requests for I/O.* This requires attention to program and application design from its inception. Retrofitting I/O reduction is usually unsuccessful.
2. *Reduce I/O wait time.* The net response time of a transaction can be dramatically affected by how long the program waits for I/O service. Tuning of the hardware is possible. For example, spreading database files across several channels, controllers, and physical DASD devices reduces contention and may reduce wait time by 50 percent. Overall system performance, for example, can be improved by placing the DDLDML, DCMSG, and load libraries on separate channels, controllers, and devices. More on that later.

Data Set Assignments

Here are a few guidelines to the placement of data sets to maximize I/O throughput:

1. *Isolate on-line data from batch data.* Because batch and on-line operate much differently, exclusive batch database areas should be kept separate from on-line. If batch operates through CV, it should have its own set of buffers.
2. *Isolate high activity datasets.* Physically locate those databases that are subject to high activity where they will not overshadow other databases of lower activity. This usually means placing such databases on channels and controllers by themselves.

   NOTE: By careful observation and tuning, mixing of high- and low-volume databases can be accomplished. In fact, this may be desirable in order to make effective use of the hardware.
3. *On-line databases require faster devices that do batch databases.* Where multiple device types are available, give on-

line systems the speediest devices with the most direct access path to the computer.

4. *The journal and log files are the heaviest used in IDMS.* Separate these files from each other and from other heavily used databases.

5. *Large application databases should be split* and placed on multiple OS files, each physically separate from the other.

6. *IDMS systems files should not share DASD space* with operating system or other on-line oriented data sets.

7. *Scratch and queue files should be isolated* from each other. Scratch buffers should be watched carefully as scratch-dependent applications are added to the system. At least four scratch buffer pages should be allocated, but six may be desirable.

33

Central Version Versus Local Mode

When should we use central version and when is local mode the best approach? This chapter will try to provide the guidelines and some techniques to aid you in making and implementing those decisions.

Central Version

Central version (CV) is that software that permits IDMS to support multiple concurrent users at the same time. It is the essence of on-line processing support. As important as multiple user handling is the backup and recovery facilities associated with CV.

Multi-User

First, let's discuss the multiuser facility. IDMS CV has the capability of supporting multiple concurrent users on-line (or batch) at the same time. The limitation on the number of users is dependent on the type of work being done. Large numbers of small, quick tasks can be performed, without performance degradation, while larger tasks require us to reduce the number of concurrent users. Given a constant machine resource and target response time, *a direct correlation exists between task complexity and number of allowable concurrent users.*

There are three variables that we can set in the sysgen that directly affects the CV environment:

1. *Maximum tasks.* This parameter defines the maximum number of concurrent tasks, *including system tasks,* that can be active in the CV at one time. This parameter should not be set lower than 10 to 15 and probably not higher than 20 to 25 for normal processing. A lower setting will allow too few users to process (the system usually requires about six tasks for itself) and a higher setting may swamp the system's resources (program and storage pools particularly). Systems using XA for the program and storage pools may be able to support a higher number of concurrent users.

2. *Maximum users.* This parameter identifies the maximum number of users that can sign onto CV at one time. Since each signed on user occupies a certain amount of storage space during the period they are signed on (even if they do no work), there should be a limit to the number who can be signed on concurrently. The number here will depend on each installation. Recommendation is to start with a small number and increase it as the system usage builds.

3. *Maximum batch tasks.* It is important to limit the batch use of the system during the prime on-line use period. It is not desirable to shut off all batch work but limiting the batch tasks to two or three will help maintain on-line performance. A long-running batch update during on-line use time can have disastrous effects on performance.

Automatic Backup and Recovery

Database integrity is of prime importance to its users. Unless the integrity of the data can be assured under all but the most catastropic conditions, confidence in the data itself will suffer.

IDMS has one of the (if not the) best backup and recovery facilities available today. Over the more than 12 years I have worked with IDMS, I can honestly say that (running under CV) I have never lost a database. There have been a few close calls, but the IDMS recovery facilities have come through.

Database recovery must be able to handle a variety of problems that can occur at any time. We can categorize these problems into three general groups:

1. *Failure of the data medium.* Head crashes are the most common medium failure although erasure of a data set has also happened to most of us.
2. *Program failures.* The abending of an update program requires that the database be restored to its condition prior to the start of the program execution. Sometimes the program detects data errors after the updating process has begun and the program itself aborts the update. Batch jobs may be canceled by the operator.
3. *Computer or operating system failure.* Power failures, even those momentary flashes of the lights, raise havoc with the computer or a terminal. Failure of a computer component is becoming a rarity but must be considered.

Each of these conditions and their side effects must be recoverable. CV provides the software facilities to ensure that IDMS can return any database to a stable condition.

The automatic recovery capability is active *only under CV.* Local mode processing must handle backup and recovery by themselves. This frequently places the DBA and operations personnel in a ticklish position. Batch updating of the database should be run under CV for enhanced integrity; yet should be run in local mode to ease contention with the on-line users.

As a general rule, *batch updating of the database should not be permitted during a time when on-line updating of the same area is likely to occur.* The possibilities of contention between tasks for records and the chance of double updating of the same record is too great.

Also as a general rule, *where practical all updating of the database should be done under CV.* This statement will raise the voices of controversy across the IDMS user community. There are those who flatly disagree with my statement, who never run *any* batch under CV. And there are those, like me, who will compromise the rule under certain circumstances. We are told rules are meant to be broken and that is true in this case.

An example: A number of years ago, an installation decided to convert a VSAM system to IDMS. The principal program of this system was a 50,000-line COBOL update program. Yes, I really mean 50,000 lines! User management was so skittish about this program that the programmers were not allowed to rewrite its logic to take advantage of IDMSs features but were told to simply replace VSAM reads and writes with IDMS DML. The resulting program was a dog! It ran so long and chewed up so many resources *that it would crash CV* almost every time it ran. So the program had to be run in local mode, on weekends.

This is an extreme example, to be sure. But it does point out the need to exercise rational thinking to balance against rules. There are too many different environments in the IDMS community for any one rule not to have an exception.

Local Mode Operation

The principal point that we must keep in mind with local mode processing is that *all database recovery and integrity requirements are our responsibility*. This means that batch updates to the database must include additional job steps to ensure the integrity of the database. Figure 33-1 illustrates a job stream logic that has been used effectively for many years.

As we see, there is additional overhead to the batch update. We *must* take a database backup before the update to have a recovery reference point. Depending on the physical size of the database, this could be quite time-consuming. (Some installations take this backup to scratch disk instead of tape to save time and operator intervention.)

Restrictions

The largest restriction of local mode processing is that *only one program* can access an area of the database *in update mode* at a time. If more than one local mode program wants to update an area, the last one there will abend. Scheduling of local updates, therefore, can be a headache.

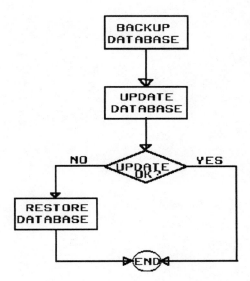

Figure 33-1   Local Mode Update Job Logic.

Advantages

Why then, you say, should I even consider using local mode? The most significant reason is resource overhead. CV has processing overhead, to perform all of those security, integrity, and task management functions, that are not present in local mode. Long batch processing will be much less expensive in local mode, assuming the run is good and recovery is not required.

Glossary of Terms

This Glossary is written for the novice IDMS user. Definitions are cross-referenced to each other by printing those terms appearing elsewhere in the glossary in italics.

access key — The *field* within a *database record* that is used a means of directly accessing the record.

access-method — The attribute identifying the software method of access to be used to update, modify, or retrieve from a file.

action code — A processing option code entered by the on-line operator to select a specific alternate function to be performed immediately by the *transaction*.

ADSG — The ADS-Online program generator product. This product combines the *data element* and *record, process*, and *map* definitions in the *data dictionary* into an executable *dialog*.

ADS/ONLINE (ADSO) — The Cullinet software product that aids the rapid development of *on-line terminal transaction* programs.

after image — The image of a *database record* after it has been up-dated by an *application program*. *The after image of the record is* written to the *journal* file to assist in recovery of the *database*.

alphabetic — The format designation of data that contains only al-phabetic characters, omitting numbers and most special characters.

alphanumeric — The format designation of data that includes all alphabetic characters, numbers, and printable special characters.

application — A computer *program* that performs a specific func-tion supporting an *enduser* of the computer. See also *transaction, software, system.*

archiving — The practice of moving seldom used data from the ac-tive *database* to magnetic tape storage.

area — The logical definition of the space within the database where record entities will occur. Areas are divided into a specified number of *pages*.

ASF — The Automatic System Facility; a tool within IDMS/R that implements the *relational* functionality.

attribute — Within the *IDD*, a specific word or term that further describes the dictionary entry. Each attribute is associated with a *class,* e.g., "ENTRY-SECURITY" is "ENTRY-UNCLASSIFIED" where "ENTRY-SECURITY" is a *class* and "ENTRY-UNCLASSIFIED" is an *attribute* within the *class*.

AUTOEXEC.BAT — A file within the *root directory* of a personal computer that instructs the computer what steps or programs to ex-ecute when the computer is turned on or *booted*.

AUTOMATE PLUS — A PC-based design and development tool, developed by *LBMS*, to automate the *LSDM* methodology.

AUTOMATIC — A type of *set* where a *member record* is automati-cally associated with its *owner* at the time the *member* record is stored in the database.

Bachman Chart (diagram) – The physical *schema* description of the database. Named for Charles Bachman, the diagram identifies the database *record* and its connecting *sets* that represent the physical database.

BAT file – Within a PC/DOS microcomputer, a special file that presents processing instructions to the computer in a designated order. Equivalent to *JCL* in a mainframe computer.

batch – (1) EDP operation characterized by the use of punched card or sequential file input and printed report or sequential file output; (2) EDP operation that processes a single job in an individual *region* of the computer.

BIND – Associate *IDMS* with the *program* accessing the *database*. See also: *BIND RECORD, BIND RUN-UNIT.*

BIND RECORD – The function that associates a location in memory within a *program's* working storage with an *IDMS record type,* permitting *IDMS* to transfer occurrences of that record type to and from the database and the program.

BIND RUN-UNIT – The function that associates *IDMS* with location within a *program's* working storage where special flags and communication data can be placed by *IDMS* to indicate the status of database activity. This function also identifies that *subschema* will be utilized by *IDMS* when supporting the application program.

BOM structure – A *database structure* that supports a hierarchy of data occurrences of the same *record type. See also: nest structure.*

boot – In a personal computer, the action that starts the computer. See also: *warm boot, cold boot.*

CALC – An *IDMS* record type stored randomly in the *database* in a location determined by the contents of its *key element(s).*

CALC key – The field that is used by *IDMS* to compute the random location *(database key)* of a *CALC* record occurrence in the *database.* CALC set Within a *database page*, the CALC set links all *records* that are pointed to the *page* by the CALC *hashing* algorithm.

CAMP – The Central Access Monitor Program of *IDMS*. This was the name given to the *Central Version (CV)* before version 5.0.

Central Version – The control program that permits multiple users of *IDMS* to share *DBMS* resources and prevent concurrent updating of the *database* by multiple users in such a way that might damage the integrity of the *database*.

chain (chain pointer) – The principal method currently use by *IDMS* to physically associate related record occurrences within the *database*. With this approach, the *dbkey* of the *next* record in the chain is physically located in a *pointer* section of the record occurrence. A *pointer* to the previous *(prior)* occurrence may also be placed in the record occurrence.

CICS – IBM's data communications monitor that provides *on-line* access to databases.

class – A basic grouping of words or terms that provide further explanation and organization of entries in the data dictionary. See also: *attribute.*

clock rule – The technique used to assign *set pointers* to *database records* in IDMS *schemas* during the early years of IDMS. No longer used to any extent.

cluster effect – The effect noted within when are stored adjacent to their owner.

CODASYL – The Conference On DAta SYstems Languages. A volunteer committee composed of representatives from the data processing industry, government, and data processing users whose task it is to recommend potential areas of standardization.

cold boot – The action that occurs when a personal computer is started by turning the power on. The cold boot process checks the status of the hardware attached to the computer before executing the *CONFIG.SYS* and *AUTOEXEC.BAT* files.

column — The *relational table* equivalent to a *data element* in a *network database*. See also: *domain*.

compound key — The *key* to a *database record* or *relational row* that consists of two or more *data elements* or *relational columns*. See also: *key, simple key*.

CONFIG.SYS — A file within the *root directory* of a personal computer that loads special programs to support hardware additions to the computer. The CONFIG.SYS is executed immediately following the hardware test on a *cold boot* and immediately upon the start of a *warm boot*.

conversational — A form of *interactive* communication between an application *program* and a *terminal* in that the application program remains active even when waiting for the operator to enter data or make a decision. Computer resources are held, preventing other computer users from utilizing those resources during the human waiting period. This mode of communication is infrequently used, the *pseudo-conversational* mode being preferred for efficient use of computer resources.

cross-area set — The process where a *set* crosses the boundary between two *areas; the owner record* is present in one area and the in another.

CULPRIT — A report writer and batch query facility marketed by Cullinet that interfaces with *IDMS*.

current (currency) — The *record* occurrence most recently acted upon by the *DBMS*. See also: *current of run-unit, current of set, current of area*.

current of area — The *record* occurrence most recently acted upon within a specific *database area*.

current of run-unit — The *record* occurrence most recently acted upon by the *run-unit* being processed by *IDMS*.

current of set — The *record* occurrence most recently acted upon within a *schema set*.

CV − See: *Central Version*.

data base − A description of the function of utilizing *DBMS* for the maintenance of information. database The physical repository of information processed by a *DBMS*.

database key − A binary number that contains the physical *page* location of a database *record* occurrence. The database key is composed of *page* and *line number*.

database structure − The formal organization of the *database* identifying the relationships between the various entities of the database.

data element − The lowest level of data definition within the database. A data element contains a specific piece of information that cannot be logically subdivided.

data entity − The highest level of data definition within the database. A data entity is the logical association of a number of *data elements* and *data groups* to form a complete picture of some information. See also: *record*.

data flow − In structured systems analysis, the transfer of data from one *process* to another.

data flow diagram − A diagrammatic technique that presents the flow of data through multiple *processes* as an aid in the effective development of *logical databases*.

data group − An intermediate level of data definition within the database. A data group consists of one or more *data elements* and/or other *data groups* that bring together logically related information. See also *data structure*.

data life cycle − A sequence of events that occurs from the time a particular data item is created until it is deleted from the *database*.

data set − The physical storage space set aside by the operating system for storing a database.

data store — In structured systems analysis, the indication of data at rest, a *database*.

data structure — Used by Gane and Sarson to describe the association of two or more *data elements*. See also: *data group*.

DBKEY — See *database key*.

DBMS — Data Base Management System.

dialog — An on-line *terminal transaction* as defined within the *ADS/ONLINE* application development facility.

DBNAME table — A table, internal to the IDMS system, that identifies alternate names to be used as *program* requests to use a *database* other than the one normally accessed.

deadlock — The condition that occurs when two or more *programs* request the same system resource at the same time.

DFD — See *data flow diagram*.

directory — Within a personal computer, a directory is a list of programs or files. Directories may be subdivided into subordinate directories, effectively organizing the data storage within a *hard disk*.

DMCL — Device-media control language. The facility that relates the *logical schema* to the physical *data files*.

DML — Data Manipulation Language. The language syntax associated with a programming language, such as *COBOL* or *ADSO*, that the language compiler or preprocessor recognizes and converts into the appropriate commands to access the database through *IDMS*.

domain — A *column* in a *relational table*. See also: *data element*.

ELEMENT DESIGNATOR — A *class* that provides the ability to associate data elements by common attributes, such as a flag, number, date, etc.

ELH – See *entity life history*.

end user – The ultimate customer of a computer *system*.

entity – In data processing, any grouping of data that represents a particular description of a real life object; a logical picture of a real world object. See also *data entity*.

entity life history – The *data life cycle* of an entity, documenting its activity from the moment of inception until it is deleted from the *database*.

entry point – An *entity* within a *data structure* that provides a point of entry into the *database*.

entity relationship – The association that exists between two *logical records* in a logical *data model*.

exclusive relationship – The relationship between three or more *data entities* where two entities may not occur at the same time.

explosion – The *set* within *bill-of-materials* database structure that connects to *nest* records and identifies subordinate occurrences of records of the same type as the *owner* of the *nest* record. For example, the owner record is *organization*. It has a nest record ORGAN-NEST. Two sets link the two. The leftmost is the *explosion* set and the right, the *implosion* set. Traversing the *explosion* set to the nest and up the *implosion* set to another occurrence of the organization record will identify an organization subordinate (a department within a division) to the first owner.

EXCLUSIVE RETRIEVAL – One of the *IDMS usage modes* associated with database access by a *run-unit*. When a run-unit attaches a database *area* in this mode, no other run-unit may access the area. This mode has the effect of locking all other users out of the area until the run-unit is complete. This mode is not compatible with *on-line, interactive* use of the database.

EXCLUSIVE UPDATE – One of the *IDMS usage modes* associated with database access by a *RUN-UNIT. When a run-unit attaches a database* AREA in this mode, no other run-unit may update or retrieve from the area. This mode has the effect of locking all other users out of the area until the run-unit is complete. This mode is not compatible with *on-line, interactive* use of the database.

external data model — The user's veiw of the data structure, optimized for simple use and ease of navigation.

file — See *AREA*.

fixed-length element — A *data element* that will always contain sufficient data to completely fill its storage space, e.g., country code is a 2-byte field and every entry to the element is always 2 bytes long.

floppy disk — The standard removable media used with personal computers. Most floppy disks are capable of storing 320k bytes to 1.2m bytes of data. Floppy disks range from 3 1/2 to 8 inches in diameter, with the most popular currently being 5 1/2 inches.

foreign key — Within a *relational DBMS*, a field within one *table* that is identical in name and format to the *primary key* in another relational table. A foreign key is used to relate two tables.

fully functional dependence — The condition where the dependent *entity requires the presence of the complete entity upon* which it is dependent; a subset of the owner entity will not suffice.

functional dependence — The condition where one *entity* is dependent on another if the dependent entity cannot exist without the presence of an occurrence of the other entity.

functional specification — A document that contains a description of all of the functions to be performed by an application software system.

group — See *data group.*

group synonym — Elements that are group names may also have alternate names. The group synonym is an alternate name by which the group element may be identified. See also: *synonym.*

hard disk — A disk storage unit where the storage media is solid and does not bend readily. The media is usually fixed in place and not removable.

hierarchical — A one-to-many relationship. This relationship may be cascaded down through several levels (an *owner* to *member* that in turn is an *owner* of another level of *member*). Within a hierarchical structure, records at one level communicate only with records at the next higher or lower level. Communication with records at the same level must be accomplished through an *owner* that joins those records that need to communicate. A subset of a *network*.

icon — A pictorial symbol displayed by the Automate picture editor and used to indicate a particular activity or process within a graphical display.

IDB — The Information DataBase; within IDMS/R, a facility that controls the access and security for multiple data files from different souces and provides a hierarchical directory for access to registered files.

IDD — Integrated Data Dictionary. The software product marketed by Cullinet, that maintains the *IDMS data dictionary*.

IDMS — Integrated Database Management System.

IDMS-DC — An expanded version of *IDMS* that marries the functions of *IDMS* and its *Central Version (CV)* together with a *teleprocessing monitor*.

implosion — The *set* within a *bill-of-materials* structure that identifies those occurrences of the record to which the first occurrence belongs. For example, the owner record is ORGANIZATION. It has a nest record ORGAN-NEST. Two sets link the two. The leftmost is the *explosion* set and the right, the *implosion* set. Traversing the *implosion* set to the nest and up the *explosion* set to the next occurrence of the organization will locate the higher level organization (a department reporting to a division).

index — A secondary path to data. Indexes are normally used to enhance the speed of data retrieval at the expense of update speed.

information modelling — A process whereby the logical relationship of information is modeled. In an information model, logical groups of data are identified and associated through relations. The information model provides the basis for the *schema* to be developed.

integrate — The association of like *data*. The process of integration brings redundant and related DATA from multiple *files* into a single *database* that is shared by several users with a minimum of redundancy of data.

interactive — The process by which an enduser of a data processing facility can "talk" to the computer *on-line*, analyze an answer, and request additional information immediately.

JCL — Job Control Language. The specialized statements that control execution of jobs on the computer.

journal — The *IDMS file* that maintains *database* recovery information.

junction record — A *record type* used to associate two other record types. See also: *structure record*.

justify — To adjust the positioning of the data within a field to the left or right edge of the field. Alphabetic data is normally justified to the left edge of the field while numeric data is justified to the right. The default may be changed by using *JUSTIFY RIGHT* for alphabetic data and *JUSTIFY LEFT* for numeric data.

key — A *data element* or *group* of data elements that defines a *database* record uniquely.

key, access — See *access key*.

key, foreign — See *foreign key*.

key, physical — See *physical key*.

language — The term used to identify the programming language used, such as *COBOL* or *ADSO*.

LBMS — Learmonth & Burchett Management Systems, a consulting firm originating in Great Britain that specializes in data management methodologies. See also: *LSDM*.

line number — The logical position of a *database record* occurrence within a *page*. When a record is stored, it is assigned the next available line number on the page. It is then physically placed in the next available space on the page and the displacement address inserted into the line number index at the bottom of the page.

line — Within Automate, a line drawn between two icons.

link — Within Automate, a line linking two icons.

logical database design — The process of defining a database structure without applying it to a physical DBMS product.

logical record — A record definition that is not concerned with the conditions of its physical use. The logical record, for example, does not consider the *area* in which it resides or the *pointers* that link it to other records. See also: *Data Entity*.

LSDM — The *LBMS* Systems Development Methodology. A database design methodology, used heavily in Great Britain and Europe for the effective design of complex database structures.

MANDATORY — A *set* condition in which once a *member* record occurrence is associated with an *owner* record occurrence, the link cannot be broken without deleting the *member* occurrence.

many-to-many — A logical data relationship in which one or more occurrences of a *record type* may be associated with one or more occurrences of another *record type*. See also: *Nest Record*.

MANUAL — A *set* condition in which the association of two *record* occurrences whose record types are joined by a *set* is determined by the logic of the supporting *application software*.

map — The definition of an *on-line* terminal display that help the *enduser* use the computer.

mapping class − A definition of the number of times a logical *entity* can physically exist within a data *relationship. The mapping classes are: One to one (1:1);* one to many (1:M); many to one (M:1);many to many (M:M).

megabyte − 1,048,576 characters *(bytes)* of memory. (This figure is the binary progression nearest 1 million.)

member − A logical *database record type* that is dependently associated with another *record type*, its *owner*.

memory − The computer's storage medium. Memory is generally either static (retains its contents if power is lost) or dynamic (contents are lost if power is removed). Memory size is measured in kilobytes (K), a kilobyte actually measuring 1024 physical memory positions.

methodology − A formal process. In this book, a formal process for the analysis, design, and development of database application *software*.

module − Within the *data dictionary*, an entity that has the capacity to store source statements for programs, tables, etc. An *ADSO process* is a form of module.

mouse − A cursor control device attached to a personal computer that is intended to speed up cursor motion, particularly when preparing graphical displays.

multilevel nest − A *nest structure* that contains or accesses multiple layers of subordinate records of the same type.

nest record − A *record type* used to present an indefinite hierarchical structure of identical *record types*. A nest record is characterized by being the *member* of two *sets*, both of which are owned by the same *owner* record. This structure permits the association of two occurrences of the *owner* record through the nest; (2) a MANY-TO-MANY data relationship in which both *owner* records are of the same *record type*.

nest structure − See *Nest Record*.

network — *Many-to-many* relationships of data. The network structure permits the physical association of data directly in the same manner in that it occurs in the "real world." In this type of structure, any record type can be associated with any other *record type*, either as *owner* or *member*.

NEXT — A reference to *set pointer* direction in *IDMS*. The next *pointer* addresses record occurrences that follow in the *set chain*.

OLM — On-line Mapping generator. The software product that assists the application developer in creating an on-line display that links the *dialog* and the *enduser*.

OOAK record — One-Of-A-Kind record. This type of record exists only once within a database. It is used to provide direct paths to one or more *CALC* records, permitting the user to locate occurrences of the *CALC* record without having to scan the entire database sequentially.

one-to-one relationship — Two *records* or *entities* have an association where one and only one occurrence of one record may exist for one occurrence of the other. Example: For each entity PERSON, there can only be one JOB ASSIGNMENT. For that JOB ASSIGNMENT, there is only one PERSON.

on-line — The term employed to mean that the *enduser* of a data processing facility is able to utilize the facilities *interactively*.

operational master — A logical *data entity* that provides an additional *entry point* into a *database*. In a physical database, the operational master corresponds to a *secondary index*.

operations instructions — The set of documents that describes to computer operations personnel the proper procedures required to operate an application software system.

orphan entry — An entry within a *pointer array index* that is no longer included in the array table. The orphan record cannot be accessed through the index.

overhead – As applied to computer software operation, the amount of processing resources required to perform system functions as compared to those necessary to perform the application *transaction*.

page – The logical subdivision of a *database area*. Pages are assigned physical sizes when they are defined within a *data set*.

pan – The process of shifting the viewing area of a diagram or picture so that another section of the diagram may be viewed on the screen.

path – The sequence of *sets* that identify the links between associated *data*.

physical database design – The process of applying a *logical database design to a specific DBMS product*.

physical key – The field within a *relational table* that is identified as *access key* for that table.

pointer – In *IDMS*, a physical binary number that contains the *dbkey* of another *DATABASE record occurrence*. See also: *chain*.

pointer array – A method to link database records together, pointer array uses a list to identify *records* that are *members* of other *owner* records. Each entry in the list is a pointer to an individual member record.

premap process – An *ADS/ONLINE process* that is executed before the display of the *map* associated with the *dialog* in that the *process* is defined.

primary key – The *attribute* within an *entity* that uniquely identifies a specific occurrence of the entity.

PRIOR – An indication of *set* direction. A *set pointer* for prior addresses the record occurrence that precedes the *current* record in the *chain*.

process – In structured analysis, the definition of a logical function being performed. In *ADS/ONLINE*, a group of source program statements that are executed by a *dialog*. *ADSO* processes are divided into *premap processes* that are executed before display of the *map* on the *terminal* and *response processes* that are executed after the display of the *map*.

program specifications – The detailed descriptions of each *program* to be developed as part of an application software system.

property – In data processing, the characteristic definition of an entity, such as size, color, and quantity.

property value – The physical occurrence of a property; the property value of color may be blue, green, or red.

proposal – A document responding to a customer *RFP*, describing the proposed software system to satisfy the customer's requirement.

PROTECTED RETRIEVAL – One of the *IDMS usage modes* for access to a database AREA. This mode permits multiple *run-units* to retrieve data from an area, but does not permit updating of the area until the run-unit operating in protected mode is completed. See also: *PROTECTED UPDATE*.

PROTECTED UPDATE – One of the *IDMS usage modes* for access to database *area*. This mode restricts updating of the database area to a single *run-unit;* general *retrieval* run-units may also access the area while the protected update run-unit is executing.

pseudoconversational – A type of *interactive* communication between an application *program* and a *terminal*. In the pseudoconversational mode, the program execution terminates while waiting for the operator to enter data or make a decision. This frees computer resources for other uses during the human waiting period. See also: *conversational*.

range – Within the *data dictionary*, the value or values associated with a data element.

record − The logical or physical representation of *data* within a *database*. The *schema* is composed of many *record types*, each of which may have an unlimited number of occurrences. These occurrences are generally referred to as records.

record format − One of the general formats used to aid in the design of a *record type*.

record type − The individual definition of a *record* within the *database schema*.

reentrant − A type of computer *program*, usually one used in *online* processing. A reentrant program is developed in such a way that the program can be used by more than one user at a time, reducing the amount of *memory* required to support multiple *end-users* of the same program.

region − The MVS operating system designation for an area of the computer where an application program resides while executing.

relational database − A database constructed by a *DBMS* that conforms to the relational concept of database development. A relational database is composed of *records* that are actually lists of related data, in *third normal form*.

relationship − The assocation between two or more *entities*. Each relationship includes an identifier and the direction of the relationship.

relationship attribute − The description of a relationship where the value of the description is based on the eligible values associated with the relationship.

requirement specification − A document prepared by the customer and/or MIS in response to a request for service from the customer. See also: *RFP*.

RETRIEVAL − One of the database access *usage modes*. This mode permits a *run-unit* to access the database *area* concurrently with other retrieval run-units and run-units operating in *update* mode.

RFP – A Request For Proposal, issued by a customer desiring computer services.

root directory – The primary *directory* of the *hard disk* of a personal computer.

row – The *relational table* equivalent to a *record* in a *network database*. See also: *tuple*.

run-unit – A unit of work within *IDMS*. Each run-unit represents a concurrently executing task that is interacting with an *IDMS* database.

schema – The logical definition of an entire *database*. The schema is the road map to the *database*.

SDLC – The systems development life cycle, from the inception of a project through the long-term maintenance of the software.

secondary index – A secondary data path to record within a *database*. See also: *SPF, index*.

secondary key – Usually associated with a *secondary index*, the key value that establishes an alternate identification of the *entity*.

service analysis – The process of identifying each function that will support a user's *application*, including *database* maintenance, reporting, and querying.

set – The term used in *IDMS* to identify the association between two or more *record types*.

simple key – A *database record key* that is composed of a single *data element* or *relational column*. See also: *key, compound key*.

single-level nest – A *nest structure* that either: 1) contains only one layer of subordinate records below the entry point, or 2) accesses only one layer of subordinate records below the entry point regardless of at what layer the entry is made.

single-thread – Software that cannot process more than one user request concurrently. Software performance is reduced when it functions as single-threaded. See also *pseudo-conversational* and *conversational*.

SMI – Space Management Interval. The original size of a *database page*, used after the pages have been expanded.

software – Computer *programs* that perform specific functions to support an *application*.

SPF – Sequential Processing Facility. Originally developed to permit users of *IDMS* to store large volumes of data in physically sequential files, the secondary index portion of the facility is the best known. The secondary index capability provides an additional access path directly to a database record.

subordinate element – A *data element* that is a part of another higher-level data element.

subschema – A subset of a *schema* that identifies a specific window view of the database, restricting the user to that portion of the database.

SVC – Supervisor Call. An assembly language routine that is supplied with *IDMS* to provide communications between *IDMS* and the operating system.

sysgen – The act of creating the control software of the IDMS system.

system – (1) An application software facility composed of one or more *programs;* (2) The operating system under which *IDMS* executes, such as MVS; (3) A version of *IDMS-CV/DC/UCF*.

system specification – The main document supporting an application software system. The specification is made up of several documents: *RFP, proposal, requirement specification, functional specification, system structure, database structure, program specifications, test plans, operations instructions, and user guide.*

system structure — The description, usually accompanied by pictorials, of the functional structure of a data processing system. The system structure identifies the software modules within the system and their interconnection.

table — 1) An *IDD* subset of the *module entity* that defines table of values used by *ADSO* maps. 2) The name assigned to a *record* within a *relational database*.

task — Within *IDMS-DC/UCF*, a single executing function. A task is normally equivalent to an *IDMS run-unit*.

task code — A unique 1- to 8-character name that identifies a *task* to be executed within *IDMS-DC/UCF*.

teleprocessing monitor — System software product that allows a *terminal* to communicate with an application *program*. *CICS* is an example of a teleprocessing monitor.

terminal — A device that can communicate with the integrated *database*, primarily *interactively*.

test plan — A formal plan prepared to coordinate the testing of an application software system.

third normal form — A level of data definition in which there is a *key data element* and subordinate data elements that occur only when associated with that key. None of the subordinate data may be repeated. This is the basic structure of a *relational database*.

tree structure — An approach to associating data within database. It is the basis of the *hierarchical* data structure. The name is derived from the appearance of the data relationships that spread out as the branches of a tree spread from the trunk.

TP — Teleprocessing, the function of communication with *database* from a remote location.

transaction — A logical unit of work for an *enduser*. The term is frequently used to define one or more *programs* or *dialogs* that execute as a group to perform a specific application task.

tuple − A *row* of a *relational table*. See also: *Record*.

UCF − Universal Communications Facility. A subset of *IDMS-DC* that relies on another *teleprocessing monitor,* such as *CICS* or *TSO,* to provide terminal handling capabilities.

usage mode − The access mode in which a *run-unit* will address a database AREA. Valid usage modes are *RETRIEVAL, PROTECTED RETRIEVAL, EXCLUSIVE RETRIEVAL, UPDATE, PROTECTED UPDATE, EXCLUSIVE UPDATE.*

user − The persons or organizations that will be utilizing the *integrated database.*

user guide − A formal document supporting the end user of an application software system.

variable-length element − A *data element* that is large enough to contain the information that it is designed to hold but which may have empty spaces (spaces or zeros) after the data has been loaded; e.g., the name of a person is 27 bytes long but the data loaded may be only 15 bytes long for a specific occurrence of the information.

VIA − One of the record *location modes* of a *CODASYL DBMS. record* store via another *record* is physically located as close to the other record occurrence as possible.

volatility period − A period of time (daily, weekly, monthly) during which an estimate of additions, changes, and deletions to the database has been made.

warm boot − The action that occurs when a personal computer is restarted through use of the CTRL-ALT-DEL key sequence; also when a personal computer is restarted by program control. A warm boot normally does not check the status of the computer hardware. See also: *boot, cold boot.*

where-used − Within a *bill-of-materials* data structure, the path that identifies a bill member as subordinate to another higher level bill member.

zoom – The process of expanding or contracting a displayed diagram or picture so that more or less of it can be seen on the screen.

Index